CW01202323

SOCIAL SECURITY FOR YOUNG PEOPLE

To Marie, Amy and Rosanne

Social Security for Young People

NEVILLE S. HARRIS
Senior Lecturer in Law
Liverpool Polytechnic

Avebury

Aldershot · Brookfield USA · Hong Kong · Singapore · Sydney

© N.S. Harris, 1989

All rights reserved. No part of this publication may be reproduced, stored in a retrieval system, or transmitted in any form or by any means, electronic, mechanical, photocopying, recording, or otherwise without the prior permission of Gower Publishing Company Limited.

Published by

Avebury

Gower Publishing Company Limited,
Gower House, Croft Road, Aldershot.
Hants. GU11 3HR, England

Gower Publishing Company,
Old Post Road, Brookfield, Vermont 05036
USA

ISBN 0 566 07029 4

Printed and Bound in Great Britain by
Athenaeum Press Ltd., Newcastle upon Tyne.

Contents

Preface ... vii

Table of Statutes ... ix

Table of Statutory Instruments ... xii

Table of Cases and Decisions of the
Social Security Commissioners ... xv

Abbreviations ... xvii

Introduction - Youth and Social Security: the Issues ... 1

PART I: *DELAYED EMPLOYMENT AND THE DEMAND FOR SOCIAL SECURITY*

Chapter 1
Patterns of Demand for Social Security ... 17

PART II: *SOCIAL SECURITY AND THE TRANSITION TO ADULTHOOD*

Introduction to Part II ... 37

Chapter 2
The Transition to Adulthood 39

Chapter 3
The Evolution of Young People's Benefits: 1911-1980 46

Chapter 4
Welfare Benefits for Young People: 1980-1989 67

Chapter 5
Consequences of Reduced Independence 104

PART III: *SOCIAL SECURITY, EDUCATION AND EMPLOYMENT POLICY*

Chapter 6
Social Security and Education 115

Chapter 7
Social Security and Youth Employment Policy 143

PART IV: *CONCLUSIONS*

Chapter 8
Conclusions 167

Bibliography 180

Index 195

Preface

This book has as central themes the continuities and transitions relating to social security for young people in Britain.

Singling out young people as a social security client group for attention might in the first instance appear somewhat indulgent. What about the elderly, lone parents or the disabled? Surely their needs make them greater social priorities compared with young people in general? After all, the period between childhood and adulthood is short. So, whatever deficiencies in social security provision for young people there may be, might they not be expected to affect a particular cohort only temporarily?

Maybe these questions should be answered in the affirmative. But with such high levels of youth unemployment in recent years and such unremitting criticism of government employment and social security policies affecting the young unemployed, an examination of social security for young people would appear to be warranted. And as these factors have drawn our attention to the young unemployed, what do we know about how the social security system deals with the transition to adulthood - which socially is made up of a number of transitions (pupil to student, trainee or worker, non-householder to householder, single person to partner/co-habitant, non-parent to parent, and so on)? It is a transition which, for some, is not as short as it might once have been.

But there is another important transition which gives a further context to this discussion - the transition of the welfare state under Thatcherism. This has particularly affected young people, whose social security entitlement has diminished to perhaps a greater extent than that of any other group and who may in the future lose more, as a consequence of further re-directing of support away from young people and towards other groups.

Our understanding of the reasons for the current status of young people in relation to social security entitlement depends on our awareness not only of the development of social security policy under the Conservatives in the 1980s, but also of certain continuities. In particular, consideration needs to be given both to the assumptions and values which have for so long underlain social security for young people and to the legal provisions in which they are reflected.

To a large extent this book is the product of doctoral research at the Faculty of Law at the University of Sheffield (completed in 1988). Some parts of the assembled material have appeared in publications by Basil Blackwell, Cambridge University Press, Debra Charles Ltd. and Sweet and Maxwell Ltd., and are included with their permission.

I wish to record my indebtedness to John Mesher and Martin Partington for their constructive advice at various stages of the work which has resulted in this book. All opinions and any errors contained herein are, of course, my own.

The law is stated as at 31 March 1989, but benefit rates and other legal changes applicable from April 1989 (where known at the time of going to press) are included.

Neville Harris

Table of statutes

1601
Act for the Relief of the Poor (43 Eliz.1, c.2)

1834
Poor Law Amendment Act (4 & 5 Will.4, c.76)

1909
Labour Exchanges Act (1 & 2 Geo. 5, c.55)

1911
National Insurance Act (1 & 2 Geo. 5, c.55)

1920
Unemployment Insurance Act (10 & 11 Geo.5, c.30)

1921
Education Act (11 & 12 Geo.5, c.51)
Unemployed Workers Dependants (Temporary Provisions) Act (11 & 12 Geo.5, c.62)

1922
Unemployment Insurance Act (12 & 13 Geo.5, c.7)

1924
Unemployment Insurance Act (No.2) (14 & 15 Geo. 5, c.84)

1925
Unemployment Insurance Act (15 & 16 Geo.5, c.69)

1927
Unemployment Insurance Act (17 & 18 Geo., 5, c.30)

1930
Unemployment Insurance Act (20 Geo. 5, c.16)

1934
Unemployment Act (24 & 25 Geo.5, c.29)

1944
Education Act (7 & 8 Geo.6, c.31)

1945
Family Allowances Act (8 & 9 Geo.6, c.62)

1946
National Insurance Act (9 & 10 Geo.6, c.67)

1948
National Assistance Act (11 & 12 Geo.6, c.29)

1956
Family Allowances and National Insurance Act (c.50)

1964
Family Allowances and National Insurance Act (c.10)

1965
National Insurance Act (c.51)

1966
Ministry of Social Security Act/Supplementary Benefit Act (c.20)

1975
Social Security Act (c.14)
Child Benefit Act (c.61)

1976
Supplementary Benefits Act (c.71)

1977
Social Security (Miscellaneous Provisions) Act (c.5)
Finance Act (c.36)

1979
Finance Act (c.25)

1980
Social Security Act (c.30)

1986
Social Security Act (c.50)
Wages Act (c.48)

1987
Abolition of Domestic Rates (Scotland) Act (c.47)

1988
Social Security Act (c.7)
Employment Act (c.19)
Local Government Finance Act (c.41)

Table of statutory instruments

1944
Compulsory School Age (Postponement) Order (S,R & O 1944 No.979)

1948
National Assistance (Determination of Needs) Regulations (SI 1948 No.1334)

1976
Child Benefit (General) Regulations (SI 1976 No.965)

1977
Social Security (Students) Regulations (SI 1977 No.619)

1980
Supplementary Benefit (Single Payments) Regulations (SI 1980 No.985)
Supplementary Benefit (Requirements) Regulations (SI 1980 No.1299)
Supplementary Benefit (Conditions of Entitlement) Regulations (SI 1980 No.1586)

1981
Supplementary Benefit (Conditions of Entitlement) Regulations (SI 1981 No.1526)
Supplementary Benefit (Single Payments) Regulations (SI 1981 No.1528)

1982
Child Benefit (General) Amendment Regulations (SI 1982 No.470)
Supplementary Benefit (Miscellaneous Amendments) Regulations (SI 1982 No.907)

1983
Supplementary Benefit (Miscellaneous Amendments) Regulations (SI 1983 No.1000)
Supplementary Benefit (Requirements) Regulations (SI 1983 No.1399)
Social Security (Unemployment, Sickness and Invalidity Benefit) Regulations (SI 1983 No.1598)

1984
Supplementary Benefit (Miscellaneous Amendments) Regulations (SI 1984 No.938)
Social Security (Severe Disablement Allowance) Regulations (SI 1984 No.1303)
Supplementary Benefit (Requirements) Amendment and Temporary Provisions Regulations (SI 1984 No.2034)

1985
Supplementary Benefit (Requirements and Resources) Miscellaneous Provisions Regulations (SI 1985 No.613)
Supplementary Benefit (Requirements and Resources) Miscellaneous Provisions (No.2) Regulations (SI 1985 No.1835)

1986
Housing Benefit (Amendment No.3) Regulations (SI 1986 No.1009)
Supplementary Benefit (Conditions of Entitlement) Amendment Regulations (SI 1986 No.1010)
Supplementary Benefit (Miscellaneous Amendments) Regulations (SI 1986 No.1259)
Supplementary Benefit (Requirements and Resources) Miscellaneous Amendment Regulations (SI 1986 No.1293)
Social Security (Unemployment, Sickness and Invalidity Benefit) Amendment (No.2) Regulations (SI 1986 No.1611)

1987
Supplementary Benefit (Conditions of Entitlement) Amendment Regulations (SI 1987 No.358)
Social Fund Maternity and Funeral Expenses (General) Regulations (SI 1987 No.481)
Income Support (General) Regulations (SI 1987 No.1967)

Housing Benefit (General) Regulations (SI 1987 No.1971)

1988

Unemployment Benefits (Disqualification Period) Order (SI 1988 No.487)
Income Support (General) Amendment No,2 Regulations (SI 1988 No.910)
Social Security Act 1988 (Commencement) No.2 Order (SI 1988 No.1226)
Child Benefit (General) Amendment Regulations (SI 1988 No. 1227)
Income Support (General) Amendment No.3 Regulations (SI 1988 No.1228)
Income Support (Transitional) Regulations (SI 1988 No.1229)
Income Support (General) Amendment No.4 Regulations (SI 1988 No.1445)
Housing Benefit (Community Charge Rebates) (Scotland) Regulations (SI 1988 No.1890 (S.178))

1989

Personal Community Charge (Students) (Scotland) Regulations (SI 1989 No.32)

Table of cases and decisions of the Social Security Commissioners

I. Cases

Carleton v DHSS (1988) C.A. (N.I.) (unreported)
Chief Adjudication Officer v Brunt [1988] 1 All.E.R. 754
Clarke v Chief Adjudication Officer, *The Times* 25.6.87; (1987) *J.S.W.L.* 378
Drake v Chief Adjudication Officer [1986] 3 All E.R. 65
Gillick v West Norfolk and Wisbech A.H.A. and Another [1985] 3 All.E.R. 403
Jones v London County Council (1932) 30 L.G.R. 455
R v Barnsley Supplementary Benefit Appeal Tribunal *ex parte* Atkinson [1977] 1 W.L.R. 917
R v DHSS *ex parte* Camden London Borough Council and Nelson, *The Times* 5.3.86.
R v Kensington & Chelsea London Borough Council *ex parte* Woolrich, *The Times* 1.9.87.
R v Secretary of State for Social Services *ex parte* Cotton, *The Times* 14.12.85 (C.A.)
R v Secretary of State for Social Services and Chief Adjudication Officer *ex parte* Elkington 22.7.86 (unreported)
Sampson v Supplementary Benefits Commission (1979) *Sol.J* 284

II. Decisions of the Social Security Commissioners

CF 38/83
CSB 15/82
CSB 176/1987
CSSB 221/1986
R(P) 3/85
R(SB) 4/81
R(SB) 11/81
R(SB) 16/81
R(SB) 26/82
R(SB) 40/83
R(SB) 41/83
R(SB) 8/84
R(SB) 8/86
R(SB) 22/87
R(SB) 25/87
R(SB) 10/88

Abbreviations

AO	adjudication officer
CAO	Chief Adjudication Officer
CPAG	Child Poverty Action Group
CSBO	Chief Supplementary Benefits Officer
DES	Department of Education and Science
DHSS	Department of Health & Social Security
DSS	Department of Social Security
EMA	Educational Maintenance Allowance

Green Paper *Reform of Social Security* (Cmnds 9517-19, 1985)

HB	Housing Benefit
HC	House of Commons
HL	House of Lords
LEA	local education authority
MSC	Manpower Services Commission
NA	National Assistance
NAB	National Assistance Board
NUS	National Union of Students
SB	Supplementary Benefit(s)
SBC	Supplementary Benefits Commission
SSAC	Social Security Advisory Committee
UA	Unemployment Assistance
UB	Unemployment Benefit

White Paper *Social Security: A Programme for Action* (Cmnd 9691, 1985)

YOP	Youth Opportunities Programme
YTS	Youth Training Scheme

Introduction – youth and social security: the issues

Social security in the United Kingdom had a budget of £47.8bn (32 per cent. of all public expenditure) and provided, amongst other things, means-tested benefits to 9 million people in 1987/88. In April 1988 the benefits system entered a critical phase in its history following the implementation of the Social Security Act 1986 reforms. These reforms, discussed in later chapters, included the introduction of an Income Support scheme, a Social Fund, and a revised Housing Benefit scheme. Although the Conservatives' social security reforms of the 1980s may well have taken the welfare state into a critical transition phase, their approach to social welfare can probably still be described as falling within the 'liberal' tradition. But there has been a discernable shift in policy to the right during the Thatcher years; a reduced role for the state in the provision of welfare is seen as desirable (under the 'New Right liberalism' : King 1987, p.110). The government's vision is of a society in Britain characterised by enterprise, freedom of choice for the individual and personal self-sufficiency. The 'culture of dependency' on welfare benefits is under attack. Public expenditure remains tightly-reined. What are the implications for the many young people who will continue to need and seek support from the social security system? This is one of the principal questions which will be considered in this book.

The latest reforms continue the rationalisation of social security which has been undertaken progressively during the Thatcher years (which commenced in 1979). Many of the reforms instituted between 1980 and 1987 produced a reduction in benefits provision for young people. Yet among the unemployed, young people became the social security system's largest client group. Meanwhile a policy of youth training has continued to be pursued vigorously and still occupies a central position in the government's employment strategy. For young people entering higher education, as increasing numbers did in the 1970s and '80s, student support has decreased in real terms, while students' social security benefits have been cut back.

In the light of all these developments it is important, as we move into the 1990s, both to reflect on the developments in young people's support which have taken place over the past decade or so and to consider what might be the future prospects for social security in this era of increasingly rapid economic and technological change and amid an apparently hostile political environment for public funding of welfare services.

The reforms introduced in April 1988 will clearly be central to much of the analysis in this book since their implications for young people are enormous, as we shall see in later chapters. When, in the Spring of 1985, far-reaching changes to social security in Britain were proposed, following a series of reviews, there was much talk of potential 'losers' and 'gainers'. The debate intensified as the date for implementation of the new scheme approached and continued after it had passed. The government suggested that around 88 per cent. of claimants would be no worse off under the changes. This figure was hotly disputed both in Parliament and elsewhere. (The Policy Studies Institute, in a statement issued in March 1988, said that it had assessed the non-losers as 52 per cent. of claimants.) But it had been predicted for some time that young people would be major losers. The government was hardly going to try to conceal the impact of the reforms on young people when the cutbacks were the product of a well-publicised, and up to a point mandated, deliberate and calculated policy.

In Green and White Papers published in 1985 the government set out its case for reform of social security. Among its arguments were the desirability of simplifying the bases of entitlement and targeting needs more effectively. As will be shown later, these aims were to be of critical importance for young people as their pursuit resulted in reduced provision for many unemployed persons aged under 25.

Before proceeding to outline the issues which fall to be considered when examining developments in social security for young people, I ought to explain what I mean by 'young people'. For the purposes of this book, 'young people' are those aged 16 or over (16 being the age at which young people can leave school and, until very recently, draw income support) but less than 21 (21 being the age at which, throughout much of the history of social security, adulthood has been deemed to start). But it has been necessary to include, at times, 14 and 15 year olds (14 was the school leaving age until 1947) and, more especially, 21-24 year olds. The latter age group are increasingly being treated as 'young people' rather than adults in the benefits system.

Choosing 'young people' as a social security client group to be studied presents three particular difficulties for the construction of a research model:

1. The ambiguous status of this age group, not just in relation to social security but in society as a whole. Thane (1981, p.6) says that '...in current British legal and administrative practice the dividing line between adults and young people is less clearly defined than might be expected'. This is said to be largely attributable to the 'apparent inconsistencies in social expectations of certain ages' (ibid., p.7). The product of this uncertainty is that young people fall to be considered under a wide variety of categories - such as dependant, non-dependant, trainee, student and employee - when attempting to define this 'dividing line' and/or reveal the extent of the uncertainty.

2. Linked very much to point 1. above, the fact that benefits provision for young people represents a highly complex area of social security law. The picture is confused by the number of changes that have taken place over the past decade, starting with the revised and heavily regulated supplementary benefit scheme post-November 1980.

3. Provision in respect of young dependants becomes tied in with that for other social security client groups. This means that in order to discuss the position of young people properly it is necessary to map out the various social security schemes in a certain amount of detail before singling out provision for young people for attention. This is not always a straightforward matter. But it is useful to examine provision in general under a scheme, to enable comparisons to be made between, for example, the entitlement of different age groups.

Despite these difficulties, an examination of young people's benefits at this juncture is, as indicated earlier, particularly apposite. It has to be appreciated that at a time of raging unemployment in the 1980s young people have been the worst affected of all age groups. For example, in October 1986 35.4 per cent. of the registered unemployed were aged 16-24 compared with 24.1 per cent. aged 25-34, 13.7 per cent. aged 45-54, and 11.6 per cent. aged 55 or over (*Employment Gazette*, Jan. 1987, p.S26, Table 2.7.). So, given the size of the social security budget as a whole, young people's benefits involve considerable amounts of public expenditure - despite the apparent beginnings of a downward trend in youth unemployment at the present time.

Various issues require examination in a comprehensive analysis of young people's benefits. These will now be outlined.

The childhood-adulthood divide

One of the central themes of this book concerns social security and the transition of young people out of childhood and into adulthood, in the context of social security entitlement. Social security law, in common with other areas of the law, has always adopted a distinction between childhood and adulthood.

Children have tended to be viewed as dependants of their families, receiving support from the state only indirectly, via provision to parents. But support for children was not a feature of early poverty relief schemes. Indeed, children were expected to earn a living as soon as they were physically able and contribute to the family's finances. Over the years, child labour has been severely curtailed, and as the twentieth century has progressed the financial burden of rearing children, increased by extensions to the period of compulsory education, has progressively been recognised in benefits provision - for example, through dependency additions to benefits such as unemployment benefit and supplementary benefit paid to the unemployed, through the universal family allowance/child benefit paid to families, and through means-tested family income supplement/family credit.

Childhood gives way to a stage in which a young person comes to be recognised as an independent individual with personal entitlement. It will be demonstrated later in this book that social security does not embrace a coherent policy in relation to the transition out of childhood and into adulthood. A distinction has been drawn between 'normative' and 'institutional' criteria for recognition of adulthood or childhood. The former define childhood in terms of stages of physiological and psychological development of the individual. The latter are based on, in particular, generalised legal definitions turning on 'the nature of the issues democratically decided in [a] society and the nature of the democratic procedures employed' (Wringe 1981, p.122). Chronological age is the principal institutional criterion on which the childhood/adulthood distinction tends to be based.

While accepting that it is difficult to know where to draw the age dividing line between childhood and adulthood in law, there are reasons for at least questioning the basis for the childhood/adulthood division which applies in social security law. In fact, given that the object of the present author's investigation has been to identify not only the benefit arrangements which have been made for young people but also the perceptions and assumptions on which they are based, an assessment of the appropriateness of the age criterion for conferment of adult status in the context of social security seems both inevitable and essential. On the basis that independence in particular, is, in psychological terms, associated with the normative side of the transition to adulthood, it is necessary to ascertain the degree of independence attributed to young people under the evolving benefits system and how the policy makers and legislators have perceived the relationship between young people and their families.

Assumptions and values

There are a number of assumptions and values underlying social security provision which are of particular significance where young people are concerned. Many of these assumptions and values are long-standing and have pervaded the benefits system more or less throughout its history. Such continuities include the principle of family responsibility and the work ethic, which are expanded upon later in this Introduction. These long-standing principles inter-act with often short-term government policies which can have the effect of giving giving greater prominence to certain values or assumptions or promoting new ones. These policies are often responses to (initially at least) short-term or immediate economic and/or social problems. Thus, so far as social security for young people is concerned, the questions which arise are: Which values and assumptions have shaped, and are shaping, provision for this age group? How have they affected provision? What impact have government policies, for example those relating to unemployment, had on the way that these assumptions and values have been applied to young people's benefits?

1. *Assumptions*

As noted earlier, the treatment of the relationship between young people and their families is a central issue in this book. Thus assumptions about the family are a particular concern. It has been said that 'many assumptions about the family...underlie contemporary social policy' (Rimmer and Wicks 1983, p.34). Since the family (in its nuclear form: Harris 1983, p.91) is still the basic social unit in industrialised society ('the family has never been rejected; it has merely changed in form': Kay 1972, p.7-8) these particular assumptions are obviously very important. Indeed,

> The entire structure of the 'welfare state' as it has evolved depends on a set of implicit assumptions concerning the responsibility which families assume, or are expected to assume, for their members and the conditions under which this responsibility must either be shared with or taken over by society (Moroney 1976, p.4).

Although assumptions in social welfare which relate to families are normally implicit, they are sometimes very close to the surface (Rimmer and Wicks 1983, p.34). One of the most obvious of assumptions relating to families with young people is also the most significant. It is the assumption that at least until young people reach a certain age or stage of entry to the labour market (often referred to in official terms as becoming 'economically active'), they are, for the most part, the financial responsibility of their families. This may be termed the *dependency assumption* relating to young people. A stage in a young person's life is eventually reached when the welfare state regards the dependency assumption as no longer applicable and confers independent (if not exactly 'adult') status on him/her. The operation of this dependency assumption is explored in this book. Also, an attempt is made to determine how far the view that 'legislation and policy sometimes assumes a model...which does not match reality' (Rimmer 1981, p.67) is applicable to the assumptions concerning young people and their families underlying many aspects of social security law.

The dependency assumption relating to young people operates within social security's mechanism for the assessment of needs - the means test - 'the harsh symbol of public welfare services in the twentieth century' (National Consumer Council 1976, p.79) which remains 'rampant' (Mesher 1985b, p.94). However, this assumption is not confined to means-tested benefits; it is also relevant to a major universal benefit - child benefit - and, indeed, runs across the full range of social security benefits.

It is, of course, one of a number of such 'dependency assumptions', of which perhaps the most fully documented is that relating to 'dependent (house-)wives'/male 'bread-winners'. It has been pointed out that the assumption that women will be carers rather than breadwinners was built into the recommendations of the Beveridge Report (despite the fact that family allowances, in being paid to mothers, made a small inroad into that assumption) (Clarke et al. 1987, Chapter 7; Wilson 1977, pp.152-4). This assumption has continued to manifest itself in the benefits system, for example in the now abolished non-contributory invalidity pension, and invalid care allowance - the relevant provisions of which (transitional arrangements in the case of the former) were found to be contrary to EEC Directive 79/7 on equal treatment for men and women in social security (cases of *Drake* (1986) and *Clarke* (1987)). Land (1987) shows that assumptions about the dependency of women are also to be found in the changes to social security wrought by the Social Security Act 1986. The 'dependent wife' issue illustrates the pervasiveness of dependency assumptions and their resistance to change. However, the dependency assumption in relation to young people, whilst no less significant, has been less commented upon. It does, however, receive brief coverage in a recent paper by Hilary Land (1987), and was considered by the Family Policy Studies Centre (1988) in its paper on the minimum age of entitlement to income support. But much remains to be said on the subject.

There are related assumptions centred more directly on *the involvement of children in the economy of the family*. Various reforms of recent years have reduced the ability of the unemployed young person to contribute towards his/her family's finances and thus his/her own upkeep. In some cases the contribution a young person is expected to make is task-orientated. Working-class girls often 'pay their way' in the home by performing domestic duties (rather more than do boys) (Finn 1984, pp.49-52). But, as shown in Chapter 2, research confirms that young people, including those who are unemployed, are, regardless of any assumptions to the contrary, expected to contribute to their upkeep. The role of income transfers within families in the transition of young family members from childhood to adulthood requires examination in order that the impact of the level of social security support for young people can be more accurately assessed.

There are, of course, other assumptions underlying legal provision for income maintenance for young people. Among these are assumptions concerning *household formation and parenthood*. The increasing societal expectations of independence for youth, discussed in Chapter 2, are in many cases being matched by a desire among young people for parenthood and/or independent households. It seems that parenting and household formation are often sub-cultural responses by the young unemployed to unemployment, reflecting a desire for improved social status which is otherwise unobtainable and for an assumption of responsibility which is a perceived feature of adulthood. So, in Chapter 4, consideration is given to benefits provision for young people living in their own households and to benefits support for couples and parents (lone or otherwise).

It should be borne in mind that the assumption that young people will remain in the family home until work brings financial independence, and that they will refrain from parenting until then, perhaps shows little recognition of the fact that young people often want to form families of their own and frequently do so. But progress towards household formation is governed by, in particular, the resources of the individual. Circumstances often dictate that young people must live in the home of one set of parents. The young unemployed frequently lack the means for independent living. But on the other hand young people sometimes have to leave home, and here state support can be of particular importance.

The issues relating to family and household formation by the young unemployed are linked not only to assumptions about families but also to those about *the transition from school to working life*. For many years one of the assumptions around which social welfare provision has been based has been that young people enter employment or apprenticeship on leaving school. It is an assumption with a firm cultural base. There has, in particular, been an 'historical expectation among large numbers of the working-class population that children earn a living as soon as they are legally entitled' (Charles 1985, p.131). When employment opportunities have been rather limited, as in recent years (but also in the 1920s and '30s), government has continued to offer minimal social security support to young people as well as placing an emphasis on training for unemployment - to provide a bridge between school and work.

In the context of the educational values of the middle-classes, the widening time gap between school and work might not be seen as a problem but rather an opportunity for education or skills attainment. Hence reduced benefits support for students in higher education, the majority of whom are from so-called 'middle-class' homes (around 75 per cent. are from social classes one and two, and only 7 per cent. have parents in manual occupations: Judd 1988; DES 1988), has been justified partly in terms of students being only temporarily short of income while on their way to relatively prosperous careers (see Chapter 6). This is an argument which middle-class parents, whose values make for a view of education as the means to advancement and self-reliance, are unlikely to feel antagonistic towards, even if they dislike the greater financial burden pressed upon them. On the other hand, it could be argued that welfare provision, like the education system, has 'never taken into account [the] material culturalism of growing up in the working-class':

> Gaining a wage to survive; hoping to enjoy some power as a buyer and consumer through the wage; going through the adolescent sexual dance and setting up the working class home in straitened circumstances ...these are the real themes of working class apprenticeship to adulthood in our society (Clarke and Willis 1984, p.11).

Clarke and Willis argue that class is one of the factors shaping the transition to adulthood; it can affect its length as well as the institutions or activities in which it is experienced.

Consideration of the assumptions concerning the transition from school to working life, and the impact of the training schemes and of reduced social security support to encourage participation in training, occurs in Chapters 2 and 7.

Finally, there is the assumption, affecting all kinds of welfare benefits provision, about the amount of money that people, and in this case young people, need to maintain what might be termed a minimum standard of living.

The questions which have to be considered are not only how the various assumptions relating to young people have coloured the benefit arrangements made for them, but also what has been the effect on young people not in employment, and on their families, of applying these assumptions to welfare benefits provision?

2. *Values*

The shape of benefits provision is determined more fundamentally and subtly by the values which underlie social security arrangements. Despite the significant changes which have taken place under the Social Security Act 1986 reforms, the revised scheme has been built on principles which have for so long, in some cases back to the Act for the Relief of the Poor of 1601, qualified the state's response to poverty. One of these, and particularly influential, is the *work ethic*, which rests on a conviction that those capable of doing so should work, for the support of themselves and their families. The work ethic manifests itself in social security law in various places.

First, there are rules under which voluntary unemployment is penalised. Similar rules apply to those refusing or prematurely leaving, a training place and they have been applied to a number of young people in recent years (see Chapter 7). The appropriateness or otherwise of these rules and of extensions to the benefit disqualification or reduction periods are considered later in this book.

Secondly, the rate of benefit, set and varied by statutory instrument, is deliberately kept below minimum wage levels so that no worker (save for those caught by the 'unemployment trap') is better off out of work. Again, the impact on young people of this aspect of provision, especially in the context of the payment of training allowances which exceed benefit rates, and the generally depressed level of young people's wages, requires consideration. But the rate of benefit paid to young people also needs to be compared with the adult rate, to see in particular whether replacement ratios (i.e. the ratio of the replacement income (while unemployed) to the normal income (when in work)) differ appreciably. It will be demonstrated that not only have young people's benefits fallen well short of those paid to adults since the introduction of unemployment insurance in 1912, but also that their replacement ratio tends to be rather lower. It could be argued that the reason for this policy of keeping young people's benefit levels at a minimum goes beyond the aim of enhancing the incentive to work and in fact relates to what some see as an attempt to lower their expectations and reinforce the subservience of youth. Youth are made to wait for release into the adult world of independence and material satisfaction - a delay to which the training schemes and their sub-wage level allowances may also contribute (Finn 1984, pp.29-31). This emphasises, perhaps, the vulnerability of unemployed youth in the public policy context.

Returning to the work ethic, the third way in which it is embodied in social security law is via the availability for work requirement, a long-standing condition of entitlement and a marked continuity. Compulsory registration at a labour exchange, signifying availability for and willingness to accept work, accompanied the introduction of unemployment insurance (under the National Insurance Act 1911) and has remained ever since, despite cosmetic changes. Such is the level of government concern about voluntary unemployment today, that perhaps not since the 'genuinely seeking work' test of the inter-war period (under which the claimant had to prove that he was 'genuinely seeking whole-time employment but unable to obtain such employment' - see Ogus and Barendt 1982, p.101-2) has there been such a positive effort to apply the work ethic through social security (see Chapter 7). Government thinking, exemplified by the decision to remove benefit entitlement from under 18 year olds, seems to have been coloured by what Dilnot, Kay and Morris (1984, pp.56-7) refer to as 'fears that incentives to seek or retain work are being blunted by an over-generous benefit system' (training being regarded as the equivalent of work). This raises the question, considered in Chapter 7, of whether these fears are, in the context of young people's entitlement, wholly justified.

The available for work condition is also applied to young claimants (subject to certain exceptions) who are filling the usually indeterminite waiting period for employment by studying for further qualifications (which can hasten entry to employment). The application of this aspect of the work ethic to those in education, particularly with regard to distinguishing between cases of availability and non-availability, has been problematical (see Chapter 6).

Another value underlying benefits provision is, of course, *'family responsibility'*. This is based on the notion that families should assume responsibility for the welfare of their members rather than looking to the state to provide for them. If this value has affected not only the development of social security in the past, but, more particularly, recent policy, the question which must then be asked is how realistic is it to expect families to provide for their young unemployed offspring? (The reader will note that we are returning here to the assumptions about families and the dependence/independence issue, discussed earlier.)

Historical context

As mentioned above, many of the assumptions within, and indeed values enforced by, the social security system today are rooted in the history of the system, and it is principally for this reason that at various points, especially in Chapter 3, there is an examination of the history of the relevant social security schemes, with particular reference to provision for young people. What will be revealed is that many of these assumptions and values have held a firm position in the social security system as a whole for at least 50 years, and in some cases since the Poor Law. Also, much of the complexity and contradiction evident in benefits provision for young people today originates from the disjointed provision, for this age group, in the post-war reforms consequent on the Beveridge Report (1942).

An exploration of relevant developments in the early decades of this century provides an opportunity to make comparisons between the state's response to similar phenomena in different eras - in the case of this study, youth unemployment in the inter-war period and in the 1970s and '80s. There are some reasons for doubting the appropriateness of such comparisons - notably the differences in the economic and political environments and in the structure of unemployment (but perhaps not in the characteristics of youth unemployment). However,

> ...this does not argue that nothing can be learned about the contemporary situation from an examination of the earlier period... there are straightforward similarities in the response of the state to the problem of unemployment among young people during the two periods (Rees and Rees 1982, p.13).

These responses have included some important developments in social security provision for young people.

Young people and the state

In both the inter-war period and, more especially, in the past two decades, there have been high levels of unemployment which have had significant consequences for families and their members, and for society as a whole. In recent years (as in the early 1930s) enormous demands have been placed on the social security system, provoking a number of government measures to ease the resultant difficulties. The emphasis on public expenditure restraint in the past decade has been particularly felt by the social security system and its clients. Young people have become major clients at a time when the system has been, and is, with the Social Security Act 1986 reforms, undergoing significant change. Many of the reforms are having, and will increasingly have, a major effect on young people's benefit entitlement, as noted earlier. Moreover, social security policy in recent years has aimed to shake some of the assumptions about the role of the state in assisting young people, especially those not in employment. Provision has tended to be minimised to inculcate a spirit of self-reliance. At the same time, the political costs of mass unemployment have resulted in forms of intervention which conflict with the traditional areas of support.

Youth unemployment levels of recent years have led to a high measure of state interference through a youth training policy. Acceptance of a life of dependence on welfare benefits by young people has been regarded as anathema by the successive Conservative administrations of the 1980s - thus leading to a measure of compulsion, via the social security system, to force the young out of idleness and into training. (This illustrates the way that government policies can serve to give greater prominence to long-term assumptions and values underlying social security provision (in this case, the work ethic value).) This element of compulsion raises questions about the freedom of young people to choose between the various options which, in theory, are open to them when they reach school leaving age.

State intervention in response to mass youth unemployment has in fact had a critical influence on the status of the young unemployed and their relationship with the state. Indeed it has been suggested that youth unemployment policies, with their 'attempted absorption of large sections of this pauperised generation' within 'institutional constraints' such as training (and one might add to this the enforced dependence of the young unemployed on their families as a result of government social security policies) reflect a 'new political definition of youth' (Finn 1984, p.60). The consequences of applying this definition will be considered later.

The nature of social security provision for young people raises broad questions about various aspects of their status. One such aspect is their ability to participate in society. This raises the question of *citizenship*. It will be demonstrated that young people's greater financial independence from the late nineteenth century onwards paved the way towards an improved status which culminated in the lowering of the age of majority to 18 in 1972. (This was to have an impact across a range of legal rights - see Latey 1967.) The age basis of rights to democratic participation may, in fact, be compared with that determining entitlement to benefits (or higher rates of benefit), particularly in view of the upward movement of the minimum age of entitlement. Wringe (1981, p.122) asserts that in setting the age of majority

> the appropriate age must be one at which the majority of individuals are judged to have attained the relevant capacities in view of the need to exclude from participation any significant numbers of those who have not.

There is a clear parallel between this argument and, for example, the official arguments presented for the age 25 split in income support rates (see Chapter 4).

It is possible that a wider concept of citizenship exists in which it is seen not merely in relation to specific legal rights of democratic participation, sexual activity, marriage, alcohol purchase, etc., but also in a more general sense in relation to the ability of young people to play an active role in society. It has been suggested that in Western Europe young people have been pushed to the edges of the social structure, largely as a result of unemployment (Fragniere 1985). There is a view which holds that the right to receive welfare benefits has the effect of 'enlarging the citizenship' of the unemployed (Street 1981, p.295). The question of citizenship for young people is discussed in Chapter 8.

I have touched on the main issues which will be explored in the chapters that follow. These issues are wide-ranging, whilst inter-connected, and are centred on a benefits system which is characterised by legal complexity and, at times, uncertainty. It was considered to be most appropriate, in the interests of clarity and contextual understanding, to look at 'clusters' of issues around broad themes before drawing the various threads together in a concluding section.

The first 'cluster' is concerned with delayed entry into employment (Part I). Here there is an examination of treends in youth unemployment and participation in further and higher education, and their effect on the demand for social security. A context is provided in which later to evaluate critically the nature and extent of social security provision for this age group.

A further, central theme is the role of social security in the transition to adulthood (Part II). Not only must the nature of this transition be understood (Chapter 2), but the impact of unemployment and social security on it requires careful examination (Chapter 5). In this context, the role of the various longer-term assumptions relating to the dependency of young people on their families, and the associated principle of family responsibility, are considered by looking at manifestations of them in the evolving social security system in the twentieth century (Chapters 3 and 4).

The third cluster is concerned with the various issues surrounding the role of the benefits system in the context of education and employment policy (Part III). Having demonstrated in Part I how, at least in terms of the numbers claiming, social security has become so important to so many persons continuing or resuming their education beyond the age of 16, it became possible to look at government responses to this area of demand and assess their implications (Chapter 6). These issues required consideration in conjunction with government youth employment policy (Chapter 7), which, as mentioned earlier, has increasingly been based on the training programmes.

The final part of the book (Part IV) contains the conclusions of this examination of social security for young people in Britain. The author sets out the principles which, in his view, ought to underlie reform of young people's benefits.

PART I
DELAYED EMPLOYMENT AND THE DEMAND FOR SOCIAL SECURITY

PART I

1 Patterns of demand for social security

Introduction

The school-to-work transition has tended to form the basis of our conception of 'youth'. At various times in the twentieth century, notably the periods of high unemployment during the past two decades and in the 1920s and '30s, this transition has become protracted. In recent years the problem has been particularly acute. Although a decline in youth unemployment in the 1990s is predicted, the fact remains that at present life without work is the immediate prospect for some 38 per cent. of school leavers (H.C. Employment Committee 1988, Annex 2) - well in excess of any corresponding figures in the inter-war years. The pressures on the social security system were different then, as was the emphasis on compulsory unemployment insurance - which is of little relevance to today's young unemployed. This does not mean to say that there is not some value in comparing and contrasting patterns of youth unemployment in both eras; for a context is provided for an evaluation of government responses, including social security policy.

Unemployment is not the only factor influencing the demand for social security. At the present time 48 per cent. of young people of school leaving age remain in full-time education (Mr K.Baker M.P., *H.C. Hansard*, Vol.140, col.308, 9.11.88). Although there are various types of support available - from educational maintenance allowances paid to parents to discretionary and mandatory awards paid to young people - there has come to be an increasing demand for social security support, largely as a result of the inadequacy of these awards.

A further factor influencing the demand for social security is the continuing development of the training schemes. Already, 16 and 17 year olds have just about lost the right to be described as 'unemployed' in any official sense, following the raising of the minimum age of entitlement to income support to 18. Further measures, relating to those aged 18 or over, are likely. Another important factor is the projected decline in the number of 16-19 year olds in the population.

Youth unemployment 1900-1939

Levels of youth unemployment

Around the turn of the century the chief concern with regard to young workers lay in their recruitment into so-called 'blind-alley' occupations such as biscuit-making, soap-making and weaving. In many such industries the number of juvenile employees exceeded the number of adults employed. A form of exploitation occurred in that 'many school leavers were being attracted by relatively high wages into employment requiring little or no skill, only to be dismissed as they reached their eighteenth birthdays and replaced by new school leavers' (Rees and Rees 1982, p.14). Thus, despite general concern about levels of youth unemployment in the first decade of the century, unemployment among 14 to 17 year olds was not considered a problem, and 'the difficulty arose in connection with the transition to more secure and skilled employment in the late teens' (Casson 1979, p.9).

After the First World War the problems associated with 'blind-alley' employment continued. During the period of widespread unemployment from 1929 onwards the phrase 'too old at sixteen' had a rather bitter significance for young people in the depressed areas. In the jute industry in Dundee one became 'too old at 18'. It was said, of the industry, that it 'offers attractive wages to boys of 14, but retains only a small proportion when they reach the age of 18' (U.A.B. 1939, p.168). In the 1920s and '30s, therefore, certain features of the juvenile labour market had changed very little since before the First World War, especially the fact that the unemployment rate among 14 and 15 year olds was much lower than among older children (Casson 1979, p.14). It was shown that at any one time almost twice as much unemployment was experienced by 21-23 year olds as by 14-17 year olds (Scottish Youth Advisory Committee 1945, para. 45). One report suggested that youth unemployment arising out of 'blind alley' work was being reinforced by the unemployment insurance scheme in that employers were faced with paying unemployment insurance contributions in respect of their young workers when the latter became 16 (Save the Children Fund 1933, p.74).

There was escalating youth unemployment in the 1920s (especially the early years - there was an improvement in the second half of the decade, before the slump in 1929). In 1929 the world economy entered recession. It soon became apparent that the employment prospects of school leavers had become very poor, and by the early 1930s there were considerable numbers of young people who had not had a steady job for several years (Casson 1979, p.13).

When analysing the statistical data on youth unemployment levels during this period, it is important to bear in mind the fact that the official unemployment statistics of the 1920s and '30s are not regarded as all that accurate. They are based on the numbers registering at the labour exchanges; but 'the coverage of the register was indefinite and unknown' and so there is 'no means of determining what proportion of the real level of unemployed insured juveniles was represented' (Garside 1979, p.529). Also, until 1934 the register consisted almost entirely of insured unemployed juveniles, but it was impossible to discover how many uninsured young people aged under 16 registered voluntarily. Until 1935, 14-15 year olds were excluded from the unemployment insurance scheme and were not included in the official unemployment figures. They were regarded as too few in number to be statistically significant - because it was assumed that most 16 year olds had obtained *some* employment in the two years after leaving school. Garside suggests that this, and the method of counting, produced a serious under-estimation of the size of the problem.

With these reservations in mind, rates calculated from figures recorded in the *Ministry of Labour Gazette* can be considered. They show that youth unemployment rose steadily from 1929-1932 and then more or less levelled off as economic recovery occurred. The rates among boys and girls (the latter in italics) were as follows: 1929 - 3.3 (*3.3*) per cent; 1930 - 6.8 (*6.4*) per cent; 1931 - 7.5 (*5.8*) per cent; 1932 - 8.0 (*6.1*) per cent; from 1933-1935 the rate stabilised at around 5 (*4.5*) per cent. (Source: Monthly return, *Ministry of Labour Gazette*, Dec. 1929-Dec. 1935.)

It has been argued that the youth unemployment rate was not bad given economic conditions at the time, and that adults suffered higher rates of unemployment (Benjamin and Kochin 1979, p.526). In 1935 the unemployment rate among persons aged 21-24 was 12.4 per cent., while the rate for 16-17 year olds was just 5.1 per cent. (*Ministry of Labour Gazette* December 1935, p.480) - although in the more depressed areas the juvenile unemployment rate was very high (see below). Overall, youth unemployment was a major feature of the economic scene at the time. The unemployment rate among juveniles in the early 1930s might have been even higher but for the reduction in the supply of juvenile labour caused by the fall in the birth rate between 1915 and 1917 (*Ministry of Labour Gazette* Nov. 1933, p.396).

Regional variations

Unemployment (including youth unemployment) at this time was disproportionately concentrated in certain regions of the country, notably the declining industrial regions. (An almost identical picture emerged in the late 1970s - see below.) This was confirmed both by official statistics and the surveys by Jewkes and Winterbottom, (1933) and Cameron, Lush and Meara (*Disinherited Youth*, 1940). Unemployment among 16-17 year olds in 1931, for example, stood at the rate of 4.1 per cent. (boys) and 2.7 per cent. (girls) in the South-East, compared with 10.0 per cent. (boys) and 8.1 per cent. (girls) in the North-East of England (*Ministry of Labour Gazette* Dec.1931, p.479). Indeed, figures for all of the Northern regions and Wales show above average recorded levels of youth unemployment.

Within regions there were also variations. A 1930 social survey of Merseyside showed that 20 per cent. of male, and 30 per cent. of female, school leavers were unemployed, and Jewkes and Jewkes' (1938) survey of Lancaster school leavers revealed unemployment rates of between 17 and 36 per cent. (cited by Sawdon, Pelican and Tucker 1981, vol.1, para.1.2.).

Save the Children Fund (1933, p.70) prepared a useful statistical breakdown of regional unemployment in two years, 1927 and 1933. In general, levels of adult unemployment were higher than those relating to juveniles. But in areas with high levels of unemployment in 1927 juveniles suffered more, pro rata. Increases between 1927-33 were suffered by both groups, but for adults the increases were greater. Variations in regions were such that, for example, in 1927 the unemployment rate among juveniles was 3.3 per cent. in Leeds, 5.7 per cent. in Bradford, 14.1 per cent. in Rotherham and 16 per cent. in Dewsbury. By 1933, juvenile unemployment in these Yorkshire towns had increased by around 25 per cent. But in the North-East it had doubled since 1927.

These regional variations, and especially the emergence of unemployment 'blackspots', were among the major conditions which determined the nature of the state's response to the youth unemployment problem of this era.

Duration of unemployment

Figures in respect of young people entering the unemployment insurance scheme up to July 1929, showing the number of days benefit drawn, suggest that unemployment was not particularly long-term (*Ministry of Labour Gazette*, Sept. 1932, p.321). Apparently, the maximum amount of benefit that could have been drawn varied between 315 and 435 days. The figures show that approximately 65 per cent. of boys and 69 per cent of girls drew not more than 100 days of benefit, and that the majority drew not more than 50 days benefit. The increase in unemployment during 1930 (above) was said to have resulted from its spread to a much larger number of individuals who became intermittently employed (sic), rather than from the lengthening of the period of unemployment among a slightly increased number of boys and girls (ibid.)

A later statistical return showed that 58 per cent. of applicants for unemployment assistance aged 30 and under had had no employment, or less than six months employment, in the previous three years (U.A.B. 1939, p.45). This entrenched long term unemployment appeared mainly to be suffered by young people who had been the victims of 'blind alley' employment, who had few marketable skills, and who, after the age of 18 had 'forgotten most of what they had learnt at school' (ibid., p.46). Casson (1979, p.28) noted a distinction between the more favourable employment experiences of skilled than of unskilled workers. When an investigation was undertaken in Edinburgh into the age at which prolonged unemployment first became a serious risk it was discovered that over 50 per cent. of cases involved the 18-22 age group (U.A.B. 1939, p.168).

Reaction to youth unemployment levels

Concern was expressed throughout the 1930s at the level of, and problems associated with, youth unemployment. Youth unemployment was blamed for increased delinquency (Rees and Rees 1932, pp.17-8); and even Save the Children Fund, which felt that juvenile crime was 'mostly due to the influence of bad companions', held the opinion that 'as unemployment gets less some decrease in juvenile crime may be expected' (1933, p.33). The U.A.B. asserted (1939, p.44) that '[t]he prolonged unemployment of young people at an age when their opportunities of obtaining work should be at a maximum is a matter of grave social concern'. The government, prompted as much by fear of disorder as by meeting the labour needs of industry, embarked on a programme of juvenile instruction and industrial transference, reinforced by social security rules (see Chapter 7).

Improved employment prospects in the mid- to late 1930s

By the mid- to late 1930s unemployment levels had fallen. In 1938 there was a slight increase in unemployment (*Ministry of Labour Gazette* 1938, p.473), but the outbreak of war in 1939 soon brought the problem to an end. The improvement in the economy from 1932 onwards had led to an increased demand for youth labour. As mentioned earlier, the fall in the birth rate in 1915-17 meant that fewer young workers were available in the early 1930s. Both factors had led to reduced levels of youth unemployment. Compared to adult workers, young workers are generally expected to be disproportionately affected by fluctuations in the economy. So there are likely to be particularly improved prospects of employment for them when economic recovery occurs. Casson observed (1979, p.29) that 'long-term unemployment among school-leavers has been a transitory phenomenon, typically emerging in the later phases of a recession and disappearing as soon as an upturn begins'. At the time of writing, there does appear to be a measure of economic recovery. Will the decline in youth unemployment such as there was in the 1930s be repeated? This question is considered later.

Youth unemployment 1939-1988

The period up to the mid-1960s

During the Second World War the incidence of unemployment was negligible. In Britain in 1944 five million people were either in the armed forces or working in munitions (Deacon 1981, p.62). In the first nine months of 1944 there were reported to have been no claims for unemployment assistance in Rugby and Reading (ibid., p.63). After the war an acute shortage of labour ensured a virtual absence of unemployment.

Between 1948 and 1966 the rate of unemployment averaged 1.7 per cent., and for much of the period the numbers of long-term unemployed were very small. Few young people were unemployed for more than a few weeks and the duration of young people's unemployment was on average far shorter than that of older age groups. For example, 57 per cent. of unemployed under 18 year olds had been continuously unemployed for not more than four weeks compared with 45 per cent. of unemployed 18-20 year olds (*Ministry of Labour Gazette*, July 1949, p.231). In 1960 only 5,100 young persons received unemployment benefit and/or national assistance. Such was the lack of concern about unemployment in general that 'little attention was paid to allegations of malingering or scrounging. Similarly, there was virtually no pressure to reduce benefits for the unemployed' (Deacon 1981, p.69). (Nevertheless, national assistance rates for young people did fall relative to wages and adult rates of assistance.)

The mid-1960s

The 1960s saw a change in this situation. Deacon says (ibid., p.70) that '[t]he idea of a turning point is always dubious and it is impossible to point to a single date on which attitudes begin to change'. Nevertheless, he cites the deflationary measures introduced by the Labour government in July 1966 as being of particular significance since they heralded not only a doubling of unemployment within four months, but also an acceptance that some unemployment would be necessary for the economy to advance. The number of young people receiving benefits rose from 7,000 in Aug. 1966 to 16,000 in Aug. 1967. Youth unemployment had, in fact, been rising steadily (but with some fluctuations) since 1962/3, and at a faster rate than adult unemployment. But the explanations for this phenomenon in the 1960s, voluntary job-changing by young workers and less financial pressure on them to hold down a job compared with other age groups, do not help us understand why so many young people came to be unemployed in the 1970s and '80s.

The 1970s

The divergence between youth and adult rates of unemployment increased dramatically after 1970. Even when there was an expected reduction in youth unemployment following the raising of the school leaving age in 1972, youth unemployment rates remained higher than adult rates. In 1971 the rates were approximately 5.5 per cent. (young people) and 3.5 per cent. (adults). By 1977 the rates had risen to 10 and 6 per cent. respectively, and in 1980 the rates stood at 12 and 7 per cent. (see Hirsch 1983, p.31). A 1978 study by the Department of Employment revealed the responsiveness of youth unemployment to changes in the economy. The research showed that an increase of one percentage point in the rate of overall male unemployment would result in an increase in male youth unemployment of 1.7 percentage points. It was found that 'as overall unemployment rises, youth unemployment worsens relatively' (*Department of Employment Gazette* Aug. 1978, p.913). Thus, once the economy entered sharp recession after 1973, 16-19 year olds made up a disproportionately large section of the unemployed.

A period of particularly rapid growth in youth unemployment occurred between 1974-77. (There was also a sharp rise in 1979-80.) The numbers of young people aged under 20 and out of work rose as follows: 80,000 in July 1974; 390,000 in July 1976; 441,000 in July 1978; and 532,000 in July 1980 (Loney 1983, p.27). This rapid increase was not confined to Britain. In the EEC as a whole the number of young people out of work doubled between 1973 and 1976 and doubled again by 1980 (Watson 1983, p.3). While considerable increases in adult unemployment rates were also being recorded, it was said that 'perhaps the most disturbing aspect of all is the speed at which the numbers of young unemployed have risen' (ibid.). Although an examination of the causes of this rapid increase in youth unemployment lies outside the scope of this book, a brief explanation can be offered. The chief factor, aside from the general effects of the economic recession, appears to have been structural unemployment:

> Those sectors which young people traditionally enter when starting work for the first time, such as manufacturing, distribution, communication...

are exactly those industries which have experienced the greatest number of net job losses in the past decade (Atkinson and Rees 1982, p.3).

By the late 1970s this problem, which had emerged in the USA in the 1950s, had taken on world dimensions. Young people in particular were affected:

> In the summer of 1977, well over a million and a half western Europeans below the age of 25 were unable to find work. Substantial numbers of these young people were well educated and possessed of valuable skills, as, of course, were many jobless young Americans. However the preponderant majority were unskilled and poorly educated (Garraty 1978, p.259).

It has also been claimed that increases in young people's wages relative to adult workers' were making young people a less attractive proposition to employers. This argument has been rejected on the ground that during a period when youth unemployment snowballed, the relative value of young people's wages remained virtually constant (Hirsch 1983, p.27). Also rejected, although not unanimously, has been any suggestion that youth unemployment has been social security benefit-induced (see Chapter 7).

The 1980s

Beyond the late 1970s, youth unemployment continued to rise, both in Britain and elsewhere in Europe. It should be noted, however, that official figures for this country have been regarded as misleading. For one thing, young people on training schemes are not included in the official statistics. Youthaid (*Bulletin* No.23, Oct. 1985, p.12) showed that while official statistics revealed a rise in unemployment among under 18 year olds from 107,800 to 197,700 over the five years between Jan. 1979-85, an 83.4 per cent. increase, the increase was from 182,000 to 490,700, or 169.6 per cent., when YOP/YTS numbers were included. Another problem is that many statistical presentations contain a combined total for the 16-19 age group, whereas in reality patterns of employment and participation in education vary as between the separate age groups within this larger group. Further, invisible, factors have included an amount of unregistered youth unemployment (Roberts et al. 1981 - see Chapter 7 below) and a high incidence of part-time employment among young people (28 per cent. of young people in one cohort study: Courtenay 1988, p.22).

Despite the expansion of the Youth Opportunities Programme the unemployment rate among 16 and 17 year olds remained the highest rate for any age group between January 1978 and October 1980 (*Employment Gazette* Jan. 1981, Table 2.15). Recorded youth unemployment continued its steep and steady rise in the early 1980s. But in 1983 new methods of calculation in Britain made effective comparisons with previous years more or less impossible (see Feb. 1985 *Employment Gazette*, footnotes to tables 2.1 and 2.2; prior to the 1983 change to 'claimant unemployed' the 'registered unemployed' figures were used). (Note that other changes in the method of calculation have contributed significantly to reductions in the recorded totals.) Nevertheless, the percentage unemployment rates for the 16-24 age group as a whole remained the highest across the range of age groups (see above).

Regional, ethnic and gender factors

It was noted earlier that in the inter-war years there were considerable regional variations in youth unemployment levels. This pattern re-emerged in the recession of the 1970s and '80s. The regions with a 'rundown economy', such as the North, Scotland, Wales and the North-East, have had the highest figures. But the rate also increased in relatively prosperous areas like London, as the effects of the recession spread. At Christmas 1984 the unemployment rate among those who had entered the labour market the previous summer, after leaving school at the age of 16, was 78 per cent. in the Northern region, 75 per cent. in Wales, 58 per cent. in the South-West and 55 per cent. in London and the South-East (*H.C. Hansard*, cols 499-502w, 23.7.84). Disparities between youth unemployment rates in different towns within the same region, which was a feature of unemployment patterns in the 1920s and '30s, has also been in evidence (Hirsch 1983, p.8).

Youth unemployment has also been more heavily concentrated in ethnic/racial minority groups. A Department of Employment survey of unemployment rates among 16-24 year olds in 1985 (*Employment Gazette*, January 1987, p.27, Table 9) offered powerful evidence of this. The unemployment rate among white males and females was 18 and 15 per cent. respectively; but among West Indians the rates were 35 per cent. (M) and 33 per cent. (F). The rates for Indians were also higher than for whites: 28 per cent. (M) and 20 per cent. (F). Among Pakistani and Bangladeshi young people (males only) the rate was 37 per cent.

Unemployment levels among young females tend to be lower than among males. But it should, perhaps, be noted that there was a greater increase in female youth unemployment in the early 1980s than among males (Atkinson and Rees 1982, p.3; Sawdon et al. 1981 vol.II, p.104), thus narrowing the gap between the rates for each group. Interestingly, recent research (Courtenay 1988) has revealed that young males are more likely to be in receipt of benefit while unemployed than young females - 71 per cent. compared with 60 per cent. (in this particular survey). (No reason for this is offered.)

Duration of unemployment

In recent years young people have faced increasingly long periods of unemployment and reliance on benefits. Between July 1974 and July 1977 the number of 16-18 year olds in Scotland who had been out of work for six months or more rose from 625 to 6,835 (Gray, McPherson and Raffe 1983, p.146). In Britain the mean duration of unemployment for young people aged under 18 was less than three weeks in Jan. 1970, but by Jan. 1977 it had risen to over eleven weeks (Sorrentino 1981, pp175-6). As many as 62 per cent. of all 16 year old school leavers in the summer of 1983, and 64 per cent. in 1984, had not found work by the Christmas after leaving (Cusack and Roll 1985, pp.1-2). In their *Second Report, 1982/3*, the SSAC noted (para. 4.11) that 23 per cent. of the young unemployed had been jobless for a year or more, many of them having passed straight from school into unemployment. Although youth training was keeping significant numbers off the registers, it was regarded as merely delaying young people's entry into long-term unemployment rather than preventing it.

There was evidence, by 1985, that rise in youth unemployment was levelling off (even when YTS take-up was ignored). Yet long-term youth unemployment remained high. The government now claims that longer-term unemployment is falling 'sharply'. It is true that in the twelve months to October 1987 the numbers out of work for six months or more fell by 281,000 (Dept. of Employment 1988a, para.3.1.). However, there were still 350,000 18-24 year olds in long-term unemployment (ibid., para.3.3.).

Youth unemployment - the position now and in the future

Up until now, the decline in youth unemployment has largely been attributable to the expansion of the training programmes. Between 1984 and 1987 the proportion of the 16 year old age group who were unemployed fell from 13.0 to 10.7 per cent. YTS participants rose from 25.0 to 27.1 per cent. over the same period, and the proportion of the age group staying on in education stayed at 45 per cent. (SDP 1985, p.35, H.C. Employment Committee 1988, Annex 2). There was a small decline in the proportion of 16 year olds in employment over this period - from 18 to 16.7 per cent. But in the first half of the 1990s there will be far fewer young people in the population (see p.27 below).

Whatever the trends, youth unemployment levels continue to be high. Recent official statistics have shown that 529,000 under 20 year olds were unemployed and drawing benefit in Jan. 1986, 460,000 in Jan. 1987, and 349,000 in Jan. 1988 (*Employment Gazettes* April 1987 and May 1988, both Table 2.7). These levels have remained well in excess of those recorded in the inter-war years and which at the time gave rise to such concern (see Middlemass 1981, p.137).

In the mid-1970s youth unemployment was seen as a temporary phenomenon linked to demographic changes (the 'baby boom' of the early 1960s) and a downturn in the business cycle heralding short-term recession. But by the early 1980s it increasingly came to be recognised that high levels of youth unemployment were likely to continue for many years. There were strong doubts about the effectiveness of the training schemes, which were regarded as palliatives for unemployment. The proportion of YTS trainees who became unemployed on leaving the scheme remained at 30 per cent. or higher between April 1983 and Jan. 1986 (Youthaid *Bulletin* Nov./Dec. 1986, p.4). Nevertheless, the youth training programmes have continued to be expanded. The Youth Opportunities Programme (YOP) affected one in eight 16 year olds in 1978-9, one in six in 1979-80, and one in four in 1980-1 (Loney 1983, p.28). A total of 1.7 million young people entered the YOP between April 1979 and March 1984, keeping them off the dole for six months at a time; 647,000 16 and 17 year olds received training under the YTS in its first six months (*H.C. Hansard* vol.68 col.219w, 22.11.84). By March 1987 66 per cent. of labour market entrants aged 16-17 held a YTS place (H.C. Employment Committee 1988, Annex 2). The total number of young people in training on the YTS in September 1988 was 435,000 - a record number (Dept. of Employment 1988b, para.6.9). The expansion of youth training has various underlying political objectives (see Chapter 7 below). Recognition of the bleak employment prospects of less well qualified young people is, however, one factor, as is the government's expressed concern about the 'skills-gap' affecting British industry. The government has said that the latter is one of the problems which the new job training scheme for the long-term unemployed is aimed at combating.

It remains to be seen whether the training programmes make any significant inroads into unemployment in the future. In any event, the recent decision to make half a million YTS places available to 16 and 17 year olds and to remove entitlement to income support from this age group makes necessary a new definition of 'youth unemployment'.

The proposed removal of restrictions affecting the employment of young people (contained, at the time of writing, in the Employment Bill 1988) should result in an expansion of employment opportunities (part-time in many cases) for this age group. But it is expected that, in the remaining years of this century, perhaps the biggest influence on youth unemployment trends is likely to be a decline in the number of 16-19 year olds - from 3.5 million in 1986 to 2.6 million in 1994 (Department of Employment 1988, para.4.6; N.E.D.O. 1988). The stock of 16-19 year olds in the labour force is expected to decline to 84 per cent. of its 1987 level by 1991. The size of the pool of young people in the labour market may also be affected by government plans for raising the level of participation in higher education (see below) and by the predicted increases in the numbers of school leavers of ethnic minority origin who will be available for employment (*Department of Employment Gazette* 1988, p.268). A further, unpredictable, factor is the impact of the expected increase in labour market entrants from other sections of the population - for example, married women.

Overall, it seems that the combination of demographic trends and the 1988 Social Security Act's increase in the minimum age of entitlement to income support will result in considerably reduced social security expenditure on young people. Nevertheless, the decline in the number of 16-19 year olds will eventually peter out. Furthermore, it seems inconceivable that these trends will, in themselves, signal the eradication of unemployment from the 18-24 age group, which constituted over one-third of benefit recipients in 1986-7.

Participation in education

Young people's participation in education has been on the increase for the past two decades, and the present government anticipates a further increase, at least in relation to the higher education sector, in the 1990s (although the main increase will be in the numbers of mature entrants). Students in higher education have been able to register for work, and draw benefit, at various times of the year. As a result of reforms in 1986-7, however, much vacation entitlement has been removed. But students are still able to draw income support or unemployment benefit in the long vacation and housing benefit (also cut back recently), although this is expected to change in 1990-91 if the proposed system of 'top-up loans' is introduced (see Chapter 6). Persons attending part-time courses, and certain others attending full-time courses but having particular personal difficulties (such as disability) or responsibilities, have also been entitled to social security if able to meet the necessary legal conditions. School leavers with no job to go to or considering whether to enter further education have also sought social security.

There has been an increasing demand for social security from young people in the above situations - especially from those whose maintenance grants are inadequate to meet their needs or where the shortage of low-rental accommodation has necessitated a move into relatively expensive private accommodation. A DES-commissioned survey discovered that in the academic year 1986-87 77 per cent. of students claimed benefits during term-time and/or the long vacation (DES 1988, para.2.11).

Participation in education has both positive and negative effects on the level of demand for social security: positive, in that, for example, students require social security support at various times of the year; negative, because in general, and with the exception of persons entitled to draw benefit while studying, full-time study signifies non-availability for work (availability being a condition of entitlement to most of the major benefits paid to the unemployed).

Government responses to demands placed on the social security system by school leavers, students in higher education and persons taking courses at further education level will be examined in Part III. So at this stage it is necessary to demonstrate the level of demand from these groups.

School leavers

In 1987, before the Social Security Act 1988 removed the right of most 16 and 17 year old school leavers to draw income support in their own right, there were 90,000 under 18 year olds who were unemployed in the year after leaving school (H.C. Employment Committee 1988, Annex 2). In the Parliamentary debates on the 1988 Act (as it became) the government explained that it was seeking to end the school-to-dole syndrome and that it believed that young people should be spending their time purposefully - in education, work or training.

In fact, the pupil-to-claimant transition had become well established. As shown earlier in this Chapter, the period 1966-80 witnessed considerable growth in youth unemployment. The SBC (1976, para.3.29) regarded this as the main reason for the rapid increase, in a two to three year period, in the numbers of young people claiming supplementary benefit (83,000 at December 1975). The scale of the increase can be appreciated by looking at the total number of unemployed 16-17 year old supplementary benefit recipients as a proportion of the total number of people receiving this benefit. In November 1967, 16-17 year olds represented 3.5 per cent. of the total (Ministry of Social Security 1967, pp.105-6), but in November/December 1975 the proportion stood at 10.4 per cent. (SBC 1976, pp.23,53).

Claims from school leavers were, not surprisingly, concentrated in certain months of the year. Eventually, in response to severe operational difficulties allegedly caused by this and the misrepresentation by a number of school leavers of their destination (by saying that they had entered the labour market when in reality they intended to continue in education), the government introduced restrictions, in November 1980. In effect, these took the form of waiting periods, of up to three months for June leavers, before supplementary benefit could be drawn. Child benefit and dependency additions to other benefits for those entitled to them were paid during these periods. For young people leaving school at Easter the waiting period was far shorter. They could draw SB from the first Monday after Easter Monday (provided, by virtue of a 1987 amendment, they were 16 by then). A number of young people had sought to take advantage of this more favourable (from the point of view of benefit entitlement) leaving date by signing on after Easter and returning to school in May and/or June only to sit examinations. It was believed that this practice had contributed significantly to the rapid increase in the numbers of young people claiming benefits as unemployed persons in the month following Easter; 8,000 Easter leavers were awarding benefit costing £1 million in 1985, but in 1986 that number had increased to 15,000 (costing £2million) (DHSS 1986b, para.9). Accordingly, the government took steps to close this 'loophole'.

The changes introduced in 1980 and 1987, referred to above, must have had a marked effect on the numbers of young people on the unemployment register, because

1. During the summer waiting period a certain proportion of school leavers would have found work and so would never have been classed officially as unemployed.

2. Those looking for, but unable to obtain work in the first few months after leaving school may have subsequently decided to take a further education course, or return to school, or join the YTS, and would not technically have been 'unemployed'.

3. Some young people who might have been expected to sit examinations in May may have had to abandon such plans before 'leaving' at Easter so that they could draw benefit. But many others would not have been on the unemployment register until September, just because they remained entered for a few examinations after Easter.

Persons in 'relevant education'

Most 16-18 year olds in non-advanced full-time education (said to be in 'relevant education' under the IS regulations) are not regarded as available for work and so are not entitled to benefit (see further Chapter 6 below). As we saw earlier, nearly 50 per cent. of 16 year olds eligible to leave school in the summer of 1986 were still in full-time education the following January (H.C. Employment Committee 1988, Annex 2). The staying-on rate in Britain is low compared with other Western European countries (Loney 1983, pp.27-8), although it has improved over the past decade. (For regional variations in staying-on rates in Britain, see *The Guardian*, 5.7.88.) One of the stated aims of raising the minimum age of entitlement to income support from 16 to 18 in 1988 was to improve this rate by removing incentives to leave education. One problem, however, is the inadequate system of awards for persons remaining in education.

For some years a certain number of young people have been able to draw benefit while studying, under the 'twelve hour rule' and 'twenty-one hour rule', on the basis that they are on a part-time course and able to show availability for work. The raising of the minimum age of entitlement to income support to 18 will have affected many in this category. It seems that in 1986-7 one-third of the 90,000 16 and 17 year olds in receipt of SB were entitled by virtue of the twenty-one hour rule (*H.C. Hansard* vol.121 cols 666-7 2.11.87) (see Chapter 6).

Students

The position in social security law of students - that is, persons on full-time 'advanced' courses (such as higher diploma, teacher training and degree or postgraduate academic or professional courses) and those aged 19 or over and on full-time non-advanced courses - has been, and remains, immensely complex. Students' entitlement to benefit, and the effects of recent reforms, are considered in Chapter 6. Here we are concerned only with the numbers of students appearing on the register of unemployed.

Following the Ministry of Social Security Act 1966 (later retitled the Supplementary Benefits Act 1966) students became entitled to draw supplementary benefit (SB) during their vacations. But by 1976 the student grant contained a sum slightly above the SB non-householder rate to cover the short vacations (SBC 1976, para.5.11). The result was that benefit was soon only being paid, in most cases, for the long vacation. This change in the rules in the 1970s was the result of 'an avalanche of claims being made during (short vacations) and the resultant pressure on the staff of local DHSS offices' (Rowell and Wilton 1982, p.179). The SBC had produced figures to show that in the summer months 'a substantial proportion' of claims for SB were being made by students. In August 1975, for example, one in twelve 'unemployed' recipients was a student (SBC 1976, para.5.10). Provided students were able to satisfy the requirement to register for work (in section 11 of the Act) they could receive benefits during the vacations, subject to the usual means test. In 1975 a total of 121,000 out of 131,000 vacation claims by students were successful, consisting of 113,000 awards of weekly benefits and 8,000 of single payments (for furniture, clothing, etc.).

Student claims for benefit were on the increase. The numbers registered at Easter 1973, 1974 and 1975 was 48,000, 73,000, and 90,000, respectively (ibid.). The reasons for the increases were said to include greater publicity for, and awareness of, the right to claim during the vacations (largely as a result of a National Union of Students publicity campaign), worsening vacation employment opportunities, and the fact that benefit levels had risen at a faster rate than student grants, relative to prices (ibid.). During Easter 1976 a record 182,000 claims were received, of which 174,000 were successful (SBC 1977, para.2.20).

The concentrated workload in certain months of the year and the need to verify that students were genuinely 'available for work' were among the problems faced by the SBC in 1975 (SBC 1976, para.5.10). When, in February 1976, changes in the arrangements for student support were announced, in particular the fact that the grant itself would include an amount for winter and

Easter vacations, it was anticipated that student claims would have a reduced impact on the administration of SB. Indeed, only 23,000 students claimed benefit during the Christmas vacation in 1976 compared with 155,000 during the same period the previous year. But there were still said to be problems in the university towns (SBC 1977, para.8.1).

When the SB scheme was reformed in 1980 the right of students to draw benefit continued. Despite changes in the way that the grant was treated as a 'resource', resulting in reduced entitlement during all three vacations, students continued to register at the end of each term. In 1985, a total of 100,000 unemployment benefit and SB claims by students in the short vacations were made; and around 180,000 students at any one time received benefit during the summer vacation (DHSS 1986, para.10). Around half the student population received SB during the long vacation (ibid., para.2). During the short vacations there were rather more claims at Easter than at Christmas: 39,008 (Easter) and 26,898 (Christmas) in 1984 and 45,231 (Easter) and 19,753 (Christmas) in 1985 (*Employment Gazette* Feb. 1985, Table 2.13 p.S35; May 1985, Table 2.13 p.S32).

As shall be shown in Chapter 6, in 1986-87 the government took measures which resulted in the termination of students' entitlement to unemployment benefit (UB) and SB (now income support) during the short vacations, in most cases. Even so, the unemployment statistics continue to include student benefit recipients. Registered student unemployment in Great Britain the summer of 1987 stood at 112,222 (July), 129,927 (August) and 139,722 (September).

From the academic year 1990-91, however, it is anticipated that most students will lose entitlement to income support, housing benefit and unemployment benefit for the duration of their course. Students will probably have to supplement their grants with 'top-up loans', although some will be eligible for 'discretionary bursaries' paid out of one of three 'Access Funds' intended for those whose access to further or higher education may be inhibited by financial considerations or who, for various reasons, face 'real financial difficulties' (DES 1988, paras 3.21-3.25). These funds will be administered by the education institutions themselves, because, according to the government, they are 'best placed to understand the circumstances of their students' (Mr K.Baker M.P., *H.C. Hansard*, Vol.140, col.306, 9,11.88). Only students who are disabled or single parents or the dependants of students will be eligible for social security entitlement (ibid., col.305). So students will disappear almost entirely from the unemployment statistics. (See further DES 1988, and discussion in Chapter 6.)

Some conclusions

Record levels of youth unemployment in the past decade have shown why state support has become of such importance to so many young people. But to what extent does unemployment influence the nature of social security provision?

It will be seen from the ensuing sections of this book that levels of unemployment, including youth unemployment, have often influenced the formulation of social security policy and law over the years. There is a strong selectivist ethos in British social security provision; and unemployment is identified as a particular contingency in respect of which state support is necessary. When unemployment is at a high level, the level 'will be tolerated politically only where those rendered unemployed... can sustain a reasonable standard of living' (Ogus and Barendt 1982, p.74). Nevertheless, often the reaction to increased demands being placed on the benefits system is a restriction of entitlement. Examples may be found in government responses to large increases in short-term registration by students, the summer 'bulge' caused by school leavers and the increasing volume of claims by unemployed young boarders (see Chapter 4). Looking further back, many of the cutbacks in benefits in the early 1930s were direct responses to the threat to the insurance fund posed by relatively sudden massive rises in unemployment (see Chapter 3).

The influence of unemployment lies not only in the way it stimulates reactive change, but also in the way that it has a major bearing on proactive social security planning. For example, aspects of the National Insurance Act 1946 were based on projections of an unemployment rate of eight and a half per cent. (Deacon 1981, p.63). Recently, the government's decision initially to retain young people's entitlement to income support (the replacement for supplementary benefit) consequent on the Social Security Reviews of 1984-85, must, in part at least, have been influenced by expectations of a decrease in the numbers of 16 and 17 year olds claiming benefit, following an extension of the YTS (see Green Paper 1985, Vol.1, para.9.27). Thus the government could, with apparent equanimity, announce that as its 'first priority' was to establish comprehensive provision for the age group, 'no changes are proposed to the eligibility of young unemployed people to benefit' (ibid.). In fact, 16 and 17 year olds' entitlement lasted for just the first six months of the IS scheme (see Chapter 7).

The way that unemployment is viewed by the general public often determines the nature of any changes to social security provision made by government, in the sense that if the political costs of reductions are too high such reductions may not be fully implemented or may be modified (as in the case of severe weather payments recently) or may not take place at all. But, it seems that rather than there being public concern that benefit rates may be too low, periods of high or rising unemployment see increased public concern at abuse (Deacon 1981, pp.84-5). The ministerial statements issued in the spring of 1987, suggesting that as there were sufficient education or training places for all those without jobs the time might have come for benefit payments to the under 18s to be scrapped altogether, would not have been made had not a sizeable proportion of the electorate been expected to support them.

PART II
SOCIAL SECURITY AND THE TRANSITION TO ADULTHOOD

Introduction to Part II

Young people in their mid- to late teens and early twenties undergo a range of transitions which take them towards and into adulthood. Some of these transitions are essentially social - from pupil to worker, non-householder to householder, financially dependent to independent. There are also the psychological and physiological changes which, although not representing neat boundaries between childhood and adulthood, characterise the ending of the former stage of development. Essentially though, 'childhood', 'adulthood' and, indeed, 'youth' are concepts which, in the way that imposed age limits determine legal status and entitlement, are based around society's perceptions and assumptions concerned with the transition to adulthood rather than any biological or psychological divide between these stages. As Clarke and Willis (1984, pp.6-7) say:

> Youth, as we know it, is the consequence of social arrangements designed to regulate the transition not of child to adult in a universal sense, but of the child to worker and citizen in *our* society, with all the appropriate habits and attitudes that are supposed to belong to such an individual.

The assumptions on which these social arrangements tend to be based, especially the dependency assumption (referred to in the Introduction), are of crucial importance. They affect the legal status conferred on young people, not least in relation to social security entitlement. As the SSAC, when reviewing the current social security position of young people, recently put it (1988, para.2.1):

> All benefit systems are built around assumptions about living patterns in society - assumptions about the borderline between childhood and independence, or the responsibilities of parents for their children, or the importance of work.

The Committee suggest (ibid.) that there can be a 'conflict between what young people - and some adults - may regard as desirable, such as increased independence from their parents, and what society is prepared to fund through the benefits system'. In Part II, therefore, I aim to consider how this particular conflict has been, and is, manifesting itself and to assess the likely consequences. First it is necessary to examine the transition to adulthood closely.

2 The transition to adulthood

It should be noted at the outset that there is no single clear dividing line in British law which marks out adult status. As Thane says (1981, p.6), '... in current British legal and administrative practice the dividing line between adults and younger people is less clearly defined than might be expected'. Similarly, Wringe (1981, p.92) refers to an 'absence of any precise and formal moment of initiation into the world of adult rights and responsibilities'. Adult status is conferred at different stages in relation to sexual intercourse (16), the franchise and jury service (18), driving licences (17), independent entitlement to social security (16 or 18), and so on. In part, this lack of clarity, or 'status ambiguity' stems from the ambiguous way that society views young people in their transition period - 'at times demanding child-like obedience, and at others expecting the self-confidence and independence of an adult' (Coleman 1979, p.8).

The ambiguity attached to the 15-18 age group, to which Coleman was referring, can continue beyond this age. For example, for students aged 18-21 'the transition from adolescence to adulthood is particularly blurred' (Nicholson 1980, p.101). Support (grants and social security) currently provided to students tends to illustrate the state's inability to decide whether or not they are adults. This support (including social security in the long vacation) is assessed at a rate intended to enable the student to live as an independent individual. But at the same time, under both the student grants and social security systems the student is regarded as being in some measure dependent on his/her parents. The grants system insists on a parental contribution, and in any event provides an inadequate level of support (see Chapter 6). The social security system classes the parental contribution to the grant as a 'notional resource' (treated as received by the student whether or not this is the case) and denies benefit in the short vacations. It should be stressed, however, that perhaps a majority of students come from middle-class backgrounds, in which some delay in the transition to adult independence may be the norm (Wallace 1987, pp. 2, 178). Only eight per cent. of entrants to UK universities presently come from social classes four and five (*Times Educational Supplement* 1.7.88).

In some respects it is understandable that legal and administrative practice should end up conferring a measure of 'status ambiguity' on young people, when one considers that there is no precise age at which young people's development brings them into adulthood. The 'wavering line between "childhood" and "adulthood"' (Thane 1981, p.7) might be expected to characterise this 'transition' period. What is happening to young people is that they are gradually renouncing their dependency as part of a process of disengagement from their parents (Coleman 1980, p.3). During late adolescence the young person is 'striving to establish a free, independent, autonomous self while still enmeshed in the web of his or her own family' (ibid., p.11). Young people who are at this stage 'tend to oscillate between adulthood and childhood' (Latey 1967, para.160). Although a young person is frequently striving for independence, times of uncertainty and self-doubt bring about a resurgence of childhood dependence in him/her. On the other hand young people tend to resent this dependence, leading to expressions of independence such as criticism of parents' ideas and values (Coleman 1980, p.4). This process is a continuous one throughout the mid-teens to early twenties.

So, in terms of young people's social and psychological development, entry into adulthood is determined not by the attainment of one particular age. As Lord Fraser said in *Gillick v West Norfolk Area Health Authority* ([1985] 3 All E.R. 402, at 410j-411a):

> It is in my view contrary to the ordinary experience of mankind, at least in Western Europe in the present century, to say that a child or young person remains in fact under the complete control of his parents until he obtains the age of majority, now 18 in the United Kingdom, and that on attaining that age he suddenly acquires independence...most wise parents relax control gradually...and encourage him or her to become increasingly independent.

The age dividing lines in law and administrative practice, which until recently perhaps were considered difficult to redraw and which have tended to remain fixed for some considerable time, are employed for reasons of administrative convenience (and/or for policy reasons, as has been the case with social security) and to signal society's approval or otherwise of certain activities among emergent 'adults'. In this latter respect they do offer a guide to young people and their families by making them more aware of the importance attached to certain stages in the transition (see Hedges and Hyatt 1985, para.6.1.1). So, although young people's birthdays are 'waymarks, but not end points in their own right' (ibid.) they are closely associated with important stages in the transition to adult independence. The most significant stages are considered to be leaving school, starting work and gaining financial independence, and leaving home; but general notions of freedom/independence and the accompanying element of responsibility are also important.

Leaving school

The age of 16 is the age that young people are free to leave school and either start work or enter training. It is the age at which young people are legally entitled to make a number of major life decisions, although freedom of choice, already weakened by inadequate educational maintenance support (Burghes and Stegles 1983, Cooper 1985) has undoubtedly been diminished as a result of the increase to the minimum age of entitlement to income support under the Social Security Act 1988 (see Chapter 7).

Leaving school has traditionally been regarded as an important step towards adulthood. The Crowther Report (1959, para.196) expressed a fear that raising the school leaving age from 15 to 16 might obstruct the expression of 'the feeling of growing independence and usefulness that 15 year old boys and girls ought to have'. The traditional importance of leaving school, from the point of view of independence, was the opportunity to enter the world of work and, through earning a wage, move away from a childishly dependent relationship with parents (Miller 1969, p.31). Parents and children still regard school as, per se, an important step towards adulthood (Hedges and Hyatt 1985, paras 6.1.1 and 6.4.1). Kallen (1983, p.28) however plays down its significance arguing that 'in the life of many young people nowadays there is no significant break between life and lifestyles while they are still at school and in the first years after they leave school'.

Entering employment or training/gaining financial independence

Less than one in five school leavers find work immediately on leaving school and only about one-third within six months of leaving (Family Policy Studies Centre 1988, p.6). For this minority, however, entering employment may be a significant and positive step:

In some ways leaving school signals the end of childhood. But a 16 year old school leaver may not have a job, and may be emotionally and financially incapable of self-support...Getting a settled job is a more solid step - not only on economic grounds...but also because it symbolises a serious move into the adult world of work (Hedges and Hyatt 1985, para.6.1.1).

Youth has been described as a transitional period during which society recruits 'potential labour-power (the child)' and transforms it into 'actual labour-power (the adult)' (Clarke and Willis 1984, p.7). Smooth progress into adulthood is to a large extent dependent upon undelayed recruitment into employment. (Loney, for example (1983, p.36), refers to the 'centrality of employment for the transition from adolescence to adult life', and Cashmore (1984, p.13) to employment 'breaking the bonds of dependency'; Price and Burke (1985, p.52) state that 'making a "normal" transition to adulthood depends on establishing and maintaining a stable attachment to the labour market'). Work brings with it financial rewards, and an accompanying measure of independence which is clearly recognised by young people (D.E.S. 1983, p.21-2). Their first regular wage would be regarded by young people as 'the starting point on the road to independence' (Catelani 1985, p.12) because it signifies the ability to support themselves.

Although financial independence is only part of a much wider process of developing from a dependent child into and independent adult, it has particular importance in the way that it enables a young person to make real choices, such as to leave home and marry. Financial resources are also important in enabling young people living with their parents to offer a contribution to them in respect of household expenditure; in so doing young people 'buy' a degree of independence (see below). Some parents believe that contributing helps young people to learn how to manage their own finances. Moreover, some take the view that as emergent adult individuals young people have a right to a degree of material independence (Hedges and Hyatt 1985, para.6.1.3). Neither social security nor the youth training allowance (the latter being received by more young people than are wages) aim to offer financial independence to young people. But both are important in enabling young people to contribute towards their 'keep'. Parents and children see such contributions as an important aspect of the transition to adulthood (ibid., para.6.2; Cusack and Roll 1985, p.2).

So far as training is concerned, despite evidence towards the end of 1987 that not all young people were sure of being offered a YTS place, the government's intention was that a training place would be available for all those who left education and did not enter employment. It had been claimed by the then Secretary of State for Employment that '[f]rom this Easter, there need be no unemployment under 18 and anyone under that age who remains unemployed will have chosen to remain unemployed' (Lord Young of Graffham, *H.L. Hansard*, vol.483, col.1334, 28.1.87). The government confirmed its guarantee of a training place for all 16 and 17 year olds during the Committee stage of the Social Security Bill 1987. For young people aged under 18 the debate on the effect of training and its allowance on the transition to adulthood may replace that concerned with the effect of work or social security; but the basic question of independence will be unchanged.

Leaving home

Personal financial resources are crucial if young people are to be able to leave home and live independently of their families. Young people with little option but to establish themselves in their own accommodation are not, perhaps, motivated by any desire for independence per se. Others will want to leave home in the normal course of events to establish an independent life (DHSS 1976, para.6.2). This is especially true of girls, who face pressure to perform domestic work for the family at home (Wallace 1987, pp.97, 158-9). Back in 1945 it was recognised that young people leave home to 'claim full adult status' (Scottish Youth Advisory Committee 1945, para.13). Significantly, perhaps, one survey in the early 1980s found that although obtaining their own accommodation was not aspired to by the majority of young people aged under 20, a greater proportion of unemployed than employed young people wanted their own accommodation (37 per cent. of the former compared with 22 per cent. of the latter: D.E.S. 1983, p.23). Indeed, among the young unemployed setting up one's own home has become part of the sub-culture of unemployment. (When leaving care it can be a necessity.)

Leaving home does seem to be regarded by young people and their families as a more important step than leaving school and even starting a settled job, because the young person has to make many more decisions and assume greater responsibility (Hedges and Hyatt 1985, para.6.1.1). The desire to assume greater responsibility is in fact another hallmark of adulthood and is recognised as such by young people ('...adulthood was perceived to imply taking responsibility for oneself, managing one's own affairs, with both positive (freedoms) and negative (duties/worries) implications...': D.E.S. 1983, p.22).

Statistics show that from age 16 upwards an increasing proportion of young claimants are classed as householders or boarders (*H.C. Hansard*, vol.72, cols 551-2w, 5.2.85). Yet it has been observed that, in general, unemployment makes obtaining and financing a place of one's own more difficult and thus delays the transition to independent householder (Jones 1986, p.55). This is part of the overall effect of unemployment on young people's attainment of independence. As society associates work with adulthood, 'people continue to be regarded as part of this group (youth), because of the difficulty of finding work and hence of leading an independent family life' (UNESCO 1981, p.27-8). UNESCO's report emphasised that while almost all societies expect young people to marry and begin having children while they are still involved in the transition to adult life, unemployment in particular was 'placing independent family life beyond the economic means of considerable numbers of young people' (ibid., p.30). Yet in Britain, at least, evidence suggests that the desire for adult status and independence provides a powerful stimulus for young people to establish families of their own (see Chapter 5).

Independence and the transition to adulthood

There is no doubt that the attainment of independence is accepted as a crucial aspect of making the transition from childhood to adulthood. A search for independence is a characteristic of adolescence; its achievement is an integral part of adolescent development (Coleman 1980, p.64). Independence has long been regarded as an ideal of youth. It is not surprising that young people want independence (Cashmore 1984, Wallace 1987 (writing about girls)) and that a degree of independence among young people has become one of society's expectations and assumptions concerning this group. (It has been suggested that 'there are powerful influences in society pulling the young person towards early adulthood and away from his or her context of dependence on the family': Fletcher 1973, p.184.) Even today, when youth unemployment has placed the social and financial independence of so many young people under threat, one of the several features of society which were much less evident than in the past is, in the words of Lord Scarman: 'the increasing independence of young people' (*Gillick v West Norfolk Area Health Authority* (1985) at 419d).

Among young people whose expression of the desire for adult independence does not extend as far as leaving home or forming a family of their own, there is still a powerful resistance to being regarded as totally dependent. Such persons tend to want to contribute towards their upkeep, as noted earlier. Although income transfers within families are difficult to trace (see O'Kelly, in Silburn 1985, p.81), it is clear that transfers from young people to parents are important to the transition to adulthood. Cusack and Roll (who carried out a survey (with 111 replies) examining young people's contributions to their parents' housing costs) explained (1985, p.5) that

> Many young people continue to live with their parents long after they have obtained an income of their own, either through social security or through work. This time is seen as very important by parents. They want their children to achieve independence. Although there is a lack of research into how exactly money is transferred within a family...money transfers do play an important role in the transition process

It is clear, therefore, that a search for independence characterises the transition to adulthood and that its attainment is regarded as perhaps the key indicator of a successfully completed transition. It is also clear that various expressions of adult independence occur during the transition to adulthood.

Unemployment and the transition to adulthood

The attainment of independence by young people is hampered significantly by unemployment (and perhaps also by being a trainee on a government scheme). What role could or should social security play in smoothing the transition of the young unemployed to adult independence?

The problem for social security in this regard is of enormous proportions. As the twentieth century has progressed, young people have, on the one hand, generally seemed to want and expect more and more independence - to a large degree supported in this desire by their parents. On the other hand, they have increasingly become economically dependent on their families for several years after leaving school or reaching the age of majority (Mnookin 1978, p.169). One reason has been increasing participation in education beyond the minimum school leaving age. But of particular significance has been the unprecedented growth in youth unemployment in the 1970s and '80s.

In periods of full employment, such as there was in Britain in the 1950s, youth is a transitory phase which leads swiftly and inexorably into adulthood and its rewards and responsibilities (Cashmore 1984). But when the level of youth unemployment is high, delay in achieving the necessary financial autonomy for household or family formation is likely to extend the period during which young people remain dependent on their families. Young people who have been unable to follow what might be described as the traditional route into adulthood via work have been 'forced back on the secondary method of income distribution - the social security system' (Finn 1984, p.32). Ideally, one might argue, social security ought to be geared towards offering a measure of financial independence to the young unemployed, especially those who need to move out of an unhappy family situation and live independently. As we shall see in later chapters, despite record levels of youth unemployment, which have caused a high level of demand for social security support, provision for young people has undoubtedly been diminished. Recent reforms in particular may be forcing many young people to remain dependent on their families, often for longer than they or other members of the household may wish, by increasing progressively the age at which independence is deemed to start. For those leaving care, who may have no families to whom they can turn for support, the situation may be particularly acute.

3 The evolution of young people's benefits: 1911-1980

This chapter covers major developments in social security from the first national social insurance scheme in Britain to the eve of the 1980 reforms to supplementary benefit. Attention is focused on provisions reflecting the various assumptions and values underlying the treatment of young people which were outlined in the introductory chapter, especially those of particular relevance to the transition to adulthood.

The period up to the Beveridge Report (1942)

The disadvantaged position of young people in the labour market resulting from the practice of 'blind-alley' employment (see Chapter 1) and ungenerous wages (compared with those paid to adults) was reflected in their entitlement under the rather narrow and limited early schemes of social insurance in Britain. The contributory scheme (the employer, worker and the government each paid a contribution) introduced in 1912 following the National Insurance Act 1911, applied to just six trades where unemployment was expected to be temporary or cyclical. It did not cover young people under the age of 16 even though the school leaving age at the time was 14. There was, however, some expectation that the school leaving age might be raised: the government had wanted to make education compulsory until the age of 17 (Gilbert 1966, p.253). The *Minority Report* of the Royal Commission on the Poor Laws (1909) had recommended prohibition of employment below the age of 15 so that young people could receive proper industrial training, which was seen as necessary at the time. The 1911 Act excluded employees aged under 17 from any entitlement to unemployment benefit and provided for 17 year olds to receive only half the adult rate. It was said that an under 17 year old could at least profit later from an accumulation of contributions when he might have greater need for the benefit (Chiozza Money 1912, p.337).

The extremely ungenerous provision for juveniles must be viewed in the context of a scheme which provided benefits for just 15 weeks in any 12 month period and at a rate of about 22 per cent. of average wages (Sadler 1983, p.19). Moreover, even young people old enough to benefit from the scheme fell outside it because they were engaged in casual labour or a non-insured trade.

The extension of the unemployment insurance scheme to munitions workers during the First World War benefited the many young people working in that industry and earning high wages in some cases (although having to work for long hours at boring and repetitive tasks) (Rees and Rees 1982, p.24). After the armistice many returning servicemen and young workers were faced with unemployment. Over half the young workers who lost their jobs at the end of the war were unable to find work (Garside 1977, p.324). By the early 1920s unemployment was at a high level (see Chapter 1). For example, in 1923 79,000 juveniles were registered as unemployed in the United Kingdom (Rees and Rees 1982, p.25). But, as shown later, young people were to benefit far less from the extension of unemployment insurance in the 1920s than older workers.

After the war and until 1921 the government paid an 'Out of Work Donation' for servicemen, who lacked contribution rights (and later, until 1919, for civilians who did not qualify under the insurance scheme). The government wanted to avoid the likely opprobrium which would have resulted from 'heroes' thrown onto the Poor Law. The Donation contained allowances for dependants. Not only did this represent a shift in emphasis towards the welfare aspect of social security, as George (1973, p.124) suggests, it also introduced a new element to social security provision for young people. From then onwards young people could be viewed either as 'dependants' - assumed to be dependent on their families for support - or as claimants in their own right. Dependants' allowances were, after their temporary inclusion in the insurance scheme under the Unemployed Workers Dependants' (Temporary Provisions) Act 1921, for the avoidance of winter hardships, made a permanent feature of the scheme following the Unemployment Insurance Act 1922. Young people were classed as dependants if in full-time education (and, later on, full-time instruction) between the ages of 14 and 16. The dependant allowance stood at one shilling until 1934 when it was raised to two shillings; it was increased to three shillings in 1935. The classification of those staying on in education as 'dependants' has continued in the benefits system up to the present day and has served to emphasise the synonymity of entering employment and attaining adult status.

In 1921 'extended benefit' (at first known as 'uncovenanted benefit') was introduced to provide a limited extension of benefit entitlement to those who had exhausted their entitlement to insurance benefits. Benefit was paid at a uniform rate, but subject to conditions and ministerial discretion. Extended benefit was paid for successive special periods the first of which was a period of sixteen weeks during the eight months from 3 March to 2 November 1921. Under the Labour government's Unemployment Insurance Act (No.2) 1924 the period for which the benefit could be paid became unlimited. However, the Labour government's term was extremely short-lived, and under the incoming Conservative administration the Minister of Labour used his discretionary power to exclude, unless hardship would be caused, 'single persons who are residing with parents or other relatives to whom, having regard to all the circumstances, they can reasonably look for support during unemployment' (Beveridge 1930, p.276 n.2). Thus many young people would have been thrown onto their families for support. According to Sadler (1983, p.19), juveniles (and married women with working husbands) were specifically excluded from benefit as part of a number of disincentives which were 'intended both to prevent abuse and to emphasise (the) temporary nature' of the benefits. This development provides a particularly clear example of the dependency assumption and the principle of family responsibility in operation.

Controversial recommendations were made by the Blanesburgh Committee in 1925 for drastic reductions in the rates of benefit paid to young people (men and women aged between 18-21 were to lose 8s. and 7s. respectively, and there were also to be new, much lower rates than previously for 16 and 17 year olds). The proposed reductions threatened to weaken further the status of young people under the social security system. The cuts were modified during the passage of the Unemployment Insurance Act 1927 by graduating benefit rates so that at age 18 males received 10s. per week, at age 19, 12s. per week, and at age 20 14s. per week (Deacon 1976, pp.52-3).

Improvements in the insurance scheme during the late 1920s did not alter the position of young people relative to others in the scheme. But the Unemployment Insurance Act 1930 did authorise the Minister of Labour to reduce the lower age for entry into the scheme to the age when compulsory education ceased, when and if that age was raised to 15 or more. At various stages in the 1920s it was anticipated that the minimum school leaving age would be raised, in the face of initially educational, and later economic, arguments in support. In July 1929 the President of the Board of Education had announced the government's intention of raising the school leaving age to 15 in April 1931 (*Ministry of Labour Gazette* 1929, p.399). It was believed that unemployment, which was increasing at a dramatic rate, could be cut drastically as a result. In the event the leaving age was not raised until 1947.

From 1930 onwards a succession of measures were taken, designed not only to reduce the drain on the insurance fund as unemployment continued to rise (see Chapter 1), but also, as economic recovery began, to prevent unemployed young people drifting into idleness on unlimited benefits. The conditions governing young people's entitlement were tightened up considerably.

The Unemployment Insurance Act 1930 authorised local education authorities which had undertaken juvenile unemployment work (see Chapter 7) to administer juveniles' benefit, give grants for courses of instruction and require attendance at instruction courses as a condition of receipt of benefit. The Minister of Labour was put under a duty to ensure that, in areas where courses were available, under 18 year olds were being required to attend as a condition of receipt of benefit.

Cuts in benefits occurred in 1931 (for example, through the Anomalies Act) (see Davison 1938, p.14). The duration of payments declined to 26 weeks and a claimant had to prove thirty contributions in the two years preceding the date of the claim (the '30 in 2' rule). There was evidence of employers of young people taking advantage of this provision rather astutely, if with unsatisfactory consequences:

> The Cardiff employer is a careful student of the Unemployment Insurance regulations and divides up the work which he is able to give among as many juveniles as possible, standing his juvenile employees off when each has qualified for Unemployment Insurance. Consequently a large increase is reported in the number of claimants for Unemployment Insurance with the minimum of thirty contributions. This may be satisfactory from the point of view of the juveniles [sic] but has involved an increase of £300 or eight per cent., in the amount paid out in the year and an increase of twenty-two per cent. in the number of individual payments, this in spite of reduced benefits and a reduction in the period over which Unemployment Benefit can be drawn by any one individual (Save The Children Fund 1933, p.272-3).

There is also evidence that the '30 in 2' rule, which had provoked considerable controversy in the late 1920s (Deacon 1976), was resulting in the disallowance of many young persons' claims for benefit. Young people in fact figured more prominently in the disallowance figures than did other age groups (Royal Commission on Unemployment Insurance 1931, p.109). Once again the dependency assumption was applied to young people - it was assumed that juveniles suffering disallowance could rely on support from relatives. Davison, reporting for the Royal Commission on Unemployment Insurance, said (ibid., p.113) that 'many a family carries on as it did in the days before State insurance, by pooling its wages and savings...' and that young single men 'suffered little'.

Even 'transitional payments', a means-tested benefit for those not qualified for unemployment benefit and introduced following the cuts of 1931 (which left one million persons cut off from benefits), were of little value to young people.

Under 18 year olds were simply not entitled to them and so could not benefit from the revised contribution conditions applicable to these new payments. (Only eight contributions in two years were required.)

Furthermore, the means test itself operated to the disadvantage of young people and their families. The public assistance committees (PACs), which administered transitional payments, applied a stigmatising 'household means test' which provides one of the best examples of the principle of family responsibility in operation. It was assumed that each household member's resources were available to meet the needs of a claimant member, if their combined resources exceeded the scale rates applied by the PACs. The presence of young people living in their parents' household posed a potential threat to the latter's benefit. The family would often be better off financially if the young person left home. In some cases there was collusive desertion; this became a serious problem for the PACs (Deacon and Bradshaw 1983, p.17). Later on, the PACs' successor, the Unemployment Assistance Board (U.A.B.), devised the 'constructive household' so that the resources of those who would normally be expected to reside in the household would also be taken into account. The household means test caused poverty and family disharmony as well as dishonesty. Young men in particular might have been, in effect, forced to leave home in order to obtain their full rate of assistance (Bruce 1965, p.240).

When the unemployment assistance scheme was introduced, under the Unemployment Act 1934, the U.A.B., which administered it, applied a means test for determining entitlement. (Unemployment assistance had a similar role to that of transitional payments, in providing support to those who were not eligible for unemployment benefit or had exhausted their entitlement to it.) This 'household means test' proved notoriously unpopular. Like the test previously applied by the PACs, it rested on the principle of family responsibility. Individual household members' resources were once again deemed to be available to meet the family's requirements. If a young person was in employment a proportion of the family's benefit was deducted: for example, 4s. of the first £1 and 10s of next £1 (November 1936 rates) if the young person was under 18. The arrangements were modified later (see Deacon and Bradshaw 1983, p.29). Such was the far-reaching effect of the household means test that, for example, in October 1938 one-third of all unemployment assistance claimants had their assistance reduced on the grounds of household income (ibid., p.26). As with unemployment benefit, independent entitlement to unemployment assistance commenced at the age of 16. Those who left school at 15 and were unemployed appear to have been treated as dependants only.

Despite the rigours of the household means test, the continuing availability of benefit and the U.A.B.'s increased generosity in 1935 and 1936 led to allegations that young people were being allowed to settle down to a life on assistance. Refusals of work were said to be growing; many young males were found not to be prepared to 'inconvenience themselves in order to become self-supporting' (Davison 1938, p.72) by seeking work in or outside their district (see U.A.B. 1939, p.47). A U.A.B. Advisory Committee conducted an investigation of applicants aged 18-29 (who numbered approximately 100,000 in October 1938). As many as 58 per cent. of them were found to have had no, or less than six months, employment in the three years prior to the enquiry and were, therefore, ineligible for unemployment benefit. It was estimated that around 25-30 per cent. of young applicants were resigned to unemployment and were unwilling to take active steps to improve their position - not so much because they preferred idleness, but rather because 'apathy and listlessness are bred...by a long period of unemployment' (U.A.B. 1939, pp.44-9).

It seems that reliance on unemployment assistance was not simply the result of its availability. Evidence suggested that the deplorably low wages paid to many young people were at the root of the problem (as well as poor employment prospects *per se*). One report, on a survey of young people's wages in 1937 (Lush 1941), concluded that many young unskilled people might have found it difficult to find work at a wage which exceeded the assistance rate. But it was argued in the report that the solution to this problem lay in increased wages rather than reduced levels of allowances 'which are recognised to be subsistence allowances' (ibid., pp.28-9). The non-householder rates, which had been increased in 1936 for all young people except males aged 18 or over by between 1s. and 2s., stood at 10s. and 9s. per week for males and females (respectively) aged 21 or over, and at 8s. for 16-20 year olds. Although wages were undoubtedly lower than these rates in some cases, unemployment assistance rates for young people were not generous, especially when one compares them with the unemployment benefit rates for males and females aged 18-20 which stood at 12s.6d. and 10s.9d. respectively. It has been suggested that low benefit rates for young people in the 1930s did not improve the rate at which employment was found but rather tended to 'increase further the misery of being out of work' (Garside 1979, p.531).

The official unacceptability of 'idleness' led to suggestions that, as with unemployment benefit, unemployment allowances should be made conditional upon attendance at a training course. This was supported by several of the U.A.B.'s Advisory Committees, based on the principle that 'from the point of view of the community it is reasonable to hold that young people in receipt of public allowances should, as a condition, keep themselves fit in mind and body'; thus,

> [e]nforcement may be necessary in a minority of cases where a long period of idleness has destroyed initiative and left the applicant without any power to rouse himself from the state of apathy into which he has fallen (U.A.B. 1939, p.50).

One way in which this might have been achieved would have been by giving the U.A.B. a power to make a deduction if the applicant failed to attend. It was argued that regular attendance up to the age of 18 might well increase a young person's readiness to attend training centres in later years. In default of this it was suggested that the solution might be to refer irregular attenders to area officers of the Board to use 'the persuasive powers at their disposal' (University of Liverpool 1938, p.14). The Board recommended a revision of the policy of granting 'unconditional allowances' to young people (U.A.B. 1939, p.52). The decline in unemployment in the late 1930s and subsequent outbreak of war obviated any need for this reform.

Returning to the development of unemployment insurance, the Unemployment Act 1934 lowered the age of entry to the scheme from 16 to 14, although no benefits were payable until the age of 16 (previously 16 years and 7 months). Juveniles were expected to pay contributions of 2d. per week. For 14-16 year olds still at school or receiving juvenile instruction (see Chapter 7), dependency additions, of 2s. per week, continued to be payable. Up to 52 weeks unemployment benefit was payable, but there was no relaxation of the '30 in 2' rule (described above).

According to the minister, the lowering of the minimum age of insurance was aimed at giving the authorities a better chance of keeping in touch with the workless (Sir Henry Betterton M.P., *H.C. Hansard,* cols 1085-6, 30.11.33). This would have aided enforcement of compulsory instruction of unemployed juveniles - compulsory for local education authorities (LEAs) who had to make provision for courses, but also for young unemployed people themselves. Section 14 of the 1934 Act empowered the Minister of Labour to make regulations requiring insured unemployed juveniles between the ages of 14 and 18 to attend courses of instruction provided by LEAs. LEAs could enforce attendance under powers contained in the Education Act 1921. Juveniles could lose their right to benefit for failing to attend at an approved course of instruction. This was achieved by making the six weeks disqualification (applied in cases of voluntary unemployment and dismissal for misconduct) permanent in such a case. The Minister said he was 'utterly opposed to anything which could be described as "dole for children"' (ibid.).

To ensure that the extension of insurance did not act as an incentive for young people to leave school at 14, the government credited secondary school children with ten contributions a year (that is, up to a maximum of 20 by the age of 16). This had been recommended, in principle, by the National Advisory Councils for Juvenile Employment (1929 - *Majority Report*). The Unemployment Act 1934 also provided for additional days' benefit for those who had paid contributions for five years (subject to their satisfying the '30 in 2' rule and certain other requirements). But every two contributions paid in respect of a person aged under 18 only counted as one for the purposes of calculating additional days of benefit (section 3(2)).

It should, finally, be noted that, as was the case with unemployment assistance, young people's unemployment benefit was very low relative to wages; the benefit/wage ratio was only 0.25. Moreover, young people's unemployment benefit was, relative to wages, only half the value of adults' benefit (Benjamin and Kochin 1979, pp.524-5). Benjamin and Kochin claim that the lower rate of unemployment among juveniles than among adults was largely attributable to the low benefit/wage ratio. (This view is disputed by Sadler: 1983, p.22.)

Young people's benefits 1911-1939: some conclusions

Overall, the early years of unemployment insurance and assistance had offered little to young people. Low benefit rates and the imposition of household means testing kept state support at a minimum for this group. So far as unemployment insurance is concerned, it seems reasonable to conclude that given the low benefit rates for persons aged under 20, the stringent contribution conditions for this age group and the gap between the age of entry to employment and the minimum age of entitlement, young people were, as Benjamin and Kochin (1979, p.525) put it, somewhat 'insulated' from the scheme. Dependency additions in respect of 14-16 year olds were paid to unemployed parents under this and the unemployment assistance scheme, subject in some cases to conditions such as the juvenile's attendance at a training course. But there was no independent entitlement until the age of 16, even though at 14 juveniles in employment were expected, after 1934, to pay contributions to the insurance fund.

There are many examples of the application of the dependency assumption relating to young people (see Introduction) during these years: for example, in the delayed entitlement to unemployment benefit and transitional payments and much lower rates of benefit for young people compared with adults. Moreover, the related principle of family responsibility, which in some respects received its most intensive application under the household means test of the 1930s, is also much in evidence. Throughout this period it was anticipated that young people, although usually productive members of the workforce and economically important, could fall back on their families for support if, for example, they became unemployed and did not have adequate contributions for entitlement to unemployment benefit. The assumed availability of support from the family lay behind the Minister's decision in 1925 to deny extended benefit to single people living with their parents.

The lower rate of unemployment benefit paid to young people compared with the rate paid to adults was presumably intended to reflect the differential between adults' and juveniles' wage rates (young people paid lower insurance contributions). However, as mentioned earlier, the gap between adult and juvenile benefit rates was wider, in proportional terms, than the difference between the groups' respective average earnings. The U.A.B.'s insistence that unemployment assistance rates should not exceed wage rates ensured a wide differential between adult and juvenile rates for this benefit as well.

The Beveridge Report and Young People

Much has been written about the reforms proposed in the Beveridge Report (1942), many of which were instituted between 1945-48. But very little attention has been paid to the position of young people under them. In fact, young people gained little under the Beveridge proposals which, if anything, served to reinforce the dependency assumption relating to them.

For one thing, the Beveridge proposals for *social insurance* were based around a contributory scheme. Such schemes, as we have seen already, are not particularly helpful to young people because school leavers who cannot find employment are left unprotected (although under the Beveridge proposals the unemployed were 'excused' Class I contributions, which were credited to them). There was to be an initial qualifying contribution condition of actual payment of 26 contributions. To be entitled to full benefit, 48 contributions, paid or excused in the preceding year, were to be necessary. Unemployment benefit was to be of unlimited duration: the Beveridge proposals were based on an assumption that for most people interruptions from work would be only temporary, so that in rare cases of prolonged unemployment it would be possible for benefit to continue in payment without diminution. There were to be safeguards against idleness, in the form of up to six months attendance by adults at a work or training centre (subsequently regarded as impracticable).

For young people, benefit was to be conditional almost right from the start. The Report made the following recommendations (in para.131(ii)):

> But for young persons who have not yet the habit of continuous work the period should be shorter; for boys and girls there should ideally be no unconditional benefit at all; their enforced abstention from work should be made an occasion of further training.

In this recommendation Beveridge reasserted a long-standing belief (1930, pp.211-16) in the need for juvenile training and the avoidance of idleness and waste of abilities.

Not surprisingly, the wide differential between young people's and adults' benefit rates was to be retained. Single adults (aged 21 or over) were to receive 24s. per week, single people aged 18-20 were to receive 20s. and 16 and 17 year olds 15s. (para.401). Interestingly, persons in this last group were to be paid 1s. per week less than the amount paid to adult claimants in respect of 16 and 17 year old dependants. Beveridge worked on the assumption that 16 and 17 year olds would be living with adults who would be able to support them. The one shilling difference was seen as

> not a matter of great importance, but is probably right, in view of the fact that boys and girls of this age will be living with older people and while those older people have earnings can be maintained in part from those earnings (para.402(F)).

Thus, in the Beveridge Committee's view, 16 and 17 year olds were not completely independent individuals but partial dependants. This view was reinforced by the Report's assumption that young people of working age would not require any allocation for rent in their benefit - 'Rent can be presumed to be covered for boys and girls by their parents...'(para.226) - since they were clearly expected to be living in the same household. By 18 some independence would have to be assumed: 'for young persons of 18-20, who will in some cases already have separate households, a larger addition, including something for rent, is needed' (ibid.).

Under the Beveridge scheme, as with the unemployment insurance scheme then in operation, employers' and employees' contributions were to be at the same rate. However, the ratios of employees' (and employers') Class I contributions to benefit paid were set to change. Under the scheme then in operation the ratios were 1:4.25 (16 year olds), 1:6.33 (17 year olds) and 1:9 (18-20 year olds). Under the Beveridge proposals the ratio was to be 1:6 in every case. This meant that 17-20 year olds would not only pay higher contributions in absolute terms but also in relation to the benefit received. Although 16 year olds meeting the necessary contribution conditions stood to gain in this respect under the Beveridge proposals, the Report stated that their rates of contribution 'may need further consideration in the light of educational policy' (para.406).

Those in the age group 14-16 were not directly included in the Beveridge plan for social insurance. The Report stated: 'No specific proposals can be made in regard to boys and girls under 16 until educational policy is decided' (para.407). The Report contemplated that school leavers (the leaving age being 14 at this time) should not remain idle and should receive appropriate training. The Report's recommendation that 'Any payment of cash benefit to them should be combined with continued supervision and education' (para.407) is redolent of the unemployment policies vis a vis this age group in the 1920s and '30s. While laying down no precise rates for 14-16 year olds the Beveridge Committee suggested that 'In so far as they work for gain, insurance contributions should be paid by them and their employers' (ibid.). Obviously a certain amount of consideration was given to this age group, but nothing very concrete or positive about them emerged from the Report, other than the recommendations on family allowances - which were to be payable in respect of those continuing their education to the age of 16, or up to age 15 in other cases (see below). Thus far, no weakening in the dependency assumption can be discerned.

Beveridge also proposed a scheme of *national assistance* which, subject to proof of need and examination of means, would provide subsistence level support to anyone whose needs could not be met under the insurance scheme. The proposals were neither very specific nor detailed. They made no mention of young people. It was clear that under the Report it was assumed that assistance would have a limited role to play as most needs would be met by an extension of unemployment insurance. But young people who were unemployed on leaving school would have fallen within the group for whom assistance would be necessary due to their inability to fulfil contribution conditions (para.371).

Finally, we must consider aspects of the system of *family allowances* proposed by Beveridge. Family allowances had been campaigned for throughout the 1920s and '30s by the Family Endowment Society/Children's Minimum Council and its chief spokesperson Eleanor Rathbone. The social and political background to their introduction is documented in Land (1975) and Macnicol (1978) (see also Brown (1984)). Since their introduction, family allowances have been pivotal to the dependent child/independent adult distinction in social security law, as shall be shown later.

Rathbone (1924, p.311) had argued that the 'age of dependency' should be 15 rather than the school leaving age of 14 if family allowances were to provide adequately for families which included persons of this age. Beveridge considered that there was a case for extending entitlement beyond the minimum school leaving age - to 16 - for those continuing their education. But he stopped short of recommending payment in respect of juveniles in their first months of paid employment, because he felt that this would have represented an unnecessary subsidy to juvenile wages (para.423). The amount proposed for the allowance, 8s., was flat rate and not graded according to age. In fact the government subsequently opted for a much lower rate, 5s. (for reasons explained by Macnicol (1980), pp.189-94).

The principle of parental or family responsibility was acknowledged by Beveridge in the recommendation that nothing should be paid for the first child of the family (para.417). However, according to Land (1975, pp.201-2), it was the expected saving as a result of this limitation (estimated at £100million by Beveridge - para.420), keeping the projected cost within acceptable bounds from the government's point of view, which lay behind this recommendation. Thus Beveridge's talk of parental responsibilities was little more than a 'convenient rationalization' (Land 1975, p.202). In fact, there had been no prior suggestion that family allowances should be limited in this way (apart from Conservative proposals, on the grounds of economy, in the late 1930s). Moreover, no other social security allowances for dependants at this time excluded the first child. Beveridge did, however, propose payment of an allowance for the first child where families were in receipt of other social security benefits. Child tax allowances were to be retained.

Developments 1945-1966

Consequent on the Beveridge Report came the Family Allowances Act 1945, the National Insurance Act 1946 and the National Assistance Act 1948. This legislation established a pattern for social security provision which, despite major changes in the period 1980-1988, has in many respects continued up to the present day. In a period of rapidly increasing independence for young people in the 1950s and '60s, the principle of family responsibility and the dependency assumption relating to young people remained firmly embedded in British social security law - although having comparatively little effect on the lives of young people at a time of virtually full employment. The dependency assumption began to have an impact when youth unemployment started to rise in the late 1960s. In common with family responsibility, it was subsequently given greater prominence (under the Conservative reforms post-1979).

Family allowances

From the National Insurance Act 1946 to the Income Support (General) Regulations 1987 child dependency has been determined, for the purposes of just about all of the major social security benefits, by reference to the provisions governing family allowance/child benefit. These in turn have hinged on the school leaving age.

In the Family Allowances Act 1945 an allowance of 5s. per week was payable in respect of a 'child'. 'Child' included any person under the upper limit of compulsory school age (Section 2(1)(a)). Under s.35 of the Education Act 1944 the compulsory school age meant any age between 5 and 15 years, with power vested in the Minister of Education to raise the upper limit to 16 years by Order in Council. The leaving age was retained at 14 by the Compulsory School Age (Postponement) Order 1944 made under s.108(3) of the 1944 Act. The Order expired on 1 April 1947 and on that day the school leaving age became 15 years. A person was also a 'child' for the purposes of family allowances if continuing in full-time education or apprenticeship, until the 1 August next following his or her sixteenth birthday (Section 2(1)(b)). There was no provision for payment of family allowances to parents of young people continuing their education beyond the age of 16.

In the first twenty years following their introduction, family allowances were an area of social policy which was rather neglected by government (see Land 1975, Brown 1984). Young people, at least, were the beneficiaries of a reform in 1956 (Family Allowances and National Insurance Act 1956) under which the allowance became payable, for those in full-time education or apprenticeship, until the age of 18 rather than the previous age limit of 16 years. The Family Allowances and National Insurance Act 1964 raised this age to 19 where it remains to this day. Thus it was assumed that young people continuing their education would be dependants. This particular reform increased the hold of the dependency assumption on aspects of social security provision. The principle of work = independence, education = dependency, may have been appropriate in this period of full employment; but its continuation and intensification in later years, when there was much unemployment, had serious implications for young people, as we shall see later. It should be noted that the Family Allowances Act's treatment of young people as dependants might have meant that extra provision for these older children, some of whom were old enough to marry and have families of their own, would have been considered necessary. However, the rate for neither family allowances nor their successor, child benefit (introduced in 1977), was age-related. (Beveridge (1942, p.75) had merely recommended keeping age-relation under review.)

National Insurance

It will be recalled that in 1934 the minimum age of entry to the unemployment insurance scheme was reduced from 16 to 14, the then minimum school leaving age. The National Insurance Act 1946 retained this link with the school leaving age, which by the time the new scheme came into operation was 15.

In the scheme, Class I contributions were payable in respect of persons who were 'gainfully employed' - at one rate for those earning at least 30s., with a lower rate for those earning less than this, dependent on age. There was no under-18 rate for persons earning 30s. or more. Presumably 15-17 year olds were assumed to be incapable of earning such wages! The rates for under-18 year olds were considerably higher than the previous rates but similar to those set out in the Beveridge Report. The age bands had been simplified to over and under 18 years. The rates of benefit were determined in accordance with this division, with under 18 year olds normally receiving 15s. (the amount proposed by Beveridge, para.401), as compared with entitlement of 26s. for a single over 18 year old with no dependants.

The 1946 Act contained a number of complicated provisions, augmented by regulations, for payment and crediting of contributions. Some of these benefited young people. For example, persons aged under 18 and in full-time education, training or unpaid apprenticeship were credited with contributions. Those aged under the school leaving age were not liable to pay any contributions, nor were their employers. Females aged under 18 were expected to pay lower contributions than males; they generally received lower wages than males.

Dependency additions were paid in the same circumstances as family allowances (see above) save that only the first (or only) child was covered. (In 1951, lower rate additions for second and subsequent children were introduced - increased to the rate for first children in 1952.) The relatively low rate of the additions, coupled with their early failure to cover second children, led to a large increase in claims for national assistance top-ups to insurance benefits (from 11 per cent. of claimants to 18 per cent., between 1948-1950: N.A.B. 1952).

Subsequent reforms to the National Insurance scheme under the National Insurance Act 1965 made little difference to young people. When an earnings related supplement to unemployment benefit was introduced it benefited few young people, not only because their wages were low but also because it was not payable to those aged under 18. As a result, young people fell further behind other recipients of unemployment benefit (UB) and increasingly looked to supplementary benefit (which had replaced national assistance in October 1966) to supplement their UB. By August 1972 as many under-18 year olds were in receipt of UB *and* supplementary benefit as were in receipt of UB only.

National assistance

The National Assistance Act 1948 introduced a national assistance scheme under the administration of a National Assistance Board (N.A.B.). The scheme was intended to provide income maintenance for those who were not protected by national insurance. The scheme was expected to have a fairly limited role due to the anticipated extension of the insurance scheme and the likelihood of virtually full employment (or very short periods of unemployment). However, increasing numbers of recipients of insurance benefits came to rely on national assistance (NA) additions to top-up their benefit so that their requirements were met.

The minimum age of entry to the NA scheme was, in effect, 16 - under a negative reference in the Act (s.7(5)):

> No application for assistance shall be made by a person who has not attained the age of sixteen years, but nothing in this subsection shall prejudice the giving of assistance by reference to the requirements of any such person as a dependant of another person.

Children aged under 16 were envisaged as the most typical category of dependant under the scheme (*Explanatory Memorandum* to the Act, para.6). Such children's needs could 'only be met as part of the needs of an adult' (ibid.).

Since the Act provided for aggregation of requirements and resources where the applicant had dependants, any possibility of young people being granted assistance in their own right would depend on, *inter alia*, whether or not they were viewed as dependants. Section 7(4) gave the N.A.B. a power to 'decline to treat as a dependant of an applicant for assistance any person who has attained the age of sixteen years' when the Board considered it 'expedient to do so'. The Board could refuse to give an applicant assistance in respect of a 'dependant' aged over 16 who refused to look for work or attend a training course (Dow 1948, p.42). The *Explanatory Memorandum* to the Determination of Needs Regulations 1948 stated that persons aged 16 or over would be able to make independent application for assistance. However, over 16 year olds could be treated as dependants (provided they consented) if, 'exceptionally', it was considered convenient. Throughout the 1950s there were, at any one time, around 5,000 young people aged over 16 who might as a matter of law have applied for assistance in their own right but who were, as the Board put it (N.A.B. 1952, p.6), 'more conveniently dealt with as dependants'.

The N.A.B. had a duty, under s.4 of the 1948 Act, 'To assist persons in Great Britain who are without resources to meet their requirements, or whose resources...must be supplemented in order to meet their requirements'. The Schedule to the 1948 regulations laid down rules for the computation of requirements and resources. No distinction was made between male and female young applicants. Requirements were divided into two main types: those other than rent, and rent. Where the applicant or his wife/her husband was a 'householder', or the applicant lived alone, the net rent was to be paid in full, 'or such part thereof as is reasonable having regard to the general level of rents in the locality' (para. 4(1)(a) Part I to the Schedule to the Regs.). Non-householder applicants were entitled to a reasonable share of the rent payable by the householder of whose household the said applicant was a member, but not if the applicant was under 18 years of age (para.4(1)(b)). Clearly not all under 18 year olds were considered to be wholly dependent on the householder, so ought they not to have been given an allowance for rent to enable them to pay a contribution towards the rent paid by the householder?

The scale rates for young non-householder recipients of NA aged 16-20 fell steadily further behind the adult (21-plus) rate between 1948-61. The rate for 16-17 year olds was 75 per cent. of the adult rate in 1948; by 1952 it had fallen to 69.3 per cent., and in 1961 it stood at 64.5 per cent. The rate for 18-20 year olds stood, as a percentage of the adult rate in those same years, at 87.5 per cent., 83.9 per cent., and 76.6 per cent. - a similar downward trend. (Source: N.A.B. Reports for 1959 and 1960.) So, while national assistance rates rose throughout this period, the overall increase in the under-21 rates was proportionately smaller than for those aged 21 or over, widening the gap between these two age groups. The increased impoverishment of those aged under 21 is emphasised by the fact that adult assistance made no ground on gross and net earnings (of male manual workers) throughout the 1950s (SBC 1976, Table 7, p.35). Indeed, Lynes reckoned (1962, p.45) that while the incomes of those in receipt of National Assistance rose in real terms between

1948-61, it was by less than the rise in incomes across the population as a whole. So, if the differential between young people's and adults' assistance was widening, the incomes of young people on assistance would probably have been falling even further behind those of workers in their age group than their adult counterparts' would have been. Nevertheless, as shown in Chapter 1, youth unemployment levels were very low during this period (which included the years of National Service). Moreover, only small numbers of young people were receiving NA top-ups to UB (1,000 in 1960: N.A.B. 1961, p.26). Assistance top-ups became increasingly important from the mid-1960s onwards.

Conclusions on developments from 1945-1966

The family allowance, national insurance and national assistance reforms of the immediate post-war period at best consolidated and at worst confounded the legal position of young people requiring income maintenance from the state. For example, for the 15 year old who had left school there was no independent entitlement to benefit, and no family allowance for his or her parents - just a dependant's allowance if the parents were unemployed. For 16 year olds there was unlikely to be any insurance benefits entitlement, because contribution conditions would not be satisfied. Under the NA scheme under 18 year olds might or might not be classed as dependants. Under the Family Allowances Act separate provisions sought to classify young people for the purpose of deciding whether or not benefit was payable. For those continuing their education beyond the age of 16 there was no family allowance support until 1956. The manner of treatment of young people as dependants under the various schemes, including NA, seems to have been based on no clear underlying policy objectives. In the reforms of 1945, 1946 and 1948 the position of the young non-employed person was all but overlooked and seeds of confusion and entanglement were sown.

A partial explanation may lie in the virtual absence of a youth unemployment problem in the years immediately following the end of the Second World War, and consequent lack of concern. Nevertheless, many of the complex and sometimes contradictory benefit provisions applicable to young people in the 1980s originate from the disjointed provision for this age group arising out of the reforms of the 1940s. More significantly, perhaps, the ambiguous treatment of young people - as adults for some purposes and children for others - became a significant feature of the law on social security entitlement during this period.

Developments 1966-1980

National assistance was replaced by another non-contributory means-tested benefit, supplementary benefit (SB), in 1966; this was the principal social security reform of this period to affect young people. There were also changes in national insurance, for example the new contribution classes introduced in 1975. The Social Security Act 1975 retained, *inter alia*, the age of 16 as the minimum age of entry to the national insurance scheme and 'starting credits'. But as the prospects of finding work on leaving school began to worsen, fewer and fewer unemployed young people became eligible for unemployment benefits, because of their increasing inability to satisfy the initial test of twenty-six contributions. The Supplementary Benefits Commission (SBC), which took over the N.A.B.'s role of administering means-tested assistance, reported in 1978 (para.7.7) that

> Young men and women who have recently entered the labour market often do not have sufficient contributions to entitle them to unemployment benefit. Hence the growth in the numbers of unemployed under 20...further swelled the ranks of young supplementary benefit claimants

So by this time the SBC was claiming (ibid., para.7.9) that the increased reliance on SB rather than UB, especially since the latter was paid to an individual for a finite period (of 12 months), meant that 'the national insurance scheme, at present levels of unemployment, has clearly failed in its original purpose of being the main source of help for people unable to find work'. In this section, I intend, therefore, to concentrate principally on developments in supplementary benefit - whose residual role, as so perceived by Beveridge, was said in 1980 to have become 'more distant than ever' (Lynes 1980, p.16).

The minimum age of entitlement to SB was 16 (Supplementary Benefit Act 1966, s.1). The SB scheme retained the assumption concerning the dependency of young people continuing in education. Persons in 'non-advanced education' - 'school...or full-time instruction of a kind given in schools' - were not entitled to benefit save in 'exceptional circumstances' (which the SBC defined as including where a claimant had a dependant of his/her own or he/she was seriously disabled). The SBC justified its policy of excluding 'non-advanced' students from benefit by arguing that they were the responsibility of their parents who could claim child benefit in respect of them (Loosemore 1980, p.496). Furthermore, these young people were not available for work (such availability being a condition of entitlement). The 'non-advanced' test used by the SBC provoked some controversy and prompted legal action (*Sampson v SBC* (1979)) before being defined in law. Students in higher ('advanced') education were also barred from benefit during term-time, but not during vacations. Changes in the basis of assessing the student grant as a 'resource' reduced considerably the opportunities for students to draw SB during the short vacations after 1976 (but see Chapter 6 below). Also, the SBC misused their discretionary power to, in effect, withhold amounts of benefit when they made a standard vacation deduction of £1 per week from students' SB (*R v Barnsley SBAT ex parte Atkinson* (1977)). Changes in the law in 1977 under the Social Security (Miscellaneous Provisions) Act 1977) put this policy onto a lawful footing.

With the Social Security Act 1980 the Conservative government took the opportunity to tighten up the provisions governing the entitlement to SB of those in education and school leavers. The latter became forced to endure a waiting period of between one and three months (depending on their actual leaving date) before SB could be drawn (SB (Conditions of Entitlement) Regs 1980 and 1981). It may be noted here that the increasing demand for SB from school leavers (see Chapter 1), although leading to consideration of the introduction of what became the waiting periods (above), did not provoke any suggestions that the minimum age of entitlement to SB should be raised. It was accepted that 'young people in this age group should be encouraged to be as independent of parents as possible and to manage their own financial affairs, making a contribution towards their keep' (*Department of Employment Gazette* 1977, p.719). In *Social Assistance* (1978) the DHSS rejected raising the minimum age of entitlement, partly because of fear of the possible social and administrative repercussions but also because any savings would have been offset by having to prolong parents' entitlement to child benefit.

In some senses young non-householders were treated as adults. Although their scale rate was lower they received an addition for household expenses - 10s. (50p.) in 1967. At first this was only paid to claimants aged 18 or over. But from 1972 16 and 17 year olds were paid it as well. The rate had risen by then to 70p. The importance of the contribution was that it enabled young claimants living with their parents to pay an amount towards their keep. This gave them a measure of independence. It also helped to make up for the much lower rate of benefit paid to non-householders than to householders. Non-householders aged 16 and 17 received just over half the householder rate; and, under the SB Act 1966, they were not entitled to the long term rate of benefit generally available to those who had been unemployed for a year or more. The disparity between 'householder' and non-householder' rates was based on the assumption that a non-householder has fewer requirements than a householder.

Young people not entitled to supplementary benefit in their own right could be treated as dependants of parent claimants. When benefit entitlement was assessed a dependant's requirements and resources were aggregated with the claimant's. Issue and adopted children of the claimant who were living with him/her and for whom he/she was responsible were included, provided such children were aged either under 16 or 16-19 and were still at school or receiving instruction of a kind given in schools. The value of any educational maintenance allowance received from the LEA was normally disregarded (DHSS 1972, para.12). When the SB scheme was reviewed by a DHSS Review Team in the 1970s it was felt that aggregation should always occur where a young person was unable to draw benefit in his/her own right, such as where he/she was aged over 16 and still at school (DHSS 1978, paras 4.25 and 8.35). This was virtually the effect of the 1980 changes (see Chapter 4).

The scale rates under the SB scheme were criticised throughout the 1970s. Wynn (1972) showed how the rates for adolescents were well below those for adults even though young people's basic requirements were, by the age of 14, much the same as those of adults. She also showed that the benefit rates for adolescents were much lower, pro rata, than those in West Germany and the USA (a fact confirmed subsequently by the DHSS (1978, para.5.17)). The relative disadvantage suffered by families with 16 year old dependants was verified by a study by Essen and Ghosian (of the National Children's Bureau) (1977, p.215). The SBC acknowledged this problem and published figures showing a clear relative decline in SB rates for 16-17 year olds over the previous thirty years - from 62.5 per cent. of the adult single householder rate in 1948, to 49.7 per cent. (of the long term rate) in 1977 (SBC *Annual Report for 1977* (1978) Table 4.9, p.24). The SBC felt that this trend ought not to be allowed to continue. By November 1980 the decline had been halted, but not reversed.

Despite a reduction in the number of age bands in the SB scales (from five to three), the separate age band of 16-17 years was retained. One of the two new systems suggested by the DHSS Review Team for the age bands had included a 13-17 years band; this would have resulted in reduced entitlement in respect of 16-17 year olds (DHSS 1978, para.5.30). In the event, the other system which the DHSS had outlined, involving bands of 0-10, 11-15 and 16-17 years, was the one chosen.

Finally, mention may be made of the introduction of child benefit to replace family allowances in 1977 under the Child Benefit Act 1975. The main aim of this reform was to achieve a merger of child tax allowances and family allowances. Child benefit, although in many respects representing a continuation of family allowances, differs from family allowances in that it is payable for the first child as well as subsequent children. In theory it is more beneficial to poorer families than family allowances because low income families pay very little or no tax and gained next to nothing from child tax allowances compared with the better-off. As mentioned above, child tax allowances were phased out. In respect of most dependants, they ceased to be available from the tax year 1979-80 (Finance Act 1979 s.1(4)).

With so many young people pursuing courses of study in higher education, whose parents had been able to claim a tax allowance for so long as their children's 'dependency' continued (with no upper age limit), the absolute upper age limit of 19 on child benefit support caused 'some anxiety on the opposition benches' because of the possibility of financial hardship among parents with sons or daughters at college or university (Ogus and Barendt 1982, p.429). The Finance Act 1977 permitted tax allowances to be paid in respect of students who were, at the end of 1976, on a full-time higher education course, in most cases (s.26). For later students, adjustments were made to the student grant.

In the 1980 budget child benefit was increased by an insufficient amount for its pre-1979 value to be retained (see Lister 1980). This provoked fears that the future of the benefit might be in jeopardy.

Conclusions on the period 1966-1980

The period 1966-80 saw the role of SB as a source of support become increasingly important. As youth unemployment levels rose (see Chapter 1) the numbers of young people dependent on SB, either as claimants in their own right or as dependants, increased correspondingly. There was a temporary decline in the numbers of 16-17 year olds receiving SB in 1973, as a result of the raising of the school leaving age from 15 to 16. Leaving this aside, the total rose from 18,000 in Nov./Dec. 1967 to 42,000 in 1972, 83,000 in 1975, and 107,800 in 1979 (Ministry of Social Security 1967a, pp.105-6; SBC *Annual Report, 1976* (1977), p.53; *Youthaid Bulletin*, No.22, July 1985, p.5). In addition to the 83,000 16-17 year olds receiving SB in their own right in 1975, there were 25,000 16-17 year old dependants of parents receiving SB (SBC 1977, Table 3.5, p.46).

The overall position was (as shown in Chapter 1) that increasing numbers of young people were not working and looked to the benefits system for total or partial support. The nature of some of the reforms to the SB system in this period indicate that the authorities did not consider it to be the benefits system's role to shoulder complete responsibility for the support of the young unemployed. At a time when society's expectations of independence among young people were high, the benefits system placed a continuing emphasis on the dependency assumption.

Overall conclusions on developments 1911-1980

There was no coherent benefits policy or provision in respect of young people throughout this period. Moreover, young unemployed people were denied independence and adult status. Compared with provision for adults, benefit levels for young people were much lower - perhaps even lower, pro rata, than comparative wage rates - and conditions of entitlement for contributory benefits were often stricter. School leavers were often left without independent entitlement to benefits. The policy of treating 16 year olds as either dependants *or* independent claimants under the national assistance scheme - 'as convenient' - illustrates the apparent difficulties experienced by policy makers in deciding how to categorise young people under the social security system. Yet when the situation demanded it, for example when youth unemployment climbed steadily in the 1920s and early 1930s, policy makers *were* able to treat young unemployed people in a special way - by, in effect, compelling them to attend instruction centres or do without the dole. To some extent the ambiguous status of young people in the period surveyed merely mirrored that in society as a whole and, more especially, in the labour market, where young people were often exploited, especially in the early years when 'blind-alley' employment was rife.

The doctrine of family responsibility and the associated dependency assumption relating to young people retained a strong influence throughout this period - being reflected most markedly in the unemployment insurance restrictions on young people in the 1920s and the household means test of the 1930s. The Beveridge Report contained comparatively little about young people (although what there was - for example in the recommendation of no rent allowances for under 18 year olds - reinforced existing assumptions). Indeed the whole period appears to be marked by complacency or indifference towards the position of young people under the benefits system. Intervention only occurred when there was a threat to social order, a massive drain on the insurance fund, or suspected 'idleness' on the part of the unemployed.

The supplementary benefits scheme, while on the face of it more generous than its predecessors, in fact maintained the suppressed status of young claimants. Furthermore, both in family allowances/child benefit and dependency additions to other benefits, provision for young people was inadequate.

These deficiencies became more visible when, at a time of raised identity for youth in society, unemployment (and especially youth unemployment) began its steep and steady rise in the 1970s. In the Chapter 4 we shall see how young people fared under the post-1979 rationalisation of social security provision.

4 Welfare benefits for young people: 1980-1989

Introduction

The long-standing values and assumptions underlying social security provision for young people and serving to promote its restriction have been extended under the Conservatives' reforms post-1979. In this chapter, the theme of independence and the transition to adulthood in the context of social security entitlement is developed under three main headings: A. Basic entitlement; B. Household formation; C. Parenthood. The broad pattern of change after 1979 is briefly described first. (Note that Family Income Supplement/Family Credit is omitted in the interests of brevity.)

The major structural reforms after 1979

The period from 1980-88 witnessed a number of major reforms. These included the introduction of a revised supplementary benefits scheme in November 1980, more regulated and less discretion-based than its predecessor; a new housing benefit scheme in 1983, later revised as part of the Social Security Act 1986 reforms; the replacement of SB, under the 1986 Act, with the more streamlined Income Support scheme and the Social Fund.

The supplementary benefits scheme from November 1980 The basic conditions of entitlement - minimum age, availability for work, and so on - were set out in the amended (by the Social Security Act 1980) Supplementary Benefits Act

1976. Specific provisions on conditions of entitlement (including rules concerning persons in education - see Chapter 6), requirements, resources, payments in cases of exceptional need ('single payments'), and so on, were laid down in detailed sets of regulations, all of which were amended many times. The administration of the scheme and the appeals system were also reformed during this period. Previously-secret guidance to benefit officers was published (in the *S Manual*). As will be seen, many of the changes in 1980 were of form rather than substance. But there were some important substantive changes (for example, in school leavers' entitlement). Increasingly in the years after 1980 additional restrictions on entitlement were imposed.

Income support and the social fund Many of the broad policy considerations governing the introduction of income support (IS) and the social fund (SF) under the Social Security Act 1986 will be considered later. The prelude to their introduction was the reviews of social security in 1984-5 - the Review of Supplementary Benefits and Review of Benefits for Children and Young Persons - followed by the Green Paper and White Paper issued in 1985.

IS, introduced in April 1988, is, like SB, a non-contributory means-tested benefit intended to provide an income safety-net for the unemployed. The basis of assessing need is, in several important respects, different to that prevailing under SB. Heating, dietary and other special needs, all of which were formerly classed as 'additional requirements' which attracted prescribed additions to weekly benefit, are now met under various premiums paid to persons falling into broad categories determined by such factors as age, family status and disablement. (For a critique see Berthoud 1988.) The category 'young people' appears in social security legislation (in this case SI 1987 No.1967, as amended) for probably the first time. But young people are among the major 'losers' under the change from SB to IS, as will be demonstrated later.

The SF has replaced the regulations-based system of single payments. Most SF payments come under a separate administrative system from IS payments. Decisions on applications for most types of SF payment are made by SF officers. A SF officer acts under guidance and directions from the Secretary of State and within the constraint of a local office budget. But s/he must exercise an amount of discretion. SF payments fall into four categories: budgeting loans (in respect of 'important intermittent expenses... for which it may be difficult to budget': SF direction 2); crisis loans (for certain types of emergency); community care grants (to 'promote community care' (SF direction 4) - for example by helping persons who have been staying in an institution or residential care, or easing 'exceptional pressures' on families); and funeral, maternity and severe weather fuel payments (which are governed by regulations). The fact that payments in the first two categories take the form of loans rather than grants has proved to be the most controversial aspect of the social fund to date.

Housing benefit Help with rent and rates has, since April 1983, been available under the housing benefit (HB) scheme, which replaced the separate systems of rent and rates rebates and supplementary benefit rent allowances. Persons wholly dependent on SB were entitled to 'certificated HB' so that their rent and rates were generally paid in full. One aspect of the reform of HB under the Social Security Act 1986 changes is that a maximum of 80 per cent. of rates is covered. There have been significant and complex changes in the method of assessing HB entitlement (such as the new tapers) which have, in fact, made the scheme simpler. Those features of particular relevance to young people will be explained in this chapter (and, in so far as they relate to students, in Chapter 6). Note that when the community charge (or 'poll tax') replaces rates - first in Scotland (in 1989) and then in England and Wales (1990) - there will be a new system of community charge rebates within the housing benefit system. Although the community charge will be payable by non-householders and householders alike, it is convenient to discuss the rebates in conjunction with housing benefits in the section on 'Benefits aiding household formation' (below). The position of students under the community charge is considered briefly in Chapter 6.

Basic entitlement

The minimum age of entitlement

The SB reforms of November 1980 did not alter the minimum age of entitlement which remained at 16 years. However, the SB (Conditions of Entitlement) Regs 1980 introduced waiting periods for school leavers to prevent, *inter alia*, those aged 16 or over who intended to continue in education after the summer vacation misrepresenting their intention and drawing benefit (see Chapter 3 above, and *school leavers' entitlement* below).

In the ensuing years the possibility of raising the minimum age of entitlement to SB, and later IS, was at various times considered both inside and outside Parliament. Although fears that it was part of the government's 'hidden agenda' for social security reform were expressed on a number of occasions, it was not really until the run-up to 1987 general election that firm proposals surfaced. A Social Security Bill, introduced in the autumn of 1987, was enacted as the Social Security Act 1988. It raised the minimum age of entitlement to IS from 16 to 18 years (s.4). The Secretary of State was granted powers to prescribe circumstances in which 16 or 17 year olds might be entitled to IS and to pay IS to an unemployed person in this age group who might otherwise suffer 'severe hardship'. An examination of the rationale for this reform and a more detailed breakdown of the relevant legal provisions appear in Chapter 7. It may be noted that this reform ran in the face of advice from the SSAC who warned against putting an extra burden on families in this way. Given the fact that 16 year olds could marry, have families, pay taxes and national insurance contributions, and leave home and live independent lives, it would be hard, felt the Committee, to justify depriving them of benefit (SSAC *Third Report, 1984* (1985), para.6.19).

School leavers' entitlement

It was noted in Chapter 1 that during the 1970s increasing numbers of school leavers registered and claimed benefit. The authorities expressed concern not only at the severe operational difficulties caused, but also at abuse of the right to benefit by young people expecting to start work a few weeks after leaving school, or going on to further education, but misrepresenting their intentions. A particular complaint was that young people signed on while waiting for their examination results at a time when the had not made up their minds about what to do next. The DHSS Review Team recommended deferment of benefit entitlement for school leavers until the end of the holiday after they left school (DHSS 1978, paras 4.7-4.9). The Supplementary Benefits Commission supported the idea of fixed dates for commencement of entitlement and were clearly attracted to the savings to be made by such a reform.

The revised SB scheme in 1980 excluded from benefit those in receipt of 'relevant education' (SB Act 1976, as amended, s.6(2)) (basically 16-19 year olds in receipt of non-advanced education - see Chapter 6). A school leaver aged under 19 was to be treated as dependant, in 'relevant education', even though full-time education has ceased, until the earliest of the following ('terminal') dates: the first Monday in January; the Monday after Easter Monday; the first Monday in September or last Monday before reaching the age of 19. Child benefit was payable up to the 'terminal date'. Changes in 1987 plugged a loophole which had enabled those leaving school before their sixteenth birthday to draw benefit earlier than those leaving after a legal leaving date (SI 1987 No.358). Note that under amendments in 1982 (by SI 1982 No.470) child benefit ceased to be payable during the vacation after a person left school if s/he entered gainful employment or a place on the Youth Opportunities Programme. This change was expected to affect about 350,000 young people and produce annual net savings of £9 million. (Its effect on additions to retirement pensions was considered in *R(P)3/85*.)

In 1987, amendment regulations (SI 1987 No.358) prevented those 'leaving' school at Easter, but returning to sit examinations and/or attend school on a part-time basis, from drawing SB from the Easter 'terminal date'. This reform, which achieved only a modest saving, had the potential to cause young people losses of up to £350 or, alternatively, to discourage them from entering for public examinations (see Youthaid 1986). It received only extremely guarded support from the SSAC (1987b). The government had argued that those registered for examinations could not really be said to have left education (DHSS 1986b).

The scale rates

The scale rates for young householders were reduced considerably following the introduction, under IS, of a new rate of personal allowance for single persons aged 18-24 years. The former classifications of householder and non-householder were abolished. There is now a distinction based on age, with persons aged 25 or over qualifying for the higher rate previously available to all adult householders (see below).

So far as 16-17 year old non-householders are concerned, the decline in their rate of benefit relative to the amount payable to adult single householders in the years 1948-80 (see Chapter 3) was arrested and stood at 48 per cent. of the adult rate between 1980-88. But the non-payment of the non-householder's housing costs contribution (see below) to 16-17 year olds after April 1983 and 18-20 year olds from April 1984 in reality widened the differential still further. Moreover, the scale rate for 16-17 year olds stood at 85.7 per cent. of the single adult non-householder rate in 1948, rose to its highest ever level of 88.9 per cent in 1971, but declined to 76.9 per cent. by 1983 (according to calculations by CPAG: 1984, para.2.7). Now, of course, the adult rate for all claimants is lower than before 11 April 1988 in the case of 18-24 year olds who might previously have been classed as householders. This fact plus the removal of entitlement to IS from most of the 16 and 17 years age group render comparisons like CPAG's (above) somewhat nugatory.

Parents in receipt of IS may be able to claim for 16 and 17 year olds as dependants. There was frequent criticism in the 1970s by the SBC of the inadequacy of the allowances for children. The SSAC has recommended an increase in these allowances, and especially in those for older children (SSAC *Third Report, 1984* (1985), para. 4.20). Figures quoted by the Committee show an increase in SB children's rates of 31.5 per cent. between November 1980-84 as compared with a 44 per cent. increase in child benefit over the same period. So there was a decline in the value of benefits for children of the unemployed on SB relative to the value of child benefit paid to those in work. Moreover, benefit rates for teenagers were based on a serious underestimation of their requirements.

The changeover from SB to IS has produced no improvement in dependants' allowances. But there is now a family premium which is payable to parent claimants on top of the basic allowances. The family premium and lone parent premium are flat rate - unlike dependants' allowances, which are age-related.

Abolition of the non-householder's contribution

Around 90 per cent. of young people aged 16-19 live as members of the household of one or both of their parents (Young Homelessness Group 1985, p.3). Under pre-April 1988 arrangements such persons were, if entitled to SB, classed as non-householders and were entitled to the appropriate rate (under SI 1983 No.1399). The effects of the 1988 reforms were discussed earlier. Noted in particular was the reduction in the level of support offered to single people aged under 25. But young people living with their parents had already been the subject of a reduction in support towards housing costs. In April 1983 new 16 and 17 year old SB claimants received £3.10 per week less than had previously been available via an allowance towards contributions to housing costs - the non-householder's contribution, which this age group lost. From April 1984 the 18-20 age group lost it as well, as did 21-24 year olds from 28 July 1986.

The non-householder's contribution had previously been paid to all young non-householders in recognition of their need to contribute towards the householder's (usually a parent's) housing costs. The basic rate of the contribution could be increased up to a prescribed maximum (£6.55 in 1982) if certain conditions were met (see decisions R(SB)*4/81*, *11/81* and *16/81*).

The effect of the abolition of these additions in the case of 16-20 year olds was increased dependence of young unemployed non-householders on their families. For parents there was an even greater onus on them than previously to provide free accommodation. The government's contention was that this loss would be compensated for by the fact that families' housing benefit would not be subject to deductions for teenagers (the 'non-dependant deduction'). Thus families in receipt of housing benefit would be no worse off (Secretary of State for Social Services 1984, para.23). But it seems to have been rather illogical to have introduced a non-dependant deduction from parents' HB in respect of offspring who were working (see below) while, in parallel regulations, providing that no rent contribution would be expected if the young person was in receipt of SB. The SSAC argued (1984, para.35) that young SB recipients 'are legally adults and if they are adult enough to pay while working, it is logical that they are adult enough to expect to bear a share of the costs even when on supplementary benefit'. It was also suggested (Youthaid 1984, p.5) that the likely saving to the government of £60 million in a full financial year was being made 'at the expense of an important family transfer' (ibid.). This refers to the transfer of resources within families, including contributions by young people towards their 'keep' - an aspect of the transition to adult independence (see Chapters 2 and 5).

The non-dependant deduction from housing benefit

The non-dependant deduction (NDD) affected about 850,000 households in 1985 (Green Paper 1985, Vol.2, para.3.71). It involves, in effect, the deduction of a set amount from a person's HB in respect of an assumed contribution towards housing costs by, for example, a son or daughter of working age living with his/her parents. The amount of the NDD, which is technically subtracted from a claimant's 'applicable amount', depends on the amount earned by the non-dependant. From April 1988 the deduction for those earning £49.20 or more per week amounted to £8.20 rent and £3.00 rates (total £11.20) and for those earning below £49.20, £3.45 rent and £3.00 rates (total £6.45) (SI 1987 No. 1971, reg.63). There is no deduction from rent rebates or allowances in respect of a single non-dependant aged under 25 who is on IS. A 'child' (person aged under 16 years) or young person (aged 16 but under 19 and in respect of whom child benefit is payable) cannot be a non-dependant (ibid., reg.3).

Criticism of the NDD surfaced both before and during the Review of Housing Benefits in 1984-5. The deduction was found to be unnecessarily large (SSAC 1984, para.28). Like the household means test of the 1930s the deduction could encourage young workers' departure from the family home, thus working against one of the most widely accepted goals of social policy, the cohesion of the family unit. It was also shown that parents were very reluctant to ask their children for the full amount of the deduction given the generally low level of the latter's earnings (Cusack and Roll 1985). Thus the effect of the NDD could be a degree of hardship, leading in severe cases to an accumulation of rent arrears (which HB was designed to prevent or alleviate) (ibid.). This was confirmed by the Association of Metropolitan Authorities and Association of District Councils in evidence to the HB Review (Kemp and Raynsford 1985, pp.5, 12). There was also the likelihood of reducing work incentives given the potentially very low wage/benefit ratio after the NDD was taken into account. In addition, it was felt to be unfair to deduct an amount from persons in receipt of HB - the poor - without making a corresponding deduction from mortgage tax relief - which benefited the better-off. Finally, there was the criticism emanating from local authorities that the NDD complicated the administration of the scheme.

Despite calls for its abolition, retention of the NDD was recommended by the HB Review Team, who expressed the belief (1985, para.4.12) that it was 'right in principle that those sharing a household should contribute to the costs if they have the income to do so'. More significantly, perhaps, the cost to the government of abolishing the NDD was estimated at £350 million. The NDD was, accordingly, preserved under the new HB scheme introduced in April 1988. The new separate rates of deduction, related to the earnings of the non-dependant, ease some of the pressure on low income families. But (on 1988-89 rates) if a family contains an 18 year old earning, say, £48 per week, a £1.50 rise in his/her earnings could result in the parents in effect losing £4.75 per week in HB. It would appear, however, that under the system of HB community charge rebates to be introduced in Scotland in April 1989 (under SI 1988 No.1890) there will be no NDD. (Non-dependants will themselves be liable to pay the community charge.)

Benefits aiding household formation

The importance of household formation to the transition to adulthood was described in Chapter 2. It is now necessary to assess the degree of support offered to young unemployed people wanting to set up home either as an expression of independence and maturity or, more importantly, because they have no 'family' home in which they can reside (e.g those leaving care).

Between ages 18-25 increasing numbers of young unemployed people live independently. For example, of those young claimants who were being paid supplementary benefit in 1985 (as boarders, householders or non-householders) the following proportion of each age group were assessed as householders:

16 and 17 year olds: 4.7%
18-20 year olds: 17.8%
21-24 year olds: 51.0%
(Source: *H.C. Hansard,* Vol.72, cols 551-2w, 5.2.85)

Although many of these young people had probably been under no pressure to leave home and were simply desirous of independence, benefits provided a lifeline to a good number of others. Social security offered the means to manage an enforced separation from their families necessitated by domestic disquiet or overcrowding, a search for work away from their home area or parental pressure requiring them to 'stand on their own feet' (Hedges and Hyatt 1985, para.6.5.3(c)). Nevertheless, as will be demonstrated, the squeeze on young people's benefits from 1980 onwards has made household formation, already hampered by the shortage of supply of rented accommodation, considerably more difficult for the young unemployed.

Removal of the householder/non-householder distinction under income support

In the assessment of SB entitlement it had always been important to determine the level of a claimant's responsibility for housing costs. Prior to the introduction of HB in 1983 his/her requirements, especially in respect of rent, were usually met by an addition to SB. But even after the introduction of HB the rule whereby a 'householder' would receive a higher amount for his/her normal requirements than would a 'non-householder' continued. From April 1987, the ordinary rate for a single householder was £30.40, and for a non-householder aged 18 or over, or 16-17 with a dependant, it was £24.35 (SI 1983 No.1399, as amended).

As shown later, in its avowed aim of simplifying the system of income support the government decided to sweep aside the relatively complicated householder/non-householder distinction. One of the reasons that the law was so complex was the fact that the distinction determined many different aspects of entitlement. The government proposed to base the distinction between entitlement to the upper and lower rates not on householder status as previously but on age. Those aged 25 or over would receive the higher rate, on the assumption that the majority of them would be living independently. Those aged under 25 would receive the lower rate; it was assumed that most of them would be living in the family home, so their requirements would not be as great (Green Paper 1985, para.2.73). (The proposals concerning young couples and young parents will be considered later in this chapter.) The government would be aiming to give claimants 'a reasonable level of help rather than to provide in detail for every variation in individual circumstances' (ibid., para.2.71). The government said that there was no point in retaining the complex distinction between householder and non-householder status in income support when housing costs were met by housing benefit (Mr A. Newton M.P., Oral evidence to H.C. Social Services Committee, 26 June 1985, Q.188). Yet in the assessment of housing benefit it is still necessary to make this distinction. No-one can deny that the age 25 split is simpler than the householder test. The government argued that it would be more easily understood by claimants, thus meeting another objective of the IS reforms (Green Paper 1985, Vol.2, para.2.70). Yet there is little evidence that householder/non-householder distinction and classifications were not generally well understood by claimants.

Another stated objective of the Social Security Act 1986 reforms was more effective targeting of need. However, one of the major objections to the age 25 split was the fact that a healthy young person aged 25 or over continuing to live with his/her parents would be 'better off, for no good reason' (Rowell and Wilton 1986, p.21). On the other hand, persons aged under 25 who became single householders would, equally, be deprived of resources. For example, 58 per cent. of 24 year old claimants were householders (including joint householders) in 1985 (SSAC *Fourth Report, 1985*, (1986) para.3.8). So when the government stated (White Paper 1985, para.3.3) that

> The abolition of the householder distinction and the introduction of the 25 age point have enabled the Government to concentrate more resources on older people - including pensioners and disabled people living in other people's households (ibid., para.3.13)

it was clear that the targeting of some groups' needs would at the expense of others' - especially young householders aged under 25.

Of course, all age dividing lines are to some extent arbitrary. Even the government has conceded that such divisions are 'open to argument at the margin' (ibid). But the main problem with the age 25 split is that it ignores social realities, namely the 'steady trend towards formation of independent households at younger ages' (SSAC *Fourth Report, 1985* (1986) para.3.9). Official statistics revealed that 50 per cent. of unemployed 21-24 year olds were paid benefit as householders in 1985. Accordingly, the SSAC did not believe that there was 'any justification for regarding age 25 as an adequate proxy for the assumption of householder status and responsibilities' (ibid., para.3.8). The age 25 split in IS personal allowance rates is one of several features, resulting from simplification, which are, arguably, 'so simple as to be crude' (Berthoud 1988, p.11).

Even with concessions being announced for couples and lone parents, there were 50,000 young people who stood to lose under the proposal (Berthoud 1986a, p.12). Those in receipt of SB before 11 April 1988 were entitled to transitional protection. In other words, their benefit would remain at its pre-11 April rate for so long as this remained higher than the under-25 personal allowance in IS. Those aged 18-24 who applied, and qualified, for IS after 11 April 1988 were entitled to a basic personal allowance of £26.05 compared with the previous ordinary householder SB rate of £30.40 (or long-term SB rate of £38.65). (Note that the IS system does not offer a long-term rate; yet, as shown in Chapter 1, many of the young unemployed are in long-term unemployment.) From April 1989 the allowance will be £27.40 for a claimant aged 18-24 and £34.90 for a claimant aged 25 or over.

Board and lodging payments

Recent government policy on board and lodging payments for unemployed young people offers one of the clearest examples of how the inter-action of short-term government policies with longer-term underlying assumptions and values has influenced the status of young people in the context of social security entitlement.

For many young people who leave home the shortage of available accommodation to rent, highlighted in a succession of reports (for example, Department of Environment 1981, Randall 1988), results in their taking up residence in board and lodgings or hostels (see Evans and Thrower 1986). Yet severe restrictions have progressively been imposed on the benefit entitlement of young people in such accommodation. Indeed, the income support changes, explained in more detail later, are the latest in a long line of what have often proved controversial legal developments concerning board and lodgings payments. The board and lodgings saga has stimulated the loudest public expression of support for young unemployed people on a social security issue since youth unemployment emerged as a major problem in the 1970s. The government reacted to the rapidly increasing expense of meeting board and lodgings charges and suspicions of abuse by introducing restrictions on entitlement - some of which, as the *Cotton* and *Elkington* cases showed, were tainted with illegality.

Background Under the supplementary benefits (SB) scheme board and lodging charges had always been met where a claimant's accommodation and meals, etc., were provided on a commercial basis. For example, the SB Act 1966 had provided for an 'appropriate' amount to be paid to a boarder. The Supplementary Benefits Commission regarded persons related to the householder (such as a son or daughter), or those simply paying their way in the household, other than as boarders - a policy subsequently incorporated in regulations in November 1980 and thereafter. These regulations (the SB (Requirements) Regulations 1980 and 1983) contained exclusions from boarder status (for those living with a 'close relative' - see reg.2(1) and *R(SB)22/87* - or residing on a non-commercial basis, certain patients, and certain others).

The 1980 Regulations (SI 1980 No.1299) provided for a maximum amount of SB for board and lodging charges to be determined by a benefit officer, being 'a reasonable weekly charge' for full board and lodging of a suitable standard. This 'local limit' could be extended by set amounts in individual cases where the claimant was infirm, of pensionable age, or receiving the long-term rate, and in certain other cases. Under a new provision in 1983 the maximum amount could be exceeded for up to thirteen weeks (previously there had been no time limit) if this was reasonable to allow the claimant time to find alternative accommodation. The 1983 Regulations (SI 1983 No.1399) introduced a system of three-tier local limits for different accommodation arrangements - essentially ordinary board and lodging, residential care homes and nursing homes.

The reform of board and lodging payments In the early 1980s there was a large increase in the numbers of SB boarders and in the amount paid out in board and lodging charges. Between 1979-84 claims per annum had risen as follows:

1979: 49,000
1981: 69,000
1982: 85,000
1983: 108,000
1984: 139,000

The annual increase between 1981-84 was around 25 per cent. (SSAC 1985, para.11). Later, following a thorough examination of claims, the government announced that over 160,000 boarders had received payments in 1984, with a total pay-out of £500 million - an 80 per cent. increase in one year (*H.C. Hansard*, Vol.100, col.1024, 2.7.86). The number of under-25 year olds claiming as boarders went up by 60 per cent. during 1983 (from 23,000 to 37,000) while the overall number of SB claimants in this age group increased by only 9 per cent. Moreover, the number of 16-17 year olds claiming as boarders at any one time was estimated to have risen from 4,300 at the end of 1982 to nearly 10,000 two years later (SSAC 1985, Appendix 2, para.8).

The government contended that these massive increases were far larger than could be explained by housing problems or unemployment (*H.C. Hansard*, Vol.84, col.49, 21.10.85). Regulations were issued in late 1984 (SI 1984 No.2034) temporarily freezing (until 1 May 1985) the local limits as 'a first step in bringing expenditure under control and responding to the increasing public concern about individual exploitation and abuse of board and lodging payments' (SSAC 1985, para.2). The regulations purported to give the Secretary of State a discretionary power to determine the limits to be applied.

The 'public concern' the government referred to was centred on reports of unemployed young people staying for long periods in seaside resorts - the so-called 'Costa del Dole' (Mathews 1986). It was alleged that landlords of seaside hotels and guest houses regarded the board and lodging limits as appealing, had been advertising for SB claimants and had attracted increasing numbers of young residents. Yet the government's evidence was disputed by members of the House of Commons Standing Committee on Statutory Instruments; and the SSAC, referring to the government's lack of evidence concerning the 'Costa del Dole' commented that 'anecdote is not a safe basis for legislation' (1985, para.32).

The government felt that another reason for making changes was what they regarded as the high rate of benefit paid to young boarders - perhaps £80-90 per week - which the government alleged exceeded what many of them could earn and represented a considerable work disincentive. According to the government, the local fixing of limits had led to the system being abused by owners - they had, through cartel-type activities, forced prices up in order to draw huge sums from the DHSS. The government proposed a national limit (allegedly set at the level of the cheapest board and lodging accommodation) varied only to the extent that the ceiling in Greater London would, at £60-70, be higher than that applicable elsewhere - £50-60. But the national limit offered no variation to meet differences in local costs and in the quality of accommodation, leading to serious doubts about the realism of a single national limit in coping with the wide variety of circumstances and costs applicable in board and lodgings.

In addition to new national limits, the government proposed special arrangements designed to recognise that only in exceptional circumstances would young people aged 16-17 be entitled to benefit as boarders in their own right. The plan was that 16-17 year olds claiming as boarders in their normal local office area (or any area immediately adjoining it) would be paid, initially, as 'non-householders'. They would be advised that only in exceptional cases (to be prescribed) would they qualify as boarders. For all unemployed people claiming outside their normal area office (apart from 16-17 year olds covered by exceptions) there were to be time limits of between two and four weeks on board and lodging payments after which payment would be reduced to the non-householder rate unless a claimant could show that householder status was justified. The proposals were subsequently modified to impose restrictions on young people *anywhere*. The time limits were deemed by the government to be sufficient to provide both a reasonable period in which to search for a job and assistance to those young people who through some personal crisis suddenly appeared, without adequate resources, in city centres. (Under the regulations that followed, a time limit of eight weeks in some areas, in addition to those of two or four weeks, was incorporated into the restrictions.) It was proposed that after the initial period had expired the claimant could not be treated as a boarder before the expiry of a further twenty-six weeks. During these twenty-six weeks the claimant would only be entitled to the non-householder rate.

There was widespread criticism of the proposals. There appeared to be little real evidence that migration of young people to the seaside for an extended holiday on the dole was taking place at all. One M.P. referred to the '"Sun" logic' behind the regulations which were 'intended to deal with abuses and scandals of large numbers of young people supposedly sunning themselves in Brighton, Bournemouth and various other seaside resorts' (Mr. Max Madden, H.C. Fifth Standing Committee on Statutory Instruments, col.10, 12.12.84). It was argued that if young people left home for board and lodgings it was often not out of choice and they should receive additional help rather than be faced by the kinds of restrictions the government was proposing (Malpass 1985, p.13).

The causes of this often unwilling departure from the family home are well known. A report on homeless young people in 1976 found that homelessness among the young

> often stems from inadequate preparation for leaving home. The family background may be such that when a crisis arises, the young person feels unable to resolve the situation except by moving out. Sometimes parents force their children to leave. In either case a hurried departure may result in an unplanned future (DHSS 1976, para.6.3).

This was reinforced by a further study, published in 1981, which identified family break-up and disputes with parents as the chief causes of young people leaving home (Department of the Environment, p.57). The new restrictions were expected to force young people out of their home areas as many were simply unable to return to the parental home. They were likely to be turned into nomads or drifters because they could 'not remain long enough in one location to find permanent accommodation or a job' without being deprived of their board and lodging allowance (SSAC 1985, para.72). But the government argued that if there was no work available in an area there was 'little case for providing an incentive to young people to settle' (Secretary of State for Social Services 1985, para.7).

The government clearly believed that many young unemployed people were moving to holiday centres or large cities with no intention of seeking work and that for those who were seriously looking for work the time periods would be sufficient to enable them to secure employment if available to them. The government felt that the fact that annual rises in homelessness (as measured by young people presenting themselves for accommodation) of around 5 per cent. in 1982 and 1983 were far below the percentage increases in board and lodging allowance claims in those years, suggested that homelessness was not the main explanation for the rapid increase in board and lodging benefit claims. But the government's apparent assumption that young people unable to remain in board and lodgings or move in with their parents could find alternative accommodation was found to be 'questionable in the light of the known scarcity of public and private rented accommodation accessible to single people, especially those dependent on social security benefits' (SSAC 1985, para.5).

It is likely that the majority of young people living in board and lodgings find them far from ideal. Most young people would prefer to live in self-contained accommodation because of the privacy and degree of independence it offers (Young Homelessness Group 1985, p.9). However, the lack of available accommodation of this kind was sending young people into low standard hostels and lodging houses. Thenceforth, young people's chances of securing *any* type of accommodation would be hampered by the proposed restrictions which, by imposing maximum periods of entitlement in any one area, would prevent young people from establishing the continuous residential qualification required both for local authority and housing association accommodation. The government was prepared to accept that improvements could be made to the availability of accommodation for young people. However, whatever its views on the future direction of housing policy may have been, it was of the opinion that 'housing problems are not resolved by making inappropriate supplementary benefit payments' (Secretary of State for Social Services 1985, para.8).

Nevertheless, the government made a few concessions following the largely critical response to the proposals. The categories of exemption were widened (and the regulations by which this was done granted the Secretary of State a power to add further categories by administrative direction). Moreover, there were to be no restrictions on boarder status for claimants aged 25 or over or those with dependent children. But the time limits for young people were to go ahead. The allowance was to be available to the under-26 age group for periods of only two, four or eight weeks (depending on area of residence) in any twenty-six week period. Board and lodging areas were drawn up, each with their own designated time limit. The new rules (SI 1985 No.613) came into force on 29 April 1985. Limited transitional arrangements applied, allowing those aged under 26 in the exemption categories to stay in their existing accommodation at their existing rate of benefit for a period of thirteen weeks. The areas and time limits were set out in a booklet, *Board and Lodging Areas*, published separately to the regulations. The 131 new areas, or zones, were phased in on 13 and 27 May, 24 June and 30 July, 1985. The first areas to be covered were, not surprisingly, the 'Costa del Dole' areas around the country's major holiday resorts.

Claims that, despite the new exemption categories, the new restrictions would lead to an increase in the numbers of young people sleeping 'rough' (Crawford 1985 p.56) were soon vindicated by reports of homeless young people being told to move on by the DHSS and of some landlords refusing to offer accommodation to persons under the age of 26 (*The Guardian* 30.4.85). Within a few months there were reports of suicide following service of eviction notices as a consequence of the new regulations, and even rumblings of disquiet on the Conservative back benches about the effects of the regulations.

But there was a successful challenge to the 1985 Regulations in the *Cotton* case, in which judgment was delivered on 31 July 1985. The regulations were considered to be illegal by Mann J. His Honour held that two important subparagraphs in the regulations (paras 6(2) of Schedule 1A and 5(3) of Schedule 2A) were *ultra vires* and void. The reason was that the power which had been given to the Secretary of State to make regulations not requiring prescribed questions to be decided by adjudication officers, tribunals or the Social Security Commissioners (under s.2(1A) of the SB Act 1976), did not, in Mann J's view extend to regulations referring to questions as to benefit entitlement of a *class* of claimant and of *general* application. The power would only have been validly exercised if the questions related to decisions on entitlement in *individual* cases. The paragraphs in question had applied limits which were of general application (*R v Secretary of State for Social Services ex parte Cotton and Waite*, The Times 5.8.85).

As a result of the ruling, Cotton, a 22 year old man from Birkenhead, was entitled to £103.30 per fortnight indefinitely instead of for just four weeks. The 1985 Regulations were, in effect, 'withdrawn'. Mr Fowler, the Secretary of State, then had two options: fresh legislation or an appeal. Meanwhile there was some doubt about whether or not the High Court's ruling was also applicable to the board and lodgings allowance maximum limits which had been introduced. Although the DHSS decided that the area allowance limits in force immediately prior to the *Cotton* decision should apply to new claimants and continue to apply to existing ones, in a case brought by Shelter at a London appeal tribunal the tribunal refused to apply the formula laid down in the 1985 Regulations.

As the Secretary of State considered which of his two options to select, M.P.s were pressing for the payment of arrears to claimants affected by the time limits. Eventually the government agreed to pay arrears. (In mid-December the Social Security Minister reported to the House of Commons that the DHSS had paid out £750,000 in arrears to 8,500 young claimants (*H.C. Hansard*, Vol.89, col.172, 17.12.85).)

On 20 August 1985 the Secretary of State lodged an appeal in the *Cotton* case. While the appeal was pending, Mr Fowler decided to invoke his other option, further regulations. But his new, temporary regulations (covering the period to April 1986) were to apply only to future claims - 'a concession to the court judgment' - that is those made on or after 4 November 1985 (*The Guardian* 22.10.85). These new regulations, containing the substance of the previous ones, were to be an interim measure pending the Court of Appeal hearing in *Cotton* towards the end of November. The government faced renewed criticism but defended the restrictions by referring to the need to preserve work incentives for young people and to reports of abuse. A special fraud investigation in Euston had apparently shown that 600 out of the 1,200 young people claiming board and lodging payments in respect of hotels were no longer living there. These figures were disputed - only ten claimants had been prosecuted.

When the regulations were laid before Parliament doubts were expressed about their legality. After consulting with the Solicitor-General, Mr Fowler withdrew them. The government put redrafted regulations before the House of Commons on 20 November 1985, five days before the Court of Appeal hearing in *Cotton* was due to commence. Mr Newton, Social Security Minister, defended the decision to introduce these regulations so soon before the appeal hearing by saying that the legal action concerned a purely technical issue (*The Times* 29.11.85). The new regulations (SI 1985 No.1835), which reintroduced the two, four and eight week limits for payment of allowances, came into force almost immediately, on 25 November 1985. They exempted existing boarders from the time limits until 28 July 1986 and introduced a new Secretary of State discretion to exempt from time limits those suffering exceptional hardship.

The Court of Appeal decision in *Cotton* was delivered on 13 December 1985. The Court, comprising Donaldson M.R., May L.J. and Glidewell L.J., unanimously upheld the decision of Mann J. The ruling affected payments made between 29 April and 24 November 1985. Many claimants were expected to have a claim for back payment of benefit. The ruling went further than the decision of the High Court in that the Court of Appeal held that both the area allowance limits and the time limits which had been applied to ordinary boarders between April and November 1985 were invalid. A few days later the government announced that it had decided not to appeal to the House of Lords. (The Court of Appeal had refused leave to appeal.) Thus another chapter in the board and lodgings saga, covering the period prior to November 1985, was at a close. There had been little gain, other than a short-term victory on technical legal grounds, for opponents of the government's policy on board and lodging allowances, although they had, at least, the satisfaction of knowing that arrears would be paid to claimants affected by the regulations. If these opponents had been expecting their Lordships to offer any comments on the motive behind the regulations, or to discuss their effects on claimants, they must have found little to satisfy themselves in the cold, grey legal argument expounded in *Cotton*. There had been some immediate embarrassment for the government after the High Court decision in July 1985. But, probably expecting defeat in the Court of Appeal, the government had already taken moves, as shown above, to ensure the future vitality of the board and lodging restrictions.

As the *Cotton* case had reached its climax, the regulations which were to cover the post-November 1985 period were made the subject of a fresh legal challenge, this time by the London Borough of Camden. Leave to apply for judicial review was granted to Camden and a claimant, Beverly Nelson. The hearing of both applications took place before Macpherson J. on 26 February 1986. The main ground on which the challenges were based was alleged failure by the government to adopt the appropriate laying before procedure in the case of the November 1985 regulations. But such failure was held not to have rendered the regulations as a whole invalid, a view subsequently upheld by the Court of Appeal (*R v DHSS ex parte London Borough of Camden and Beverly Nelson*).

In June 1986 Mr Newton, Social Security Minister, announced that apart from an improvement in the amount paid to couples, no increase in the board and lodging allowance was to be made in July 1986 when other social security benefit rates were raised. Those aged under 26 who were already living as boarders would not be subject to the two, four or eight week time limits - i.e., transitional protection would continue indefinitely. But from 28 July, new claimants would again be subject to these limits unless they fell within one of the exemption categories (*H.C. Hansard*, Vol.99, cols 1069-70, 18.6.86).

The legal battles were not over. On 22 July 1986, in the case of *Elkington*, Simon Brown J. in the Divisional Court declared *ultra vires* the Temporary Provisions regulations introduced in November 1984 (SI 1984 No.2043) to 'freeze' the local limits until 1 May 1985 and give the Secretary of State power to determine the limits to apply (thus ending the purely local fixing of limits) (*R v Secretary of State for Social Services ex parte Elkington*, 22 July 1986). The result of the decision was that the previous (1983) version of the regulations applied to the period between November 1984 and April 1985. Those who had claimed during this period were thus entitled to the difference between the frozen limits and what would be judged by adjudication officers to have been reasonable charges for board and lodging at the time. Arrears were payable to between 17,000 and 35,000 people (*The Times* 6.3.87).

Meanwhile further evidence on the effects of the changes came to light. A survey of homeless young people in London showed that the board and lodging regulations had exacerbated poverty and vagrancy - 18 per cent. of the 123 persons surveyed were forced to sleep rough after losing their accommodation and 30 per cent. used part of their food allowance to pay for their accommodation. Moreover, 26 per cent. were unaware of the exemptions in the regulations (W.E.C.V.S., 1986, p.1). The survey, carried out in December 1985 and January 1986, also confirmed the inability of most young board and lodging claimants to return to a family home; many cited 'family or relationship problems' as the reason for this. Moreover, some gave as their reason the fact that they had previously been in care, which in may cases would have resulted from family tension or break-up. Similar findings emerged from a survey by the Social Security Policy Inspectorate in August 1985; 44 per cent. of boarders aged under 26 were living in board and lodging because of disagreements or disputes with parents or relatives. Research by the Policy Studies Institute revealed that few young people returned home after the April and November 1985 changes. But equally, although some claimants roamed around the country it was 'apparently not an army of them' - less than 10 per cent. actually moved to another area (Berthoud 1986b, paras 94-102).

Board and lodging payments under income support From 11 April 1988 and until 10 April 1989, board and lodging payments are administered wholly under the income support (IS) scheme. Those in board and lodgings or hostel accommodation are entitled to an accommodation allowance and the IS personal expenses allowance (£10.30 for a single claimant aged 18 or over - those with a child receive £11.50 plus a child allowance). The accommodation allowance is subject to a maximum limit. For hostels the maximum is (and will continue after 10 April 1989 to be) £70. For ordinary board and lodging there is a limit of between £45-70 depending upon the area in which the accommodation is situated. The limit is extended by a set amount for those with dependants. In calculating the allowance, amounts for meals not covered by the accommodation charge are included. In limited circumstances only, the maximum accommodation allowance can be extended if below the actual accommodation charge (Schs 4 and 5, SI 1987 No. 1967). From 10 April 1989 the accommodation charge for board and lodgings will be met through housing benefit. (IS will still apply in hostels.)

One problem for young boarders resulting from the reforms is that the amount of money they may have left to cover ordinary living expenses - clothing, travel, entertainment, etc., - will be very small indeed. The government claimed that the changes would mean that

> people in bed and breakfast - particularly young people - would no longer have more spending money than others in their age group. This removes one deterrent to their settling down in more permanent accommodation, and taking up employment (DHSS 1986, para.13).

But the Policy Studies Institute argued that 'the credibility of the benefit calculation will be at risk if it is seen to be more sensitive to the date of claimants' birthdays than their needs' (Berthoud 1987, para.11).

A further problem, at least under the IS based provision after April 1988, has been that apart from those living in a hostel, the long-term sick or disabled, those entitled to transitional protection, and those within other categories of exemption, claimants aged under 25 have been subject to the two, four or eight week time limits that existed previously (and applied to under 26 year olds under SB - see above). (There is a residual Secretary of State discretion to offer exemption in cases of exceptional hardship.)

A further problem, highlighted in 1988, has been the payment of the allowance two weeks in arrears. A consequence of this has been that many claimants have been experiencing difficulty in securing accommodation because landlords often insist on payments in advance (Randall 1988). The government announced, in October 1988, that, where possible, claimants would receive their allowance in the first week after claiming.

From 10 April 1989, the accommodation charge for board and lodging accommodation will be met via housing benefit rather than income support (SI 1988 No.1445). Transitional protection will be provided so that those who are in receipt of a board and lodging allowance under IS before this date and who will be entitled to less benefit following the changeover, will suffer no diminution of benefit (ibid., Schedule 1, Part II). One purpose of transferring the accommodation charge from IS to HB is to bring support for those in and out of work and living in board and lodging into line, thus removing any advantage that the unemployed might have in terms of a slightly higher level of SB/IS support. The government has also been concerned that by the provision of a 'nominal breakfast' a landlord could recoup a relatively generous amount in rent via the occupant's SB/IS board and lodging allowance (DHSS 1986, para.8).

No secret has been made of the fact that this change, like others relating to these payments, is aimed at keeping an area of public expenditure under control. The government has said that the objectives of reform of this kind include the simplification and rationalisation of benefit arrangements, to ease administration 'and ensure effective controls on claims and expenditure' (ibid., para.9; cf. SSAC 1987a, para.10). The government is also concerned that the level of payment made available is related more closely to the standard of accommodation offered (ibid., para.8). It is anticipated by the government that there will be a downward adjustment in many cases, as a result of local authority assessment of housing benefit for boarders. Local authorities will consider 'the reasonableness of rents charged and whether any restrictions on benefits would be appropriate' (ibid., para. 12). Young claimants will, however, benefit from the abolition of the controversial time limits from April 1989.

Board and lodging payments: some conclusions The government believed that the restrictions (in 1985-86 in particular) would bring charges for board and lodging down to a realistic level, thus halting snowballing public expenditure on this part of the social security system, and would ensure that the many young people who, in its view, ought to have remained with their families until they had attained true economic independence, would return home. The government could claim that as a result of the concessions made, especially the widened exemption categories and discretionary powers to offer help in cases of real hardship, opportunities for independent living for those who really needed it were being provided. Moreover, transitional protection had been offered to allow those affected time to make other arrangements.

But attacks on the government's failure to give consideration to the reasons for so many young people moving into board and lodging accommodation, and especially their unwillingness to turn the issue into one of housing need instead of merely benefit entitlement, have proved difficult to counter. The board and lodging benefit restrictions undoubtedly increased the numbers of young homeless people (evidence emerged of landlords only taking in young people exempt from the restrictions: Parish 1986, p.17). As young people failed to return 'home', the government's policy resulted in extra pressure for over-stretched local housing authorities (whose responsibilities towards the young homeless are in any event limited by the restricted concept of 'priority need' in Part III Housing Act 1985: see Parish 1986, p.9) and voluntary agencies.

These stern measures affecting so many young people were introduced despite the fact that board and lodging allowance expenditure represented only one per cent. of the total social security budget and despite the known housing difficulties experienced by young people, which the government has mostly failed to acknowledge. The government should take heed of Berthoud's comment (1986, para.126) that

> Supplementary benefit is the sweeper-up behind the failure of all kinds of other policies; that is its role... And if neither the public nor the private sectors can satisfy the demand for housing among single people, supplementary benefit has to deal with that problem too.

Housing benefit for young people (except students)

HB in respect of rent and rates The highly complex housing benefit (HB) scheme was reformed in 1988. But the basic purpose of the scheme has not changed. Housing benefit, which is means-tested and administered by local authorities, is intended to provide assistance with rent and/or rates on premises occupied as a home. The 1988 changes, along with the introduction of income support, have affected entitlement. For example, although HB recipients have never been entitled to help with water charges, these were covered by SB but are not covered under IS. Furthermore, the IS personal allowances are, in effect, used in the assessment of HB (for the purposes of which they are called 'applicable amounts'). (This has resulted in reduced HB entitlement for many young people - see below.) This change was introduced because the government was convinced that a measure of simplification would be achieved if the methods of calculation of the HB needs allowance and IS personal allowances were harmonised and HB assessed with reference to net income like SB/IS (whereas formerly it was calculated with reference to gross income). Another important change has been the introduction of a maximum entitlement of 80 per cent. of eligible rates. This ceiling has affected both those in receipt of IS (who, under SB, would have been entitled to HB covering rates as well as rent - via 'certificated' HB) and those on low incomes whose eligibility depends upon, *inter alia*, their satisfying an income test (the former 'standard' HB category). (Note also the changes concerning the non-dependant deduction, discussed earlier in this chapter.) The latest change is the community charge rebate, necessitated by the introduction of the community charge in Scotland in April 1989 (see below).

In calculating HB entitlement maximum HB is reduced by a set percentage of the amount by which the claimant's income exceeds his 'applicable amount'. Separate 'tapers' for allowances or rebates in respect of (i) rent, and (ii) rates, have been used. The operation of these tapers has determined the amount of HB payable to those not entitled to maximum HB. There were suggestions that the separate tapers should be replaced by a single taper for rent and rates. The HB Review Team (1985, paras 2.21-2.35) saw this as advantageous, in terms of simplifying the benefit. But the idea was generally found to be unsound (see Kemp and Raynsford 1985, p.122) and the government later decided to retain separate rent and rates tapers (although the tapers were changed and are currently set at 20 per cent. for rates and 65 per cent. for rent).

What has been the effect on young people of these reforms? Now that the IS scale (allowances plus premiums, where appropriate) represents the threshold (persons on IS being entitled to 'maximum housing benefit'), the reduced IS entitlement of householders in the 18-24 age group as a result of the age 25 split in IS personal allowance rates means that this age group has also suffered reduced HB entitlement since April 1988, even without the new 80 per cent. ceiling on rates rebates which affects claimants in general. Although the government promised that IS rates would be adjusted to help claimants find their 20 per cent. contribution towards their rates, this can hardly be said to have happened with regard to 18-24 year olds living in their own households, whose IS rates have, of course, been reduced. (Persons claiming before 11 April 1988 have been entitled to transitional protection.) Qualifiers for IS nevertheless have (subject to certain conditions) their rent met in full.

Earners aged under 25 qualifying for HB (an estimated 200,000-250,000 people in all) will also receive less HB support than they might have done previously (see Lewis and Willmore 1985, pp.9-10). A 65 per cent. taper in respect of rent allowance/rebate was introduced under the HB (General) Regs 1987 (SI 1987 No. 1971). The effect of this steep taper is that on a rent of £15.30 per week a 19 year old would lose all entitlement at a wage of just £67 per week (at April 1988 benefit rates).

It should be noted that young people previously in board and lodgings, whose entitlement has run out (but remember that the board and lodgings allowance time limits are abolished in April 1989), are excluded from HB (ibid., reg.8).

Thus a conclusion which can be drawn from the above changes in the assessment of HB is that further barriers to independent household formation by young people have been erected.

Community charge rebates Mention may be made here of the system of rebates in respect of the community charge in Scotland from 1 April 1989. It is highly likely that there will be an almost identical rebates system for England and Wales when the community charge is introduced there in 1990. Discussion of these rebates does not really belong in a section on benefits aiding household formation since the charge that will be paid by most of the population, the personal community charge, falls equally on householders and non-householders alike. But it is convenient to include such discussion here, because community charge rebates will be administered under the HB system.

Domestic rates will be abolished in Scotland with effect from 1 April 1989 (Abolition of Domestic Rates Etc. (Scotland) Act 1987, s.1). They will be replaced by (i) the personal community charge (ss.8 & 9) (ii) the standard community charge (s.10) (iii) a collective community charge contribution (s.11). The standard community charge is essentially payable by people with second homes. The Local Government Finance Act 1988 provides for an identical scheme for England and Wales from April 1990.

The level of the personal community charge (PCC) is to be determined by local authorities in accordance with their expenditure needs (s.9). This may mean that residents in run-down urban areas where local authority services are in greatest demand could find themselves having to pay a relatively high charge - which will exacerbate the poverty suffered by many of them, including young people (see British Youth Council 1988, para.3) (but there are rebates - see below). A person is liable to pay the PCC if aged 18 or over and 'solely or mainly resident in the area of a local authority' (s.8). There are special provisions dealing with students' liability (see SI 1989 No.32 and pp.124-5 below). The charge is not payable by an 18 year old in respect of whom child benefit is payable (s.8(8)(a)), and there other categories of exemption. A register will be kept of persons liable to pay the charge.

The collective community charge (CCC) is actually levied on the owner or certain tenants of designated premises (generally lodging house accommodation or houses in multiple occupation - see Scottish Office 1988, p.22) who, in turn, must collect from residents of these premises a 'collective community charge contribution' in respect of each day these residents spend in residence at the premises (s.11(11)). Such residents are, basically speaking, those persons who are likely to be on the move and residing in one place for very short periods of time - making it impracticable to attempt to collect the personal community charge from them. One of the main criticisms of this charge is the administrative burden put on those who run hostel-type accommodation, to keep detailed records of who has stayed in the accommodation and for how long and the amount of any CCC contribution paid (s.11(14)). This administrative burden could push up the costs of running crisis accommodation which generally operates on a very tight and limited budget.

In many respects entitlement to the community charge (CC) rebates will be virtually identical to the rest of housing benefits. This is not surprising given that CC rebates will be part of the HB system. Section 24 of the 1987 Act (above) provides for the payment of rebates under regulations made under the Social Security Act 1986 (see SI 1988 No.1890 (S.178)). (Schedule 10 of the Local Government Finance Act 1988 amends the Social Security Act 1986 so that similar regulations may be made for England and Wales.) As with HB at present, there will be no rebates in respect of water charges. As was the case for rates under HB, there is a ceiling of 80 per cent. on PCC and CCC rebates (reg.46(1)). (Note that IS recipients are to be compensated for their liability for 20 per cent. of the CC by extra benefit.) The taper (see 'Housing benefit' above), which for rates was 20 per cent., will be 15 per cent for CC rebates purposes (reg.47). The income support personal allowance rates and premiums will continue to be used in determining a claimant's 'applicable amount' (reg.7 & Sch.1).

The system of community charge rebates in Scotland will offer claimants little more than the HB rates rebates system in operation until April 1989 (apart from the reduction in the taper from 20 to 15 per cent.). The reduction in support for young people under the IS reforms of April 1988 will continue to have an impact on this age group. But young people will probably be even worse off once the community charge is introduced, since they will be liable for at least 20 per cent. of what may be a substantial charge, whereas previously they may have had no rates liability at all (for example, if they were non-householders) or were required, under perhaps a tenancy, to pay only a proportion of their landlord's rates liability. The CC rebates system will not be at all generous to young wage earners. Taking the government's estimated average CC for England and Wales had it been introduced there in 1988/89, no rebate would be payable to a single person aged under 25 with a net income of £52.98 or more (see CPAG 1989). (There is also one glaring anomaly, concerning 19 year olds still at school. These young people will be required to pay the CC even though they are not entitled to IS in their own right and their parents are not entitled to claim child benefit or dependency additions in respect of them - see Chapter 6, note 1.)

Single payments/social fund payments for furniture and household equipment

Introduction Many young people who leave home permanently are in their mid- to late thirties and in secure employment. Often they have left to set up an independent home with a partner. But as we saw earlier in the context of board and lodging payments, there are many young unemployed people in their late teens or early twenties left with little option but to set up home - because of overcrowding in the family home, family tension, the need to look for work in another area, their release from custody or their coming out of local authority care. For such people, rented accommodation in public and private sectors tends not to be readily available. Private landlords are usually reluctant to let accommodation to young, single unemployed persons - whose benefits tend to be low. But when accommodation *is* made available, an immediate need, the extent of which will depend upon whether the accommodation is fully or partly furnished or (as is most likely) unfurnished, is for furniture and/or household equipment. Even if the young claimant is on good terms with his/her family, he/she will probably find that they can spare few, if any, items.

Before November 1980, a payment could be made to a claimant whose exceptional need(s), in the opinion of a benefit officer, justified it. After clothing and footwear, the highest number of claims was in respect of furniture and household equipment. The average award for furniture/equipment in 1977-78 was just under £40, although in some case multi-item payments totalling £200 were made (SBC *Annual Report for 1977* (1978), para.11.11, and *1978* (1979), Table 15.4). This demonstrates the importance of what were then known as furniture exceptional needs payments (ENPs) to claimants (of whom young people became an increasingly large proportion in the late 1970s and early 1980s - see Chapter 1). When a new, regulated system of single payments was introduced in November 1980 and rationalised in the ensuing years, young people faced increasing barriers to household formation as the availability of furniture and household equipment payments decreased. The replacement of the single payments system with the social fund in 1988 resulted in yet further obstacles being placed in their path.

Single payments 1980-88 Prior to November 1980, payments for furniture and household equipment were part of the system under which the SBC exercised discretionary power under the SB Act (1966, and, subsequently, 1976) to make lump sum payments in cases of exceptional need. Categories of 'exceptional need' were not laid down in the Act. However, guidelines, set out in the secret 'A' Code, suggested that officers were to make payments in cases where existing items could not be repaired or where they were required for the first time, if necessary to bring a claimant's furniture up to what the SBC regarded as the 'normal minimum standard'. Basically, payments would only be made for 'essential' items. The overriding conditions for payments related to the necessity for claimants to be moving into unfurnished accommodation. Generally the Commission did not favour making payments to claimants if they were not disabled, pregnant or caring for dependants, or had not recently left prison or care, unless they would have had to remain in accommodation that was a risk to health and no suitable furnished accommodation was available in the area (SBC *Annual Report for 1977* (1978), para.11.11).

As the number of ENPs made in respect of furniture and household equipment grew (an increase from 77,000 to 145,000 single item ENPs from 1975-78: *SBC Annual Report for 1978* (1979), Table 15.4), calls for rationalisation emanated from some quarters (for example, the DHSS Review Team (DHSS 1978)). The Department was concerned about the disproportionate time and expense involved in the administration of claims for ENPs.

The replacement of ENPs with single payments in November 1980 involved, initially, a change in form rather than substance. Although the provision of payments was now governed by regulations, the substance of the 'A' Code guidance was incorporated into them (SI 1980 No.985). The list of 'essential' items of furniture and household equipment, and whether the amount of payment should be the cost of a new, reconditioned or secondhand item, were prescribed. Young people who had recently become tenants or occupiers and who did not have a particular item (or a safe one) were only entitled to a payment if, for example, leaving prison or care, or moving to improve job prospects, or out of work for six months or more and having poor job prospects. Those who had not become tenants or occupiers (after 1984 licensees were included: SI 1984 No.938) recently could also qualify for a payment, but again only in tightly defined circumstances.

In the case of both recent and longer-standing tenants/occupiers there was an additional condition attached to some of the grounds for a payment - the old 'no suitable alternative furnished accommodation in the area', or 'SAFA', rule. Perhaps the majority of the claims made by young people were based on one of the grounds to which the SAFA condition was attached - especially that of being out of work for six months or more and having poor prospects of employment.

It became apparent that this rule was being applied rather restrictively, even though there were doubts about its value in the light of evidence resulting from surveys in Birmingham, London and Manchester, which confirmed that there was very little accommodation available to the unemployed (CHAR 1984, PP.86-106). Benefit officers believed that the law put the onus of proving that there was no suitable alternative furnished accommodation available in an area on claimants. This view was upheld by a Tribunal of Commissioners in *R(SB)8/84*. The claimant would have to show that s/he had made proper efforts to secure furnished accommodation and had been unsuccessful. S/he could not simply rely on general evidence of the non-availability of such accommodation. Circular *S/8/84*, issued to adjudication officers after the decision, recommended that officers require claimants to supply sources of information about addresses tried, reasons for rejection and other information. In most cases evidence of perhaps fifteen rejections would be demanded.

Despite complaints that the regulations, and the SAFA rule and its interpretation in particular, had made it more difficult for young people to set up home (e.g. Crawford 1985), the government was convinced that work disincentives would be created if those on social security received help not readily available to those on low incomes. Furthermore, there was the belief, expressed by Dr Rhodes Boyson M.P. (*H.C. Hansard*, col.1190, 10.5.84), that any relaxation of the rules 'would... encourage people to move away from the family after the slightest argument and would be costly'.

It was in the context of the reforms to board and lodging payments between 1984-86 that furniture and household equipment grants found a more central place in the debates on benefit support for young people living away from the family home. This was not surprising, as the principles involved were the same. Both board and lodging payments and single payments for furniture and household equipment provided either necessary help to enable young people to establish an independent home when their personal circumstances demanded it, or, as the government viewed it, encouraged young people to leave home prematurely, when they could quite reasonably be expected to remain with their families.

At first the government, whilst acknowledging the difficulties of applying the SAFA rule, appeared to be awaiting the findings of the Social Security Reviews before instituting reforms in this area. But even after planning for the social fund was well in hand (proposals for it having been revealed in March 1985), the government felt compelled to embark on urgent selective reform of the single payments system. Here again is a tie-in with the reform of board and lodging payments, because once again mounting claims and concomitant expense were the main reasons for the government's new restrictions, although high administrative costs were another important factor. Although the amount paid out in single payments amounted only to about 4.5 per cent. of total SB expenditure in 1985-86, single payments accounted for 48 per cent. of all decisions in that period (SSAC *Sixth Report, 1986/7* (1988), para.2.3.3) (and 49 per cent. of appeals in 1985). Overall, furniture payments had increased in number from 135,000 in 1979 to 250,000 in 1981 and 654,000 in 1983. Also, the number of claims per thousand claimants had risen over this period, from 47

(1979) to 67 (1981), 98 (1982) and 150 (1983) (SSAC 1986 (Secretary of State's Statement) para.29).

The government argued that it was the 'open-ended nature of the regulations' that had led to continuing growth in the number of claims for single payments generally (SSAC 1986, para.28) (cf. Allbeson and Smith 1984), although the category chosen to illustrate this, furniture payments, was somewhat atypical. The number of furniture grants had increased by 75 per cent. in 1983, while clothing and footwear payments had declined in number (SSAC *Second Annual Report, 1982/3* (1984), para.9.26).

There were predictions that any tightening-up of the conditions for the granting of single payments would result in real hardship, as the demand had risen because of the existence of a growing unmet need. It seemed to some that the government was intent on attacking the 'symptoms (increased public expenditure) without fully analysing the causes' (SSAC 1986, para.45). Nevertheless, the Single Payments Regulations were amended (by SI 1986 No.1259) with effect from 11 August 1986. In the run-up to this date, welfare rights agencies, Citizens' Advice Bureaux and many local authorities urged claimants to lodge claims before the restrictions came into operation.

The amendments resulted in a much shorter list of essential items of furniture and household equipment. Items such as dining furniture, easy chairs, storage units, curtains and floor coverings were no longer included. These items could, however, be claimed (along with any other 'non-essential' items) as 'miscellaneous furniture and household equipment', although here too there were very stringent conditions. These conditions meant, in effect, that most young people, other than perhaps those leaving care or prison, would not qualify for a payment (at the prescribed rate of £75 for the claimant plus £50 for each additional member of the 'assessment unit' (basically those family members treated as one unit for benefit assessment purposes)). Regulation 30, which provided a long-stop discretionary power to make a single payment in cases where such a payment would provide the only means of avoiding serious risk to the health or safety of a member of the assessment unit, was amended so that 'miscellaneous items' payments appeared to be excluded from its scope. Later on it became clear (by virtue of the decision in *R(SB)10/88*) that the change had only partly had this effect on regulation 30 (although a Northern Ireland decision, binding only in Ulster, suggests that it had the full effect: *Carleton v DHSS* (1988)). The amendment regulations also resulted in claims being barred if a payment had been awarded to the claimant previously or where the need for an item had arisen because of the claimant's failure to take care of such an item.

Although the new regulations had resulted in removal of the SAFA rule (above), there were now many new obstacles to household formation. Apart from exceptional cases, the items for which a single payment might be available were restricted to a cooker, heater and a bed, and then only if the claimant had been in receipt of benefit for twelve months. These restrictions came on top of those relating to board and lodgings payments, discussed earlier. Changes were also made to the rules governing payments for items of bedding, which at one time had been less restrictive than those concerning furniture and household equipment. Overall, the single payment reforms of 1986 had, in Youthaid's words (*Bulletin* No.28, Sept./Oct. 1986, p.4) 'struck a major blow against the independence of unemployed young people'.

The social fund   Since 11 April 1988, young claimants, indeed a majority of claimants, have faced further obstacles in their quest for furniture grants. On that date the social fund, for which provision is made in the Social Security Act 1986 (as amended) came into operation. (A small part of the fund, relating to funeral and maternity payments, had in fact been introduced in April 1987.) The fund (briefly outlined in the introduction to this chapter) represents a return to a more discretion-based system, such as prevailed before November 1980, although SF officers are obliged (by s.33(10) of the 1986 Act) to take account of, *inter alia*, guidance issued by the Secretary of State. Furthermore, the availability of payments is likely to be affected by the fact that the fund has a limited resource allocation (£203 million in 1988-89); also, offices must keep within their SF budgets. Another new limitation is the fact that many of the payments take the form of loans, the exceptions being those involving 'community care', funeral and maternity expenses, and cold weather payments, for which there are grants.

The government has consistently argued that loans are more equitable than grants because they place claimants and low income earners on an even footing - both have to budget carefully to meet their needs for items such as furniture, clothing, and so on. In this respect, the government contends, loans are better at maintaining work incentives than single payment grants. However, as the SSAC has pointed out (*Fourth Annual Report, 1985* (1986)), it may be both unreasonable and unrealistic to expect claimants to meet the cost of loan repayments for essential items from very basic levels of social security income. In their *Fifth Annual Report, 1986/7* (1988, para.2.3.7), the SSAC mentioned specific items of furniture and household equipment, including beds, cookers and heaters, as warranting, in specified circumstances, grants rather than loans. It is interesting that in a National Association of Citizens' Advice Bureaux study in May 1988 the overwhelming majority of actual or potential applications to the social fund were for furniture (NACAB 1988, para.10.1), illustrating the continuing need for extra payments, on top of weekly benefit, to cover the cost of these items.

The SSAC has commented (1987c, para.5) that unless IS personal allowances are adequate to meet the essential daily needs of claimants, the social fund will be 'overwhelmed'. In fact, much of the research into the initial effects of the introduction of the fund revealed that far fewer applications were made than were anticipated - although there are various plausible hypotheses put forward to explain this: the 'take-up' campaign before single payments were abolished, reluctance of claimants to claim - partly through fear of the unknown and more particularly concern about whether they might be able to afford repayments, ignorance of the right to claim, and possibly pessimism about the likelihood of being successful (around two-thirds of applications in one sample were turned down: NACAB 1988). A combination of these factors was probably the cause of the low take-up in the first three to four months of the fund reported across the country. Many offices 'under-spent' their fund allocation, although subsequently there were signs that take-up was beginning to increase.

Young people are bound to suffer particular difficulty as a result of the change to a system of loans, as repayments will have to be found from a lower rate of benefit than was paid before 11 April 1988. The difficulty has been compounded by the fact that one of the criteria to be borne in mind by SF officers when deciding whether or not to advance a loan is the likely extent of the claimant's ability to repay it. There is also the fact that claimants are expected to exhaust all other avenues - charities, for example - before turning to the fund; in other words, in most cases claims for social fund payments are to be regarded as a last resort. A further obstacle for young people (but not really a new one) is that in the case of budgeting loans (but not community care grants - available, for example, to those coming out of residential care) the claimant must have been in receipt of IS (or been the partner of someone in receipt of IS) for at least twenty-six weeks at the date of the award (SF direction 8).

Young people are also likely to adversely affected by the new 'priority' categories introduced to assist officers in the distribution of the social fund. Although the guidance (set out in the *SF Manual*) makes it clear that for budgeting loans a need for essential items of furniture and household equipment (not defined in the guidance) has 'high priority' (paras 3017-18), and for non-essential such items 'medium priority' (para.3019), this is stated to depend on the circumstances of applicants. The consultation document on the fund made it clear that single applicants and couples without children would have 'lower priority' than families (DHSS 1987b, para.5027). The Secretary of State's guidance is less specific, but indicates that priority should be given to cases where refusal could cause hardship or risk to health. It is clear that, in general, young people will have more difficulty in establishing priority than other applicants, even where a community care grant (CCG) is being considered. They are certainly not a high priority for a CCG where the ground is 'moving to more suitable accommodation to be able to remain in the community' (*SF Manual*, paras 6331-45). They are, however, likely to be awarded a CCG if the ground is that they are moving out of institutional or residential care. But even in such a case, the grant would not be in respect of furniture unless the young person was rejoining the 'family' household (ibid., paras 6326-27).

In conclusion, the social fund is unlikely to have improved prospects of independent household formation for young people. Indeed, it is likely to have become more difficult for young people to set up home. The introduction of the fund follows quite a long line of reforms, considered earlier in this chapter, which have put pressure on the young unemployed to remain in their parents' home and on their parents to accommodate them.

Family formation

Introduction

As a 1981 UNESCO report, *Youth in the 1980s*, put it: 'Youth is not only formed within families; it forms families'. Despite the government's recent insistence that adulthood should, in effect, be regarded as commencing on a person's twenty-fifth birthday, many young couples marry and/or set up home together well be before this age. Some young people have children; and as we shall see later, parenthood among the young unemployed tends to occur more frequently than amongst those continuing in education or obtaining work, often reflecting a desire for a measure of 'adult' social status which is otherwise unobtainable.

Many births to teenagers are, in fact, illegitimate. There were 11,995 illegitimate births to 16-17 year olds in 1985 (OPCS figures). In a good number of cases, probably the majority of them, these children are cared for by a lone parent (nearly always the mother). Lone parents in general often live in another person's household (approximately 50 per cent of them: SBC 1976, p.44), and this is particularly true of teenagers. In one survey a majority of 17 year old single mothers were found to be living with their mothers (Roberts et al. 1985, p.190). Nevertheless, all young parents embarking on family formation without a wage need help. Similarly, young unemployed couples without children often suffer hardship as a result of poverty. They have few opportunities to acquire any wealth, especially if one partner or both of them have not had a job since leaving school, and so experience difficulty both in finding a deposit for a privately rented flat (local authority housing being in generally short supply) and in paying for household equipment.

Young unemployed people with children, whether living in couples or as lone parents, face particular financial hardship and need all the help the state can provide, including adequate social security support. Although it is sometimes suggested that there are financial advantages to having a child if unemployed, Roberts et al. (1985, p.193) found that 'teenage parenthood is far more likely to aggravate than solve the problems associated with unemployment'. One of the reasons put forward by the DHSS Review Team in *Social Assistance* (1978) for not recommending an increase in the minimum age of entitlement to SB from 16 to 18 was that certain needy groups, such as teenage parents, would be excluded from entitlement (para.4.3). Both the SBC in the 1970s and the Conservative governments of the 1980s have acknowledged the extra needs of families. The government claims that a variety of its recent reforms, including the new family credit scheme and income support family premiums, reflect its desire to help families. However, the freezing of child benefit in 1987 and 1988 appeared to offer a contradiction to this stated commitment.

There is a potential area of conflict surrounding social security policy vis-a-vis young couples and parents. The dependency assumption underlying the age 25 split in IS personal allowances rests on the presupposition that young people will remain dependent on their families until their mid-twenties; their families will be expected to accept a measure of continuing responsibility for them. Yet young people who are still young enough to be classed as 'children' (or as 'young people', in some cases - for example housing benefit) by the state do sometimes become parents, with families of their own to care for. In such cases they ought no longer to be regarded as 'dependants'. On the one hand the government might perceive an interest in minimising the rate of benefit paid to young unemployed couples - to discourage family formation before work is obtained or the officially determined age of 'adulthood' (arguably now 25 in relation to social security) is reached. On the other hand, once young people have families of their own, their needs and those of their children cannot be allowed to go unmet.

Supplementary benefit and young couples and parents

Under the post-November 1980 supplementary benefits system a standard (and not age related) amount was allowed for the normal requirements of a couple (married or living together as husband and wife). (The 1987 rates were £49.35 ordinary rate and £61.85 long-term rate.) There was no 'non-householder' rate for couples, on the assumption that nearly all couples would be householders. Couples with a child or children received the appropriate dependant allowance.

A lone parent's requirements depended upon whether or not s/he was a householder. However, lone parent non-householders aged 16 or 17 received the adult (18-plus) rate. This had also been the position prior to November 1980, under an exercise of the SBC's discretion (Finer 1974, para.5.255). It meant £5 per week benefit on top of the basic rate. However, young parents were not excluded from the staggered abolition of the non-householder's contribution between 1983-86 for those aged under 25 (above).

Yet in some respects young parents have been treated as a special case. For example, they have been excluded from the time limits (due to be abolished in April 1989) applicable to under-26 year old (or under 25 under IS) claimants of board and lodgings payments, as have those who are (or whose partners are) pregnant (SI 1987 No.1967, Sch.5, para.16(4)(a) and (c)). They have been, and still are, granted exemption from the restriction on entitlement, for reason of non-availability for work, for those in 'relevant education' (ibid., Sch.1, para.10). (A parent who is a 'student' would have to be a lone parent to qualify on the ground of having a child to care for: ibid., para.1.) Also, many parents aged under 18 are lone parents who have, at least, benefited from one parent benefit (£4.90 in 1987-88, but treated as a resource for SB purposes), and from an earnings disregard higher than that for other parents (initially £6, compared with £2-4 for others - later £4 plus half the amount of any net earnings between £4-20). They qualified for the SB long-term rate after 52 weeks in receipt of a 'prescribed allowance', i.e. one in respect of which, because they were lone parents, they were not required to be available for work.

Income support and young couples and parents

As discussed earlier in this chapter, the proposals concerning young people and income-related benefits set out in the 1985 Green Paper on Social Security provided for one level of personal allowance for those aged 25 or over, and another, lower, rate for 18-24 year old claimants, regardless of householder status. All lone parents of whatever age were to receive the higher-level allowance plus the new family premium and any other additions to which they were entitled (such as dependency additions and the new 'lone parent premium'). So far as young couples (married or unmarried) aged under 25 were concerned, the proposal seemed to be that they would be entitled to the lower level personal allowance even if they had children to care for, although they were to receive the family premium. The effect of the reforms on young couples with children would have been neutral; but those aged 24 would, nevertheless, have received significantly less (around £10 per week less) than those who had reached their 25th birthday, even though their needs might have been the same. For young couples with children the payment of the lower rate was seen as particularly inappropriate when so many of them, 95 per cent. according to Youthaid's figures (Lewis and Willmore 1985, p.4), lived as householders. Also, the abolition of the long-term rate of benefit would mean that the family premium might not, by itself, compensate for the reduction in IS for householders aged 24 or less.

Many of the responses to the Green Paper were critical of the treatment of young parents under its proposals. The House of Commons Social Services Committee (1986b, para.35) argued that the proposal that lone parents be paid the higher, age 25-plus, rate of allowance should be extended to cover couples. The Board for Social Responsibility of the General Synod of the Church of England (1985, para.7c) could see 'no justification for paying a lower rate of income support to young people under 25, particularly in the case of married couples with children', saying that the Green Paper contained 'unrealistic assumptions about the nature of family life'. The SSAC, in disapproving of the age 25 split in personal allowance rates (for reasons which were discussed earlier in this chapter), argued in favour of some relaxation of this rule in the case of young couples - who were nearly always householders. The Committee felt that it was anomalous to offer the higher rate to lone parents but not to couples, and that the proposals ran counter to the government's avowed aim of supporting families (SSAC *Fourth Annual Report, 1985* (1986), para.3.10).

The government subsequently decided to extend the age 25-plus rate of IS to all couples aged 18 or over, in recognition of the fact that claimants aged under 25 living as couples are likely to have established an independent lifestyle; moreover, those with children would have equal family responsibilities to their counterparts aged 25 or over (White Paper 1985, paras 3.10-3.11). The Income Support (General) Regulations (SI 1987 No.1967) provide for the following rates of personal allowance and premiums (April 1989 rates in brackets):

Personal allowances:

A. Lone parent: under 18 - £19.40 (£20.80); 18 or over - £33.40 (£34.90)
B. Couple, both under 18, no children - £38.80 (£41.60)*
C. Couple, both under 18, child(ren) - £38.80 (£41.60) plus dependant(s') allowance(s)
D. Couple, one aged under 18, no children - £51.45 (£54.80)**
E. Couple, both aged 18 or over, no children - £51.45 (£54.80)
F. Couple, one or both aged 18 or over, child(ren) - £51.45 (£54.80) plus dependant(s') allowance(s)

* Since 12 September 1988 (and by virtue of SI 1988 No.1228) claimants in category B will get the couple rate only if both are entitled to IS even though under the normal minimum age of entitlement of 18 (introduced by the Social Security Act 1988). Only those falling within prescribed categories (IS (General) Regs 1987, reg.13A) or where the Secretary of State has awarded benefit to avoid severe hardship (Social Security Act 1986 s.20(4A)) will be so entitled (see Chapter 7 for details). The assumption would be that both partners would be capable of receiving training and a training allowance on the YTS. If the female partner is pregnant she will be entitled to £19.40 (£20.80) in IS, but her partner would receive no IS. This will also be the position if one partner qualifies for IS on any other ground and the other does not. (Note that in both of the last two cases the non-qualifier might have short-term entitlement to IS - during the child benefit extension period (see Chapter 7).)

** Generally, a couple in category D will only be entitled to the single person rate to which the older partner is entitled - £26.05 (£27.40) if aged 18-24 or £33.40 (£34.90) if aged 25 or over. If the 16 or 17 year old partner would qualify for IS if s/he were single (see above), the couple will be entitled to £51.45 (£54.80).

Premiums:

A. Family premium £6.15 (£6.50) and Lone Parent premium £3.70 (£3.90)
B. None
C. Family premium (as in A)
D. None
E. None
F. Family premium

The differences in the rates paid to parents and couples across the six categories above illustrate just how artificial the age dividing lines in income support allowances have become. An unemployed couple without children would have no guaranteed right to IS if both members were aged 17; but within twelve months their entitlement would have risen from nothing to £54.80 (rate from April 1989). If, instead of both being 18 their ages were 19 and 17 they would be entitled to £27.40 (rate from April 1989). A couple both of whom are aged under 18 and who have a child will receive nearly £13 per week less than a similar couple who have reached the age of 18.

Despite the fact that they are now one of the few categories of claimant entitled to IS in their own right when aged 16 or 17, unemployed lone parents aged under 18 (especially the minority who do not live with their own parents) have not been left in a particularly advantageous position under the IS reforms; and there is still no extra help for pregnant single women (of whatever age) on IS until they have had their babies (apart from the social fund maternity allowance: see below). The National Council for One Parent Families (1985, p.49) believes that single women who are pregnant should receive a special 'pregnancy premium'. The inadequate financial help for young single pregnant women who lack family support has been highlighted by the SSAC (*Fifth Report, 1986/7* (1987), para.2.2.4)

In fact, the Income Support (General) Regulations 1987 provide (Schedule 1A) that a pregnant woman aged 16 or 17 is entitled to IS even though under the normal minimum age of entitlement. However, it would appear that entitlement without the need to be available for work only applies in the case of such a woman while she is incapable of work by reason of pregnancy or during an eighteen week period beginning eleven weeks before her expected week of confinement (Sch.1A para.1). But by the end of this period she would normally have had a live birth, and so would continue to be eligible for IS - either as a lone parent or as a member of a couple (if treated as responsible for her child) (Sch.1A para.1; Sch.2 para 1(3)(a)(i)).

Under-16 year old mothers: income support, the social fund and child benefit

An assumption that family support - emotional, practical and financial - is available governs the treatment of under 16 year old mothers under the income support, social fund and child benefit schemes. The position of very young mothers under social security law is interesting and touches on the whole dependency/independence issue. According to OPCS figures, the numbers of live births to under-16 year olds rose steadily between 1982-85. In 1985 there were 1,390 such births (although there were as many as 4,000 in 1977).

The major costs associated with caring for a young baby are met by maternity expenses payments, available as a grant under the social fund since 6 April 1987 (SI 1987 No.481) and before then as a supplementary benefit single payment. Although the April 1987 rate was criticised as being wholly inadequate and well below the total amount previously available under the single payments system (see SSAC *Fifth Annual Report, 1986/7* (1988), para.2.3.16) it was raised by only £5 in April 1988, to £85. A maternity expenses payment can only be granted to a person who has been awarded IS or family credit. Under-16 year old mothers and mothers to be have no independent entitlement to such a payment because they are below the minimum age of entitlement to IS (and, for all practical purposes, family credit).

During the Committee stage of the Social Security Bill in 1986 M.P.s rejected a proposed amendment by Jo Richardson which aimed to give under 16 year old mothers independent entitlement to IS and a maternity payment. The National Council for One Parent Families had campaigned for such an extension of support, arguing (1985, p.23) that it was 'extremely illogical...that their health needs and the health of their babies should be overlooked simply because they are under 16'.

The Finer Committee in 1974 (Vol.1, para.5.156) had also favoured granting special financial support to under 16 year old mothers in view of the additional burden placed on families. The Committee had also recommended that the extensive use made by the SBC of their discretionary power to award the adult non-householder rate to young single parents aged under 18 who were caring for their children should be expanded to cover all such parents by *right* (ibid., para.5.255). It is not clear whether under 16 year olds in receipt of the proposed allowance were to receive the adult SB rate. The Finer Committee's recommendation was not acted upon, but provision was made for all lone parents by an addition to child benefit for such persons from 4 April 1977.

Returning to income support, and to Jo Richardson M.P.'s proposed amendment to the Social Security Bill, the government was convinced that the correct avenue of support for the very young mother was via her parents' benefit. Many M.P.s disagreed with Ms Richardson's argument that young mothers were inadequately provided for by the benefits system or their families, and the amendment was defeated.

Under the social fund the maternity payment will be awarded to the girl's parent if the parent is on income support or family credit. There is no provision in respect of under-16 year old mothers being cared for in local authority homes (because of family break-up and/or other problems). Not only will they not receive a payment in their own right, they will presumably not receive one indirectly either, as they are not members of a household which includes a person in receipt of IS or family credit. However, their babies' needs will hopefully be met by local authority social services.

There are clearly several arguments involved in the question of whether direct entitlement to benefit should be offered to under 16 year old mothers. They are clearly unavailable for work - by law they must receive 'efficient full-time education' (Education Act 1944, s.36). Moreover, some might argue that direct entitlement would be tantamount to condonation of under-age parenthood. Nevertheless, it is sometimes pointless allowing moral considerations to colour judgement about matters of social reality, as the House of Lords recognised in *Gillick v West Norfolk and Wisbech A.H.A. and Another* (1985).

If under-age parents bring up their children themselves they will, following the birth, immediately be faced with the enormous responsibilities of parenthood - including financial responsibilities. The direct provision to them of IS and the maternity payment is desirable. Direct provision would allow young mothers or mothers to be, able to follow guidance on how best to use the money from parents (with whom most of them will be living), to receive a valuable introduction to the financial responsibilities of parenthood. It is worth recalling the Crowther Committee's reference thirty years ago (albeit in a different context) to the 'feeling of growing independence and usefulness that 15 year olds boys and girls ought to have, which is often closely connected with the amount of money they have to command' (Crowther 1959, para.196).

The real question centres not only on whether mothers aged under 16 years should enjoy independent entitlement to social security support but whether, alternatively, it should be assumed that their babies will be the grandparents' responsibility. The law could, at least, seek to distinguish between cases where the grandparents have assumed responsibility and those where they have not. There may be inherent difficulties in this, but the alternative is a blanket rule which although administratively tidy prevents recognition in law of the actual locus of responsibility for the girl's child.

The Child Benefit Act 1975 (section 1) states that child benefit is payable to the person (no minimum age being specified) 'responsible' for the child - either
(a) the person who 'has the child living with him...'; or
(b) the person 'contributing to the cost of providing for the child at a weekly rate which is not less than the weekly rate of child benefit payable in respect of the child for the relevant week'
(s.3(1)). A person claiming under (a) has priority over someone claiming under (b) (Ogus and Barendt 1982, p.432). In practice, what tends to happen is that

child benefit (and one parent benefit) is paid to the young mother; but it is possible for her and her own parent to agree to nominate the latter as the person 'responsible' for the child, for child benefit purposes. It could be asked why the law governing income support and the social fund could not be similarly flexible.

In any event, it seems anomalous not to provide the maternity payment to under 16 year olds when the law already recognises their responsibilities in related benefit areas. They have, as already stated, an independent right to child benefit, are legally obliged to maintain their child, and until 6 April 1987 when it was abolished (by s.38 Social Security Act 1986) were, apparently, entitled to the maternity grant of £25 paid under s.21 Social Security Act 1975.

The Conservatives' social security reforms 1980-88: some conclusions

Young people's entitlement to social security has been reduced progressively since 1980. A variety of clear policy goals, many based on ideology but more often than not motivated by expediency, have been pursued - these are considered in Chapter 7 and the Conclusions (Chapter 8). Expediency is illustrated by, for example, the response to the massive and rapid increases in the total cost of meeting board and lodging allowance claims and the introduction of the age 25 dividing line for IS personal allowances. Ideology is reflected in, for example, the notion of social fund loans - to encourage self-reliance and reduce dependency on the state.

There remains a continuing emphasis on family responsibility - as reflected in, for example, the non-dependant deduction in housing benefit. Furthermore, a dependency assumption (see Introduction) has influenced most of the policy developments affecting young people described in this chapter: delayed entitlement for school leavers, removal of the non-householder's contribution, restrictions to board and lodging payments for young people, and so on.

The chief overall characteristic of the period, so far as social security for young people is concerned, has been much reduced independent entitlement, with unemployed under-25 year olds facing more and more obstacles to independent household formation. The consequences for those concerned of the enforced dependence of young people on their families are considered in the next chapter.

5 Consequences of reduced independence

Reforms to social security from 1980 onwards have helped to normalise the protracted transition to adulthood experienced by unemployed youth. As enforced dependence by young people on their families has increased, their independence, shown in Chapter 2 to be such an important feature of the transition to adulthood, has been eroded. A succession of reforms, discussed in Chapter 4, have, in effect, pushed back the age at which adult independence among the young unemployed is deemed to start. The impact of the reforms on young people is all the greater for having occurred at a time in the post-war era when young people have acquired greater independence and citizenship, and improved legal status, through, *inter alia*, a reduction in the age of majority.

The importance of social security to the unemployed cannot be over-stated. Where young people are concerned, a solid system of financial support could, in theory, ameliorate some of the effects of being in the 'limboland' of unemployment and aid the transition process. But this is not an aim of the Conservative government's social security policy, and the nature and extent of social security provision for this age group reflects that fact. In fact, as we saw in Chapter 3 (and see Cusack and Roll 1985, p.4), social security has never been expected to provide the means whereby young people make the transition to adulthood.

The training schemes, on which such an emphasis has been placed by the government - to the extent of removing income support entitlement from most 16 and 17 year olds because training places are available and they do not need to be 'unemployed' - have become a dominant feature of this transition for many.

Yet they too offer little independence to young people, at least in the short-term. (In the long-term some young people will benefit from improved employment prospects as a result of participation in the training programme.) Most trainees feel that the training allowance provides an inadequate reward for their efforts in the workplace (Horton 1985; DES 1983). Although the YTS allowance is fifty per cent. higher than the IS rate for under-18 year olds (the few who still qualify for IS), or seventy-five per cent. higher in the case of most 17 year olds, it is well below most wage rates for young people. Furthermore, the YTS allowance does not vary in accordance with the needs of applicants. (However, since September 1988 there has been a 'top-up' to allowances paid to trainees on the Employment Training scheme (for persons aged 18 or over), who can receive £10-11.95 per week more than their benefit entitlement while on the scheme.)

It has to be understood that any view which holds that social security or the training allowance should offer a measure of financial independence to young people runs counter to the government's preoccupation with family or parental responsibility - manifested in, for example, their arguments surrounding the age 25 divide in IS personal allowance rates, and the restrictions on young people's board and lodging payments. As Malpass has argued:

> the present Government has made no secret of its intention to shift the burden of responsibility away from the state onto the family. The changes mean that parental responsibility now continues up to the age of 25 (Malpass 1985, p.13).

It could, however, be argued that in addition to the direct enforcement of family or parental responsibility, the social security system has always indirectly forced the young unemployed into some degree of dependency; low benefit levels have tended to keep them in some measure economically dependent on their parents. Young people's benefit payments have deliberately been kept well below adult rates to reflect the differential that exists between young people's and adults' wage rates. This was certainly true in the inter-war years (Benjamin and Kochin 1979, p.524); and the differential between these groups' benefit levels, which was little affected by the Beveridge Report, has barely changed over the post-war period. But it is not only the relativities that have remained constant. It has also been shown how, especially in recent years when youth unemployment levels have been so high, benefit rates for young people (and education allowances) have been so low that young people have been forced to depend on their families for support as a matter of necessity (Longfield 1984, p.23). In one survey, 61 per cent. of unemployed 17 year olds referred to 'financial problems - lack of money, being "skint"' (Roberts et al. 1985, p.63). Not surprisingly, another survey found that unemployed young people struggled to afford the typical 'keep' contribution of £10 per week and that many were, in fact, forced to borrow money from their parents (Coffield et al. 1983, p.333).

CPAG, in their submission to the Social Security Reviews (1984), reported on the findings of a West Midlands survey of unemployed 17-21 year olds (by the European Centre for Work and Society): 65 per cent. of those interviewed had said they 'couldn't manage' or 'could only just manage' on the amount of benefit they received. CPAG commented (Vol.1, para.7.7) that recent cuts had merely exacerbated an enforced dependence, and that shortage of money was 'making any alternative transition to adulthood very difficult for them'.

While internal forces (psychological and emotional) as well as those which are external to the individual (peers, teachers, parents and society) govern the transition process, the external forces can have a particular influence in either accelerating or slowing down the process (Coleman 1980, p.2). Social security policy in recent years may well exemplify the latter, in acting 'as a brake, holding the adolescent back from the freedom and independence which he or she believes to be a legitimate right' (ibid.). Whether the YTS and its training allowance has counter-balanced this at all is difficult to assess. Hedges and Hyatt (1985, para.6.16) in fact found YTS trainees to be 'somewhat in limbo so far as perceived independence is concerned' and Schostak (1983, p.145) viewed youth training as extending childhood dependency on adults. There is a clear warning, in the view expressed by a majority of parents in Hedges and Hyatt's survey (1985, para.6.4.1), in the context of restrictions applied to young people's benefit entitlement:

> ...young people start to become independent when they leave school (if not before), and are no longer appendages of the family...(They) will not learn to behave responsibly unless they are treated responsibly.

It is now necessary to give closer consideration to the effects that the 1980s reforms may be having on young people and their families.

Enforced dependence and reduced independence: effects

A. Transfers

One consequence of the reforms may have been changes in the way that resources are transferred within families. Young people may be expected to participate in such transfers. An important aspect of young people's independence is, as noted in the Introduction and Chapter 2, their ability to contribute towards their upkeep, although it is recognised that in families containing unemployed young people money tranfers are operating in both directions - from both parents and children (Cusack and Roll 1985, p.5; Youthaid 1984; Wallace 1987, pp.94-6). It could be argued that measures like the removal of the SB non-householder's contribution, now in effect incorporated in parents' housing benefit, or the increase in the HB non-dependant deduction, have at least revealed some acknowledgement of the importance of income contributions within families, and that such moves serve to strengthen family stability by ensuring that all money is 'pooled' to meet family needs. But the imposition of financial arrangements such as these, which represent a 'transfer of control over resources from teenagers to parents' (Bradshaw et al. 1987, p.15) and a reduction in those resources, could be having a damaging effect not only on young persons' progress to adult independence but also on family unity (see below).

It has been suggested that the Social Security Reviews of 1984-85 'revealed glaring gaps in our knowledge of financial arrangements between parents and their children' (Bennett and Tarpey 1985, p.31). Certainly there seems to be a lack of official recognition of the true importance of income transfers within those families whose members include young unemployed benefit recipients. But further research, to add to the information gathered by Cusack and Roll (1985) and Hedges and Hyatt (1985) is necessary to determine the precise nature and extent of these income transfers. It ought, perhaps, to have been undertaken as part of the Review of Benefits for Children and Young People in 1984-85.

B. Poverty

There is no available evidence of the extent to which families may have been directing more of their resources towards young people within them to compensate the latter for their progressively reduced social security entitlement. But it is almost certain that the reduced financial independence of young unemployed people will be placing an additional burden on families. Indeed, whole family units may well have been plunged into a deeper state of poverty as a result.

One particularly marked feature of unemployment patterns is that unemployment tends to run in families (Roll 1986, p.13). Research indicates that perhaps more than half of the unemployed aged under 25 have families with either a parent, brother or sister, or more than one of these, unemployed (White 1985, pp.39-40). One survey of young people concluded that at greatest risk of unemployment are those from high unemployment areas, from poor families, often with unemployed or lone parents (Roberts et at. 1985, p.210). Forcing young unemployed people to depend more heavily on their families is likely to increase family poverty. It seems that this effect may have been glossed-over or ignored by those responsible for cutbacks in young persons' social security benefits in recent years:

> The hard reality which must be faced by those who promote policies which cut benefit levels for young people and assume that parents can take more and more of the strain is that such young people are likely to be

disproportionately concentrated among families that are already hard-pressed (Evason 1985, p.39).

C. Household formation

But the problems do not end in poverty per se. As mentioned above, young people forced to depend on their families because benefit support is inadequate are far less likely to be able to leave home and live independently (with consequential pressure and tension - see below). As stated in Chapter 4, many recent social security reforms have produced major constraints to household formation among young people. The SSAC (1988, para.2.20), while acknowledging that perhaps the majority of 18-24 year olds are not fully responsible for their own housing costs, expressed 'regret' that the lower rate of IS (and housing benefit) for this age group 'will make it difficult for young men and women to leave home, whether to seek work, to escape domestic tension or simply to establish their independence'. It has been suggested that in this way unemployment 'may affect family structure by differentially foreclosing options in household formation among young adults' (Murphy and Sullivan 1986, p.216). Thus there are important social consequences arising out of the reduced independence of young people, not least because this reduction runs counter to a social trend in which young people are increasingly moving away from the parental home before marriage and cohabitation - signifying 'the emergence of a period of extra-familial independence among young adults' (Harris 1983, pp.221-2). Moreover, household formation has become, among young people, an important sub-cultural response to unemployment - setting up home (see Banks and Ullah 1987, p.75).

It has been the availability of benefits which has enabled many unemployed young people to live independently in Britain. (In many other European countries, for example West Germany and Norway, such support is not available to this age group.) Now independent household formation is becoming much more difficult for the young unemployed. Yet household formation remains, as stated earlier, an important aspect of the transition to adulthood (Jones 1987). Any barriers to it, resulting not only from unemployment but also from the rationalisation of social security provision, must surely have consequences for this transition.

D. Family formation

In Chapter 2 it was shown how young people who were unable to find work in the years after leaving school failed to enjoy the measure of adult status conferred on their contemporaries in employment and earning a wage. The fact that a significantly higher proportion of unemployed than employed young people have children of their own suggests that one of the consequences of this status denial has been attempts by some young people to increase their status, as well as perhaps their social security income, by entering parenthood. Recent research confirms this trend (Coffield et al. 1986). Amongst unemployed girls parenthood is particularly favoured as a means of acquiring status; in one survey approximately twelve per cent. of such girls gave birth to at least one child within two years of leaving school at the age of 16 (Banks and Ullah 1987, p.62). This offers further evidence that parenthood amongst the young unemployed is a sub-cultural response to unemployment. For many young unemployed females parenthood may in fact offer the only route to independent status while living with parents or elsewhere (Wallace 1987, p.164). It can provide a means of countering the enforced dependence on parents inflicted by the present benefit arrangements.

It may also be noted here that while social security legislation has raised the starting age for adult independence the Law Commission has recently (1988, paras 7.5-7.11) recommended abolition of the requirement for parental consent for the marriage of a 16 or 17 year old. The Commission acknowledges that 'many already live away from home and...couples increasingly live together before or instead of marriage'.

E. Tension within families

Wynn (1972, p.324) argued: 'The social consequences of concentrating hardship more particularly in families with dependent adolescents are imponderable but probably very expensive'. One potential consequence in particular appears to be an amount of stress in intra-familial relations. CPAG (1984, para.7.9) told the Review of Benefits for Children and Young People of their concern about this effect of enforced dependence of young people on their families. One factor here is that, as noted earlier, parents of unemployed teenagers often will themselves be unemployed. Roll (1986, p.13) has suggested that 'families tend to become unemployed together but unemployed families are less likely to stay together'.

Forcing young people to remain at home with parents, as, for example, the board and lodging benefit reforms must have done, may be a particular cause of stress. As shown in Chapter 4, returning home is not an option for many young people living independently, and family tension was, for many, a cause of leaving home in the first place. The SSAC (1985, para.92) commented: 'Relatives and friends may well be willing to help in an emergency, but not to provide a permanent home for someone who can contribute very little for his keep'.

It has to be realised that there has been an historical expectation among many members of the working class that children earn a living as soon as they are legally able (Charles 1985, p.131). The continuing inability of many young people aged 16-25 to find employment means that the social security system could be given a positive role in going some way towards meeting this expectation. At present, however, it seems that the system is being taken in the opposite direction, increasing some of the problems affecting the families concerned. Writing in 1984, Glennerster predicted that further measures reducing or removing benefit rights from young people would 'impoverish as well as prematurely break up many families' (p.25).

F. Psychological effects on young people

What of the effects, on young people, of enforced dependence? Apart from the poverty referred to earlier, reference has been made to 'the frustration of prolonged dependence on parents' (Crowther 1959, para.196) and to 'faltering and frustrated steps towards adulthood' (Swain 1985, p.v) resulting from unemployment. It has been suggested that lack of money, or even boredom, are not the main problems since

> surviving with a shortage of cash is part and parcel of adolescence for many youngsters... having to cope with boredom and lack of money are not experiences restricted to worklessness during youth (Bloxham 1983, p.114).

But poor self esteem, or even embarrassment (Roberts et al. 1985, p.63), resulting from lack of one's own funds, might cause young people to 'avoid awkward, competitive or novel social situations', thus denying them 'opportunities to progress in... social skills' (Bloxham 1983, p.122). This might also be a contributory factor in relation to the well documented psychological health problems of unemployed young people (Banks et al. 1984, pp.334-5; see also Platt 1985). Research by Banks and Ullah (1987) shows that the principal cause of lower psychological well-being among unemployed 16-18 year olds, compared with their contemporaries in employment, is unemployment *per se*; but problems concerning money and housing are also significant factors. (Note that unemployed females across all ethnic groups suffer more anxiety and depression than males: ibid., p.43.) It could be argued that when real jobs are so scarce social security policy should aim to prevent all of these problems rather than, as it is presently doing, reinforcing them.

Conclusions

Paradoxically, at a time when a long-standing policy of prolonging the dependence of the young unemployed on their families is being most intensively applied, there have been government statements concerning the need for a social security system which encourages 'self-reliance' (Green Paper 1985, Vol.2, para.2.70) and supports families. The government wants social security in the future to be based 'on twin pillars of provision - individual and state - with stronger emphasis on individual provision than hitherto' (ibid., Vol.1, para.13.1). The government's policy involves a partial transfer of responsibility for the support of the unemployed from the state to the family, even though many families do not represent the 'standard' model and often contain one or more adult members who are unemployed. Such families are often unable to shoulder an increased financial burden.

The contradiction evident in a social security policy which is based on supporting families whilst encouraging self-reliance is well known. George (1973, p.124) argued that

> social security often walks the tightrope between its wishes to support the family and its fear lest the help it provides undermines either the very family virtues that it wants to foster or other social values that override family considerations.

Similarly, Parker (1982, p.357) has referred to the problem, which confronts the state, of 'how to support families sufficiently to ensure their widespread continuity without, at the same time, seeming to encourage the weakening of the very responsibilities it seeks to encourage'. The question which must, therefore, be asked is whether this balance has been achieved where social security support is concerned. Evidence of the drive towards increasing young people's dependence on their families suggests that it has not, and also that the consequences for families and young people may be damaging.

The assumption that young people can and should remain in some measure economically dependent on their parents until they enter employment is a 'dependency assumption' which has always underlain British social security policy. We saw in Chapter 3 how in the 1920s, for example, the government excluded from unemployment benefit single persons living with parents to whom they could reasonably look for support. Moreover, the Beveridge Report recommended that unemployment benefit for 16 and 17 year olds should be paid at a rate of one shilling less than the dependant's allowance, because it was assumed that persons of this age would be living with parents, who could, in part, support them. This was also the reason for not incorporating a rent element in their benefit (Beveridge 1942, paras 226 and 402f). This dependency assumption has, over the years, been an influential factor in keeping the rate of supplementary benefit paid to 16 and 17 year olds well below the rates paid to older persons and maintaining the less favourable qualifying conditions for insurance and other benefits where young people are concerned. But, as shown earlier, families now seem to want and expect young people to have more independence than in the past. Ironically, the government too wants to foster greater self-reliance (as mentioned above) as well as greater independence among young people (Mr John Moore M.P., *H.C. Hansard*, Vol.121, col.656, 2.11.87). Yet at the same time the government has been prepared to cause dependence (on families) to increase.

Dependence of young people on their families may be as much a result of social security policy as a factor influencing it. Dependency assumptions have shaped the policy, and the policy has created, or increased, the dependency. But such assumptions, or, more importantly, the way they are incorporated into social security policy, may no longer be wholly appropriate, if indeed they ever were. The policy may be hampering the transition of a number of young people to adulthood, because the attainment of independence, especially financial independence, enabling young people to leave home and to satisfy personally their material and psychological needs, is an important part of this transition. Enforced dependence of young people on their families has the potential to upset family relationships by causing poverty and stress. It may also produce psychological problems for young people.

Closer attention should be paid to the real needs of young unemployed people in their important stage of personal and social development. There ought to be a clearer understanding, on the part of policy makers, of the importance of a measure of financial independence during the transition to adulthood; this should be reflected in social security and in training and student support schemes. Financial dependence ought not to be allowed to stand in the way of normative physical and emotional detachment from parents.

Even if every effort were made to reflect the true nature of the transition to adulthood more accurately in social security provision for young people, it would still be necessary to decide, as the SSAC (*Sixth Annual Report, 1988*, para.2.12) put it: 'At what point... should young people be regarded as independent, with a right to assistance from the state in their own right?' This is a critical decision for policy makers. The SSAC (ibid., para.2.17) feel that it is 'generally right for the benefit system to reflect the fact that at 16 or 17 the vast majority of young people will be living with their parents', but that such a general assumption should not be applied in such a way as to deny provision to 'the very small minority who, for good reasons, do need to live independently'. Thus it is not perhaps *where* you draw the line, but rather *how* you draw it that is the crucial question. The dependency assumptions concerning young people, which are increasingly evident in social security in Britain, should give way to a set of arrangements which permit true differentiation between individual young claimants' actual need for adult independence.

PART III
SOCIAL SECURITY, EDUCATION AND EMPLOYMENT POLICY

PART III

6 Social security and education

Introduction

Over the past ten to fifteen years students have increasingly looked to the benefits system to supplement their grants as the latter have shrunk progressively in real terms and as vacation employment opportunities have declined (see Chapter 1). Also, as unemployment among young people in general has risen to reach unprecedented levels, the availability of benefits to those studying part-time has provided a useful, if rather restricted, educational opportunity. Nevertheless, the relentless search by the successive Thatcher governments for ways of reducing both the role of the social security system and dependence on it, has resulted in the benefit rights of those in education being considered a prime target for rationalisation. Yet it may be that these consecutive governments have failed to recognise the true importance of social security as a means of support for persons pursuing courses of study after reaching school leaving age. Even the government's most recent proposals on student financial support, which involve 'top-up loans' to supplement grants (see below) and the removal of benefit entitlement during a student's course from 1990-91, seem to be based on an underestimation of the importance of social security support to a significant number of students.

It is convenient to arrange discussion of benefits and education into two sections : <u>one</u> governing 'students' - 16-18 year olds attending a full-time course of 'advanced' education, and persons aged 19 or over attending a full-time course of study of whatever academic level; and <u>the other</u> concerning persons aged 16-18 in full-time education which is not 'advanced' (known as 'relevant education' for IS purposes). Such a division occurs (although with a less than clear boundary in places) in the legislation concerning IS, child benefit and housing benefit. As the rules are discussed two particular features will emerge: first, the immense complexity of the provisions; secondly, and related to the first, the continuing difficulty caused by making entitlement to benefit in this context, as many in others, conditional upon availability for work. The chief theme of this chapter is the impact on educational opportunity of the changing provisions.

Reform of students' benefits

There was, as shown in Chapter 1, a growing demand for supplementary benefit (SB) from students in the 1970s and '80s. The number of claims continued to rise despite changes in the method of calculating students' SB in 1976 which had resulted in reduced vacation entitlement. In 1985, 100,000 short vacation claims for unemployment benefit (UB) or SB were made (SSAC 1986a, DHSS Note, Appx.2). The government announced in 1985 that it believed it to be

> right in principle to return to the situation which existed before the introduction of supplementary benefit in 1966 with students being helped through the grants system, by their families, and by their own earnings in vacation (Green Paper 1985, Vol.1, para.9.28).

The government pointed to the disproportionate cost of administering benefits to students. The DHSS estimated that it cost £1 to pay each 65p of SB to students during the short vacations (SSAC 1986a, Appx.2, para.2). Housing benefit was similarly expensive to administer, especially since claims had frequently to be reassessed during the year (see below).

In 1986 the government embarked on a programme of reform of students' benefits. As in the case of other areas of young people's benefit entitlement, there was a cutback in support. The chief reform involved removal of short vacation benefit entitlement from virtually all students. There was criticism not only of the substance of the reforms but also their timing. Although a review of student support had been instituted by the government, the reforms were introduced long before it was concluded. When the government announced formally its intention of seeking an increase in higher education participation rates (DES 1987) it had still not made its plans on student support known. In July 1988 the government postponed any announcement on reform of student support, which many expected would involve the introduction of loans to replace part of the student grant.

Opponents of the government's planned reforms to students' social security benefits, and its longer-term view that students should not be supported by the social security system, pointed to:
1. The decline in the value of the student grant (by about 20 per cent. in real terms between 1979-86) (SSAC 1986a, para.64)
2. The fact that the increased responsibility placed on parents by the grants system - via the parental contribution (which rose from 19 per cent. in 1980-81 to 35 per cent. in 1985-86: ibid., para.18) - had in fact been shunned by many of them, with the entire contribution being paid in only about 50 per cent. of cases where a contribution was required (House of Commons Education etc. Committee 1986a, Q.153)
3. The reduced opportunities for vacation employment (the proportion of students finding such employment fell from 80 to 54 per cent. between 1975 and 1982: NUS 1986, para.6.14) or part-time work (House of Commons Education etc. Committee 1986b, para.27), despite the availability and relative cheapness of student labour (see Ball 1988). It was said that 'now that it is more difficult to find work it is not surprising that students should claim benefit instead' (SSAC 1986a, para.29).

Thenceforth students were to lose much of their entitlement, with only a modest increase in the student grant as compensation. Not only might there be hardship, there would be a real threat to educational opportunity. But in a period of rationalisation of social security, students' benefits were, from the government's point of view, an obvious candidate for reform.

A. *Supplementary benefit/income support*

The reforms, most of which were introduced in 1986-87 (see below), did not alter the basic principle, which had applied under the SBC's discretion prior to November 1980 and which became enshrined in regulations thereafter, that students were/are not entitled to SB/IS during term-time because they were/are not regarded as available for work, such availability being a precondition of entitlement. There are categories of exemption for students from the availability requirement; they have remained fairly constant since November 1980, and currently enable lone parents, the disabled, and certain others, to draw IS while on their course (SI 1987 No.1967, Sch.1).

A person aged under 19 can only be a 'student' for the purposes of this area of the law if, *inter alia*, taking a full-time 'advanced' course. The definition of 'advanced' course has changed over the years, but has continued to refer to degree courses, teacher training courses, higher national diploma courses and others above 'A', Scottish 'higher' or BTEC national level (SI 1987 No.1967, reg.61). A person aged 19 or over and taking a full-time course (whether 'advanced' or not) at an educational establishment is also a 'student' (ibid.).

Prior to the introduction of IS on 11 April 1988, 19 year olds were (by virtue of a 1987 amendment - SI 1987 No.358, reg.6) able to draw SB while in full-time non-advanced education in the same six exceptional sets of circumstances as 16-18 year olds in such education. Since then, these exceptions have applied to 16-18 year olds *only* (see 'Relevant education' below). However, some 19 year olds living independently (those with no parents, or estranged from parents, or those whose parents are unable to support them for prescribed reasons, such as ill-health) were granted transitional protection following a government 'climbdown' (see SI 1988 No.910). Those 19 year olds who now stay on at school/college to complete their (full-time) non-advanced courses will, in addition to not being entitled in their own right, not be classed as dependants - possibly leaving their parents, if unemployed, in considerable hardship (see *Welfare Rights Bulletin*, No.85, Aug. 1988).

A person can only be classed as a student for IS purposes if attending a *full-time* course. (A barrister was held not to be a student during his pupillage but was, in any event, deemed to be unavailable for employment: *R(SB)25/87*.) 'Full-time' education is not defined in the regulations, but has been considered by the Social Security Commissioners. *R(SB)40/83* and *41/83* hold that when deciding whether or not a course is full- or part-time the emphasis should be not merely on the number of hours taken up by study per week but on a wider set of circumstances such as the nature of the course and how it is described by the college or local education authority, although the description can be disregarded if there is compelling evidence to the contrary. In *R(SB)40/83* it was held that 'full-time' relates to the course and not to the student. (The IS (General) Regs 1987 (SI 1987 No.1967, reg.61) reinforce this emphasis on the 'course': see Mesher 1988, p.108.) In *R(SB)41/83* Commissioner Heggs said it was relevant to consider the period prescribed for the completion of the course. The Commissioner also suggested that neither the claimant's intentions, nor his perception of the nature of the course, were material. A similar approach was taken by Commissioner Penny in the later (although earlier reported) decision, *R(SB)40/83*. The Commissioner suggested that a student's reasons for undertaking his/her course, and his/her willingness to accept employment at any time, are irrelevant (cf. *CSB 15/82*). The approach taken in *R(SB)40/83* and *41/83* received an endorsement in *CSB 176/1987*, in which a 22 year old man attending a Law Society Finals course, on which tuition amounted to eleven hours per week, was held to be a student. [1]

The entitlement of someone who is pursuing post-graduate research has been somewhat uncertain, but it is probable that as such a person is 'attending a full-time course of study' (SI 1987 No.1967, reg.61) s/he is a student for IS purposes. The presumption must be that if registered as a 'full-time' student by the institution concerned s/he will be a student for IS purposes.

As mentioned earlier, a major area of change in relation to students' benefits has been their entitlement during the short vacations. In the 1970s the SBC had adopted a liberal approach:

> ... so long as the students' grant fails, during vacations, to provide the minimum level of income which Parliament has laid down in the supplementary benefit scheme for society generally, and insofar as students are able to satisfy the normal qualifying conditions, the Commission sees no justification for excluding them from a right that is available to others (SBC 1977, para.2.25).

Following the *Atkinson* (1977) case (see Prosser 1979), legal rules were introduced to legitimise SBC policy of taking into account as a resource both the part of the student award notionally allocated to maintenance during the short vacations and, more importantly, the parental contribution (even if not actually made - i.e., treating it as a 'notional resource') (Social Security (Miscellaneous Provisions) Act 1977, s.14; and SI 1977 No.619). The grant (including the parental contribution) was treated as an income resource equal to the adult non-householder rate of SB plus the non-householder's contribution (see Chapter 4). Those living away from home during the vacations were able to draw benefit, but it amounted only to the difference between the householder rate of benefit and the deemed income resource (above). Those living at their parents' home usually lost out on resource grounds. The fact that the student grant (and assumed parental contribution) did not cover the summer vacation period meant that unemployed students were usually entitled to benefit for this period; this entitlement was left intact by the 1980 SB reforms. The rather complex SB provisions from November 1980 stated that a person on a full-time course was not a student when not attending his/her course nor 'engaged in a programme of studies' (SI 1981 No.1526, as amended by SI 1984 No.438). This basically meant that s/he was not a student during the short vacations.

When deliberating in 1986 over possible reforms to the rules governing students' benefit entitlement, the government was less concerned about the complexity of the provisions than about the disproportionate expense in meeting claims (referred to above). In the 1985 Green Paper the government had said that it would be reviewing benefit arrangements for students in the light of its proposals on student grants, when published. The government's decision shortly thereafter to proceed with the reforms in the absence of the promised paper on student support was a major source of criticism.

One change was actually to beneficial to students. Travel expenses and special equipment costs, previously disregarded only under a construction of a provision dealing with miscellaneous disregards (see *R(SB)8/86*), were specifically disregarded under the regulations, which also provided for a disregard of a set amount (initially £187, £210 from April 1988) in respect of books and certain categories of equipment. Most of the changes were, however, detrimental to students. First, students were deemed to receive the full grant throughout the grant-aided period (including the short vacations) (SI 1986 No.1293) even though some students did not receive a grant or the full parental contribution. Secondly, under an amendment aimed more specifically at removing SB entitlement during short vacations, 'student' was redefined in the regulations so that a person was deemed to be on his/her course, and thus a student, throughout the period spanned by it, other than during the long vacation (unless a student's grant covered the full twelve months) (SI 1981 No.1526, amended by SI 1986 No.1010). The rules have been incorporated into the income support scheme (SI 1987 No.1967, reg.61).

The government has justified its removal of all short vacation entitlement by suggesting that students, by embarking on a course of study, have taken themselves out of the labour market (SSAC 1986a, Appx. 2, para.3). There is an obvious contradiction when another of the government's arguments is considered - that students should seek vacation or part-time employment to supplement their grants. In fact, course requirements often prevent students from accepting temporary work (see *The Times*, 19 June 1986).

Another of the government's arguments, that payment of benefits to students amounts to a subsidy to higher education, raises a broader issue. It touches on the whole basis of student support, which has emanated from two sources - the DES (grants) and DHSS (benefits). There has not been a co-ordinated approach, involving the two departments, to the question of student support. Reductions in the value of the grant have led to continuing demands being placed on the social security system by students. Payment of benefits may well represent a subsidy to higher education but this seems inevitable. As the SSAC (1986a, para.21) said, if the students' grant is below the normal level of means-tested benefit 'then social security must bear part of the burden of supporting students in higher education, however inappropriate that may be'. The House of Commons Education, Science and the Arts Committee has suggested (1986b) that while it might be right, in the long term, to remove student support from the benefits system, it would be wrong if the government attempted to make substantial savings in expenditure by withdrawing benefit without compensation in terms of an improved grant. Only a £36 increase in the grant for 1986-87 was made. This was regarded by the opposition as 'miserly' compensation for the loss of short vacation benefit entitlement (Mr M. Meacher M.P., *H.C. Hansard*, Vol.99, col.1042, 18.6.86). Even with the increase in the grant, there was a net saving of £20 million as a result of the student benefit reforms.

B. Unemployment benefit

Here the government's main aims were, once again, to reduce the administrative burden (each £3 of benefit paid cost £1 to administer) and to avoid double provision from public funds resulting from the fact that a student qualifying for UB would have received his/her full rate of benefit, not offset by the maintenance element in the grant for the short vacation periods. The government also doubted whether a student could genuinely be available for work 'during a short vacation lasting only three to four weeks, and including several bank holidays' (SSAC 1986a, DHSS Note, Appx.2, para.13). This is a curious argument in view of the government's stated belief that students should in part support themselves by their own earnings in vacation instead of relying on benefits (Green Paper 1985, Vol.1, para.9.28).

The government's proposal was that a student would not be entitled to UB during Christmas and Easter vacations. Despite criticism from a 'significant minority' of the SSAC (1986a, para.36) to the effect that 'to deny students a benefit earned from their own contributions would be a violation of the contributory principle', the proposed amendment was introduced (SI 1986 No.1611). For a claimant a day is not to be treated as a day of unemployment if on that day s/he is 'attending a full-time course of education'. Persons are treated as attending their course during the short vacations (SI 1983 No.1598, reg.7). Note that students, like other young people, will now have to meet the more stringent contribution conditions for short-term benefits like UB introduced via the Social Security Act 1988.

C. Housing benefit

Within the package of benefit reforms affecting students which were first announced in January 1986 were planned restrictions to housing benefit (HB) aimed at saving £16 million per annum. In July 1986 regulations (SI 1986, No.1009) were made which, *inter alia*, had the effect of disentitling students in halls of residence (other than those where the university itself was the lessee) to HB, and of requiring students' income to be averaged across the whole of the grant-aided period (thirty-eight weeks) so that income remained constant, for HB assessment purposes, at different times of the year.

Conservative M.P. Mr Robert McCrindle claimed that housing benefits 'were never intended to prop up students in the way that has become familiar in the recent past' (*H.C. Hansard*, Vol.100, col.1033, 2.7.86). Certainly, few could have expected that by 1986 over half the student population would be claiming HB during term-time and short vacations (SSAC 1986a, Appx.2, para.2; see Chapter 1). Such was the demand in Manchester that the local authority's housing benefit office devised special student claim forms (see Carver and Martin 1987, para.4.2). In a survey commissioned by the DES, covering the academic year 1986-87, housing benefit was received by 43 per cent. of undergraduates not living in the parental home (DES 1988, Annex B, para.7); others may have been entitled but did not claim. The SSAC (1986a, para.15) explained that the reasons for the proliferation of claims from students included a change in the economic climate affecting students, and, in particular, a contraction in the privately rented housing sector, increases in rents and prices, a decline in the value of the student grant, and an increase in the size of the parental contribution (which, as mentioned earlier, is often not paid in full). Escalating hall fees were another factor (*Times Higher Educational Supplement*, 28.2.86).

A number of arguments in favour of reform of students' housing benefit were advanced by the government, some of which had emanated from the Housing Benefits Review of 1984-85. The Review Team had argued (1985, para.4.8) that 'the present arrangement whereby students can look to two sources of help with housing costs is both wrong in principle and unnecessarily complicated in practice'. The Review had highlighted the disproportionate difficulties presented to the administrative authorities by student claims. Nearly all student claims for HB had to be reassessed 'at least six times a year' (ibid., para.4.6). It was said to be costing £3 to deliver each £5 of HB to students (H.C. Standing Committee B, *Social Security Bill*, col.1906, 30.4.86). The HB Review Team felt that speedy abolition of students' HB would not be possible and urged, as a preliminary measure, exclusion of assistance during the grant-aided period, with an appropriate adjustment to the grant. Accepting that this would leave the authorities with continuing difficulties in the summer months, the Review Team urged 'complete exclusion' as the overriding goal if simplification of the scheme was to be achieved.

The government's proposals meant cutbacks. But concessions were promised. For example, £11 million was to be spent by disregarding the amount included in the grant for books and travelling expenses (which had previously been disregarded in calculating entitlement to SB but not HB). There was also to be a £36 increase in the student grant, as mentioned above. But this was not felt to measure up to the HB Review Team's call for an improved student grant to offset reduced HB entitlement. The SSAC (1986a, para.64) highlighted the fact that while students paying the highest rents, mostly London based students, would sustain significant losses, up to 140,000 others would receive a 'windfall unrelated to their needs'. NUS calculations (1986, para 5.2 and Technical Annex) suggested that some students could lose several hundred £s a year.

Discussion of the background to the HB reforms must, at this point, give way to a brief run through the main changes, now consolidated in the new HB scheme under the Housing Benefit (General) Regulations (SI 1987 No.1971).

1. Changes have been made to the entitlement of students living in accommodation provided by educational establishments. Those paying rent to such an establishment are now excluded from eligibility for rent allowances,

and, if rates are paid as part of the rent, rate rebates as well. (If they pay rates direct to the local authority students remain eligible for rates rebates.) The government had been concerned that increases in hall fees were often met by HB; absorption of increased hall charges by HB gave universities no incentive to keep down their costs. An exemption was incorporated, governing accommodation which a student rented from his/her university, polytechnic or college where the institution had rented it from a third party - usually in response to the increase in student numbers and decline in privately rented accommodation. These 'head lease' schemes were described by the SSAC (1986a, para.42) as demonstrating 'an imaginative approach to the student accommodation problem'. The exclusion from HB does not apply where institutions are simply acting as intermediaries between students and private landlords. (See SI 1987 No.1971, reg.,50.)

2. Proposals which would have left some grant-aided students worse off in HB terms, by treating them as receiving the accommodation element in the student grant, were particularly unfair on those who had commenced their course with the belief that HB might be available as a means of support. The government allowed a period of adjustment, as a concession to students living away from home (see Secretary of State for Social Services 1986, para.10). No deduction was made until the end of the student's course, or April 1988 (by which time the government expected the vast majority to have completed their studies), whichever was the sooner. Students on courses of more than three years' duration, or having to repeat a year of their three-year course, clearly failed to benefit from this concession.

3. The deduction of the accommodation element in the student grant in the assessment of housing benefit also applies in cases where the claimant is not, but his partner is, a full-time student, whether or not a grant has been awarded (SI 1987 No.1971, reg.52).

4. Changes have been made concerning HB entitlement in respect of property not occupied in the long vacation. The government believes that 'it cannot be right that housing benefit should [be paid to] large numbers of students for accommodation in which they do not live - perhaps for over three months' (Mr A. Newton M.P., *H.C. Hansard*, Vol.100, col.1021, 2.7.86). The general rule now is that full-time students renting accommodation mainly in order to attend their place of study are not eligible for HB during any period of the long vacation when they are absent from it. HB entitlement is not affected, in respect of any benefit week, by absences of less than the full benefit week or by absences occasioned by the need to enter hospital for treatment (SI 1987 No.1971 reg.48).

5. Mention has already been made of the proposed disregard, for income assessment purposes, of the elements in the student grant for books and travel. This change was welcomed by the SSAC and was introduced in the academic year 1987-88.

6. A further proposal, now implemented, concerned averaging the accommodation element in the student grant over the full grant-aided period (38 weeks) instead of over term-time only (30 weeks in the case of universities), even though the student grant contains no accommodation element for the vacations. Averaging of the accommodation element for HB purposes has resulted in considerable simplification, for local authorities only have to assess students' housing costs once in respect of the 38 week period instead of up six times per annum. It was expected that students would continue to be eligible for HB in the short vacations, provided they were still paying the full rent, and that averaging would not produce significant benefit reductions. From 1 September 1987 a student's eligible rent was reduced by a weekly amount of £17.80 (London) or £13.60 (elsewhere) throughout the 'period of study', which in most cases runs to the day before the start of the summer vacation (SI 1987 No.1971, reg.51). These deductions (increased in 1988) do not apply to students in receipt of IS and those in a few other categories, and in any event only apply to 'full-time' students.

(Note that the *vires* of the regulations which first introduced the changes in point 6. above, SI 1986 No.1009, was unsuccessfully challenged by a non-grant-aided student: *R v Kensington and Chelsea L.B.C. ex parte Woolrich and Another* (1987).)

7. In common with SB there have also been amendments to the provisions governing covenanted income.

HB community charge rebates From April 1989 in Scotland and April 1990 in England and Wales students will become liable to pay the community charge (CC). (See pp88-90 for an outline of the CC system.) Students will be expected to pay a proportion of the personal community charge (PCC) for the area in which they reside during term-time (Abolition of Domestic Rates (Scotland) Act 1987 s.8(4)). When the legislation was before Parliament as a Bill, there was a view which held that students should be granted complete exemption from liability to pay the CC because most students do not pay rates and there would thus be an extra burden placed on them (or, in effect, their families). But full exemption has not been granted, although students' liability for the PCC will be limited to a 'prescribed percentage' (s.8(5)) - which has now been set at 20 per cent. Students will not be liable for a collective community charge contribution (which, in basic terms, is payable by persons living for in certain types of communal accommodation - see Chapter 4), but will have to pay the PCC (and 20 per cent. of community water charges). (Students' halls of residence are expected to be classed as 'domestic subjects' - residents of non-domestic premises for rating/CC purposes are exempt from the PCC: s.8(8)(d)).

CC rebates will form part of the HB system, as explained in Chapter 4. Under the regulations, a student's grant income is to assessed for CC rebate purposes in the same way as for rate rebates etc. under the HB system at present (above) (SI 1988 No.1890, reg.38). However, *full*-time students are only liable for 20 per cent. of the PCC (also the position in England and Wales from 1990: Local Government Finance Act 1988 s.13), and it would appear that they will, in effect, be outside the rebate scheme (see M. Howard M.P., *H.C. Standing Committee E*, col. 652, 11.2.88., and CPAG 1989). Nevertheless, the rules relating to grant income are necessary for cases where the claimant is a partner of a registered student (reg.50) and perhaps in relation to persons studying part-time and receiving some kind of educational grant or award.

The 1988 White Paper on student support

The long-awaited White Paper on student support, which followed a review, was finally published in November 1988 (DES 1988). The review had confirmed what many had been saying for some time (set out earlier in this Chapter) - that student grants were inadequate, having fallen in real value by around 20 per cent. since the present system's introduction in 1962, and that the problem had been compounded by increases in the proportion of the grant expected to be made up by parental contributions, coupled with a failure by many parents to pay the contribution in full. But the review also confirmed the mounting cost of the mandatory awards system; at £829 million in 1986-87 it cost the government more than treble as much as in 1962-63 in real terms (ibid., para.2.4), although this was largely the result of huge increases in the numbers of people entering higher education. The government stated that while it intended to increase the amount of support available to students, in part because of its commitment towards improving participation in higher education rates, it wanted to reduce the burden on parents and the taxpayer.

The solution, assuming the necessary legislation is enacted, is to be a system of 'top-up loans', introduced in 1990-91 and amounting to £420 on average (at current rates). From that year, the amount of the mandatory award, including the parental contribution, will be frozen. Only the size of the available loan will be increased, in line with inflation. Such increases in the loan only will continue until the year in which the mandatory award (including parental contribution) and loan are about equal, which at a constant annual rate of inflation of three per cent. would be in 2007-8. (Note that the 'top-up loans system will not apply to postgraduate students nor to those aged 50 or over.) Repayment of the loan will normally begin in the April following the end of the period of study. The length of the repayment period will probably be extendable to take account of the level of income in the student's chosen career. The loans will be interest free, but the level of the outstanding debt will be adjusted each year to take account of inflation.

The government states that the loan facility is intended to provide support throughout the year - 'at a level which will make it unnecessary for students to look for supplementary support from the benefits system' - up to the start of the long vacation following the end of their course (DES 1988, para.3.7). Accordingly, the government will end the right of students to draw housing benefit, income support, or unemployment benefit until they have completed their course. As shown in earlier discussion, there are, in fact, several reasons why the government wants to take this step. These were reiterated in the White Paper: the 'disproportionate administrative problems' posed by student claims for housing benefit and income support (ibid., para 2.11); the need to promote 'self-reliance' and 'economic awareness' through loans rather than benefits (ibid., para.3.30) and make students take a 'step away from the dependency culture' (Mr K.Baker M.P., *H.C. Hansard*, Vol.140, col.306, 9.11.88); and the argument that 'the benefits system is intended to serve social and not educational purposes' (ibid., para. 2.12). The government acknowledges that its sponsored survey of undergraduate income and expenditure revealed that many students get into debt (almost half expected to have debts outstanding at the end of the year surveyed) and that 'students need access to additional support towards their living costs' (ibid., para.2.15). However, the government does not believe that extra support should come from the taxpayer, through increases in the mandatory award, nor by asking parents to contribute more. Furthermore, the government 'rejects the principle of student dependence on benefits' (ibid.). The government believes that the extra support must come from top-up loans.

In addition, the government promises to introduce three 'Access funds', each of £5 million a year - one for students already within the loans scheme, another for postgraduates (not covered by the scheme), and a further fund for students aged 19 or over in further education. The funds are to be administered by higher and further education institutions for their own students. The proposals concerning these funds are somewhat vague, but it would appear that the funds are intended to help those whose access to further or higher education, or, perhaps whose continuing involvement in such education, would be inhibited by lack of finance. The budget for these funds, totalling £15 million, is tiny compared with the £829 million spent on student maintenance in 1987-88.

Not all students would, if the proposals are made law, lose benefits entitlement in 1990-91. Some, in particular those who are single parents or disabled would continue to be eligible. So would the partner of a student who is in receipt of income support or housing benefit (ibid., para.3.28). It is not clear, however, whether or how the aggregation principle will be applied. The government gives a hypothetical example and states that the partner would be eligible for benefit 'subject to the conditions applying to all claimants' (ibid.). This implies that in the case of a student with a partner the grant might be taken into account in full as a resource for IS purposes, subject to certain disregards (Income Support (General) Regs 1987 SI 1987 No.1967, reg.62(2)) and spread over 52 weeks of the year as at present. Students in general would, depending on their circumstances, still be able to claim refunds for dental charges and perhaps prescriptions, and draw child benefit.

Given the availability of the new possible sources of support referred to in the White Paper, what impact might the removal of entitlement to welfare benefits have on students? The government states that the top-up loans 'will more than compensate the average student claimant of benefits for the loss of entitlement' (DES 1988, para.2.30). In the survey of student income and expenditure carried out for the government as part of its review of student support, 58 per cent. of undergraduates received social security benefits during the long vacation, at an average of £193 per student. Throughout the year as a whole, 43 per cent. of undergraduates not living in the parental home received housing benefit, the average received being £211, or, in London, £296. As these are average figures, it would appear that a certain number of students - those entitled to and receiving more than the average amount of benefits - may not be 'more than compensated' for the loss of entitlement by a loan of around £420 for those living away from the parental home and outside London (or £460 for non-home based students living in London).

The National Union of Students (NUS 1988) allege that problems in obtaining responses from those living in the private-rented sector were encountered by those carrying out the survey of students' incomes and expenditure. The survey was, therefore, weighted towards those living in halls of residence - who lost eligibility to HB in 1986. As a result, the NUS claim, the survey under-estimates the degree of reliance on welfare benefits by students. Moreover, on the basis that the proportion of the loan covering the summer vacation is £110 (non-London student living independently: £420 minus £310 (amount of loan in final year of course, which excludes summer vacation) = £110), whereas up to £383 IS is presently payable, many of the students from poorer backgrounds would be considerably worse off. They would receive no benefit, and would be unable to rely on additional parental support. London-based students paying high rents, up to £50 per week in some cases, would certainly not find that the loan available compensated for loss of benefit; the NUS calculates that they could be up to £1,500 a year worse off as a result of the changes.

Comment

In the absence of a major overhaul of the grants system at the time, many of the 1986-87 HB, UB and SB reforms were premature in their introduction, as well as potentially damaging in their effect. The particularly detrimental effect on students paying the highest rents, and on non-grant-aided students, show that many of the reforms were inequitable as well.

The feasibility of removing of student support from the benefits system, which the government says it intends to do, remains uncertain. SB/IS and HB have been designed to cater (although they do not always do so adequately) for individual needs, reflecting a claimant's particular circumstances (although rather less so since the introduction of IS in April 1988). It was the prescription of such needs and circumstances which led to such a detailed and complex SB scheme after November 1980. So far student grants have not been geared towards so sophisticated a system of assessment. The grants system will have to contain far more flexibility if it is to be able to respond effectively to the individual needs of particular students, for example in relation to housing costs, in which there are wide variations. It is by no means clear that the reformed student support system envisaged by the 1988 White Paper would meet this objective.

Aside from greater flexibility, there is an immediate need to increase the size of the grant (the maintenance element of which stands at £2,425 in London, £2,050 elsewhere, in 1988-89 for students not living with their parents during term-time) to compensate students and their parents adequately for the cutbacks in benefits which have occurred so far. At the end of 1986, the House of Commons Education, Science and the Arts Committee (1986b, para.25) concluded that such an increase was required as a matter of urgency, but the government disagreed. Now the government says that it accepts that students need more financial support, but believes that students should be required to repay the extra amount - which will, in fact, not be all that much extra in view of the freezing of the level of the grant and parental contribution at their 1990-91 levels.

Perhaps what is needed is a change of attitude on the government's part. In the White Paper (DES 1988, Annex D), the government tries to demonstrate that the personal rate of return to students who take a higher education course, in terms of enhanced future earnings potential measured against earnings foregone while studying, outstrips the social rate of return on public investment in higher education. It seems that there is a belief that because '...most students are on their way to relatively prosperous careers' (Sir Keith Joseph M.P., *H.C. Hansard*, col.1002, 12.3.86) they are somehow less deserving of outright state support. The government also feels that it is undesirable that, in expecting social security support, 'students should learn to depend upon a wrong understanding of the reciprocal obligations of the citizen and the state' (DES 1988, para.2.12). But it could be argued that the government should accept that students are equally as deserving of state welfare benefits support as any other impecunious citizens. (Inadequate levels of support have resulted in debt amongst many students; 64 per cent. of students in one recent survey were in debt by the end of the Christmas term: Carver and Martin 1987, para.4.1.) As the House of Commons Education, Science and the Arts Committee said (1986b, para.23):

> ...the use of welfare benefits arose because students were able to show, within the rules applying to the public generally, that they were suffering from hardship and were therefore entitled to benefit.

The argument that because students are heading for relatively prosperous careers they should not expect total state support seems spurious because it ignores what students will put into society, and not just in terms of tax payments, even if it is consistent with the self-reliance philosophy embodied in the notion of student loans and, indeed, in many of the Social Security Act 1986 reforms. Ironically, so far as self-reliance is concerned, the expected increase in young unemployed persons' dependence on their families consequent on the 1986 Act reforms (Chapter 5 above) is likely to be matched by reduced independence for students as a result of many of the reforms discussed earlier in this chapter.

It is worth recalling the government's stated aim of a system of financial support for students in higher education: 'to remove financial constraints on their ability to study and their choice of course or institution' (DES 1985, para.3.10). The recent cutbacks in students' benefit entitlement seem, in the light of what has, or rather what has not, been happening to students' grants, incompatible with this. A considerable degree of concern has been expressed about the effect of the level of support on incentives to study. This concern has grown since the government announced its plans to remove students' social security entitlement and introduce top-up loans. Loans could act as a disincentive to enter higher education, especially for those young people from less advantaged sections of society whose parents are less likely to perceive the value of higher education and may be apprehensive about the young person incurring a loan repayment commitment. The government defends this argument by quoting statistics which it argues demonstrate the increasing use of credit facilities by unskilled manual workers. This increase, says the government, shows that the argument that 'the introduction of a loan element will compound the disincentive involves an unproven cultural assumption' (ibid., Annex G, para.5). But the government's own assumption about the effects of the introduction of the top-up loan (and removal of benefit entitlement) on incentives to enter higher education seems also to be based on an unproven assumption.

Over the years, and particularly over the past few, students have been largely uncompensated victims of governments' social security rationalisation. Any rethink of student support, including benefits provision, must surely aim to secure its improvement for all students who are left, through no fault of their own, with insufficient resources on which to manage. Assuming students' social security entitlement is to disappear, it would be a great pity if it were not replaced by another form of additional support which is equally responsive to their needs and at the very least makes up the shortfall in income. The proposed 'top-up loans' scheme is unlikely to fit the bill in this regard.

'Relevant education' and the twenty-one hour rule

Those in full-time education who are not classifiable as 'students', because they are persons aged 16-18 not in advanced education (see above), are in what the law describes as 'relevant education' - a phrase used in the legislation since November 1980 and now contained in the IS (General) Regulations (SI 1987 No.1967, reg.12). Save in prescribed circumstances, a person is not entitled to IS if in 'relevant education' (s.20(3)(d)(ii) Social Security Act 1986) (see below).

The provisions concerning persons in relevant education, which include a concession in respect of those meeting certain conditions and taking a part-time course of less than twenty-one hours per week (the 'twenty-one hour rule'), are complex and are based around a continuing precondition of entitlement - availability for work. As we shall see, it is assumed that most of those continuing in education, either at school or college, are not available for work. A dependency assumption will also apply: persons in relevant education will not be entitled, save in prescribed exceptional circumstances, to draw benefit in their own right, but may be classed as dependants if their parents claim IS and as children for child benefit purposes (SI 1976 No.965, Regs 5-7). (Note that in the case of 19 year olds still at school there is a peculiar anomaly [2])

The raising of the minimum age of entitlement to income support from 16 to 18 for most young people, from 12 September 1988, has undoubtedly reduced the overall importance of the 'relevant education' and 'twenty-one hour' tests applied to 16 and 17 year olds taking courses. In most cases only 18 year olds will be directly affected by the provisions. But it will be important in some cases for 16 and 17 year olds to be shown to be still in relevant education, so that if their parent claims IS s/he will be entitled to a dependant allowance for a 'young person' (SI 1987 No.1967, regs 12, 14 and 17(b)). (Note also that some 19 year olds, not classed as 'students' because their course is part-time, may, if in non-advanced education, still have their availability for work judged under the twenty-one hour rule.) Although the recent changes to 16 and 17 year olds' IS entitlement have reduced slightly the significance of the twenty-one hour and relevant education rules, it is important to realise that over the years these rules have had enormous implications for the educational opportunities of the young unemployed.

'Relevant education'

Only a 'child' (person aged under 16) or 'young person' (aged 16-18) can be in 'relevant education' for the purposes of income support entitlement (SI 1987 No.1967, reg.12). 'Relevant education' involves full-time (more than twelve hours per week) education which is not 'advanced' education (above). This means that 16-18 year olds at school or college and taking GCSEs, National level vocational courses such as BTEC, 'A' levels, and so on, are in relevant education if receiving more than twelve hours instruction per week. Persons on the YTS are not in relevant education.

Only in certain prescribed circumstances can a person in relevant education be entitled to income support:

(i) if s/he is responsible for a child; or

(ii) is severely mentally or physically handicapped and because of that would be unable to gain employment within the following twelve months; or

(iii) is without a parent or person acting in place of a parent; or

(iv) lives away from and is estranged from a parent or person acting in place of a parent; or

(v) lives away from a parent (etc.) who cannot provide for him/her financially and is chronically sick or mentally or physically disabled or in custody or prohibited from entering G.B.; or

(vi) in the case of persons aged 18 or over only, is taking or completing a course under the twenty-one hour rule (below) (SI 1987 No.1967, reg.13).

Note that in relation to (i)-(v) above, 16 and 17 year olds are eligible for IS by virtue of falling with the categories of exception to the age 18 minimum age of entitlement (ibid., reg.13A, Sch.1 para.10, Sch.1A para.1).

A person leaving school or college will remain in relevant education until s/he is 16, or until his/her next 'terminal date' (the first Monday (i) in January, or (ii) after Easter Monday, or (iii) in September). Persons who leave school at Easter and who, at that time, remain entered for public examinations in the summer, will be classed as in relevant education until the next terminal date after the examinations. This rule was introduced in 1987 to prevent pupils from leaving school at Easter and drawing benefit while not truly available for work because of their plans to take examinations in the early summer. However, those who, having left school, decide not to attend the examinations, are also barred until the appropriate terminal date. These rules concerning school leavers have ceased to be relevant to independent entitlement for persons aged 16 or 17 because of the raising of the minimum age of entitlement to IS from 16 to 18 (see Chapter 7 below), although they will determine whether a young person is a dependant for the purposes of his/her parent's IS entitlement (where relevant) and entitlement to child benefit.

Reference was made earlier to a twelve hour rule for determining whether or not the weekly hours of instruction are sufficient to constitute 'relevant education'. The twelve hour rule dates from August 1984 when it replaced the rather unsatisfactory fifteen hour rule (actually just a policy rule adopted by the authorities). The rigidity of the fifteen hour rule, under which hours of homework were included in the claimant's hours, was criticised by Commissioner Bowen in *CF 38/1983* (the *Mc Cormack* case), and the rule was considered unfair in the way that it penalised endeavour (see, for example, '"Fined" - The Eager Student', *Liverpool Echo*, 1.2.84, and 'Student Loses

Benefit for Doing Homework', *The Guardian*, 2.2.84). In 1984, amendment regulations (SI 1984 No.938) introduced the twelve hour test under which time spent in private study is ignored when calculating the claimant's hours. The need to calculate time spent in private study had been a cause of sometimes sour relations between the DHSS and schools and colleges (Pelican 1983, p.53), and had led to difficulties of interpretation. The exclusion of private study etc. from the calculation from 1984 brought the twelve hour rule into line with the twenty-one hour rule.

The twenty-one hour rule

> The 21 hour rule... was introduced to help people who wanted to do something useful in their spare time while they were unemployed and looking for a job. We would all accept that that is a sensible objective. In the world as it is now, there is no merit in those who are young and unemployed and genuinely unable to find work being forced to spend their time in idleness when it would be possible for them to engage in some study of a kind which might help them in the longer term. The 21 hour rule was designed... to assist in that purpose (Mr A. Newton M.P., H.C. Standing Committee B, The Social Security Bill, cols 577-8, 4.3.86).

The twenty-one hour rule was developed out of a concession introduced under the SBC's discretion in 1971. Young claimants attending college for not more than three days per week were granted supplementary benefit provided they were prepared to give up their studies if offered suitable employment. Around this time the level of youth unemployment was becoming more noticeable. Concern was expressed by the general purposes committee of the National Youth Employment Council in 1971 about trends in the rate at which summer school leavers were finding employment. It was reported (*Department of Employment Gazette*, September 1971, p.818) that

> The Committee... sympathised with the view that young people were much better off taking courses of further education rather than wasting time until a job became available. They were aware of the difficulties that arise when people on such courses claim unemployment or supplementary benefit, but asked for consideration to be given to finding ways to encourage young people to take such courses rather than be unemployed

According to the DHSS (Memorandum to the H.C. Education, Science and the Arts Committee, 1983), the concession for people in part-time education was the SBC's attempt to draw a distinction between young people who had chosen to pursue their studies through sixth form or further education college and perhaps beyond and whose primary commitment was to the world of education and those unemployed youngsters who had completed their formal education but wished to do some formal study or training while seeking work

The rule was revised a few times between 1977 and 1979. The amount of permitted attendance was changed from three days to twenty-one hours spread over five or six days a week. Claimants had to continue signing on while studying and be prepared to leave their course if a job became available (DES *Memorandum 4/77*, 1977, and *4/77 Amendment No.1*, 1979).

In November 1980 the rule was built into the new, regulated, SB scheme. A further condition was introduced, that a person must not have given up a job or full-time course in order to attend the part-time course. (Also, those aged 21 or over had to have been in receipt of benefit and available for work for at least twelve months prior to the start of the course.) The twenty-one hour rule also applied to persons attending a course of instruction or training analogous to a course for which a training allowance would be payable. Further reforms to the rule occurred in the period after November 1980 (see below).

The development of the twenty-one hour rule appears to have been influenced by a guarded approach by the benefit authorities towards support for persons pursuing courses. The DHSS has argued (H.C. Education, Science and the Arts Committee 1983, Q.730) that social security support for persons in *full-time* education arises only indirectly, in the course of providing family support:

> being in education in your own right is not one of the contingencies which social security benefits are provided for. So *we* look after people between 16 and 19 as part of a family, when they are in education (in other words, either by paying child benefit to their parents or dependency benefits if their parents are on some sort of social security benefit), but we do not provide student support as such.

For those pursuing their education on a *part-time* basis the role of social security has been less certain. The Supplementary Benefits Commission recognised that here 'the division between the worlds of education and employment' is 'less clear cut' (DHSS, *Memorandum* to H.C. Education, Science and the Arts Committee 1983, para.4). Persons in part-time education often regard themselves as available for work and thus entitled to be regarded as unemployed for benefit purposes. While believing on the one hand that 'the element of choice and suitability involved in the decision to continue in education makes it unlike contingencies covered by social security', the Department has had to acknowledge (ibid., paras 3 and 4) that if young people taking part-time courses were to be treated as not available for work this would impose a penalty on those unemployed youngsters who (make) the effort to do something constructive with their time... while seeking work

But despite the fact that the SBC and DHSS were prepared to make a 'concession' to enable some young people in part-time education to receive benefit, there was still a degree of disquiet about whether the social security system should offer support to persons in education at all - a disquiet which surfaced in the debates in 1985-86 concerning the policy, intimated in the 1985 Green Paper, of removing student support from the social security system. So it is against a background of reluctant acceptance of responsibility for support of persons studying on a part-time basis that the policies and provisions have developed in the form of the twenty-one hour rule, which is considered by the authorities as '...a very special case. Although it is a very small bit of *our* system, it is the bit which impinges more on the education system... than any of the others' (H.C. Education, Science and the Arts Committee 1983, Q.731).

Yet the way that the twenty-one hour rule had been structured led to difficulties as soon as it came to be applied in its context of education. The rule stated that a person should be 'attending... for instruction' on a course for not more than twenty-one hours per week. The Chief Supplementary Benefit Officer (CSBO), having taken legal advice, advised that hours in class and lunchbreaks, homework and unsupervised private study time be included (CSBO 1982a). This interpretation caused considerable disquiet, not least because it resulted in many young people being deprived of entitlement. There were also practical difficulties - what about young people studying at weekends when they would not normally be available for work (Rust 1982)? Including hours of private study that might be undertaken at home seemed to be stretching the interpretation of 'attending' beyond reasonable limits.

As had perhaps been expected, a Tribunal of Commissioners held that the CSBO's guidance had been incorrect (*R(SB)26/82*). The hours to be counted were the hours of instruction in the classroom, time spent on compulsory field work or outings which were an integral part of the course, and time spent on compulsory and predetermined periods of private study on the premises. Although the Commissioners did not dismiss as irrelevant any classification of the course (as full- or part-time) by the institution concerned (a factor later deemed particularly relevant to determinations, in *CF38/1983*), they held that tribunals were entitled to weigh precise evidence about hours of attendance given by the claimant against a general statement by the school.

Following the decision, amendment regulations (SI 1982 No.907) were introduced. The major changes, so far as the twenty-one hour rule was concerned, were: first, that 'part-time course' was defined as involving not more than twenty-one hours instruction or tuition including supervised study or practical work but excluding meal breaks or unsupervised study whether on or off the premises of the educational establishment(s) involved; and secondly, that a three month qualifying period, which had been promised by the minister, was introduced. This qualifying period would be applicable to persons of all ages, replacing the twelve month qualifying period which had applied to those aged 21 or over. Claimants had to have been unemployed and in receipt of benefit for three months before they could become entitled under the twenty-one hour rule. Furthermore, the course followed after the qualifying period had to be different from that taken during those three months. Antony Newton M.P., Social Security Minister, emphasised that it would be possible, during the three month qualifying period, for young people to undertake a certain amount of part-time study provided they could demonstrate that they were available for work (*H.C. Hansard*, Vol.23, cols 198-9, 10.5.82). The amount of study allowed was in fact anything less than fifteen hours per week, the maximum amount under child benefit rules before education would be classed as 'full-time'.

Particular concern was expressed about the likely effects of the introduction of the three month qualifying period; for although unemployed people aged 21 or over stood to benefit from the abolition of the twelve month qualifying period applicable to them, it was said that younger claimants in particular would now

> 'not be eligible for the twenty-one hour concession until December, a time when colleges do not normally begin courses and when it could well be too late for youngsters to profit by any course leading to a qualification in that academic year' (SSAC 1982, para.8).

A report, *Studying on the Dole* (commissioned by the Department of Employment) (Pelican 1983), recommended (p.15) abandonment of the three month qualifying period. Courses could then be allowed to run from September right through to the following summer, with no adverse effect on benefit entitlement nor educational quality (which had been affected by the need to condense courses to below the fifteen hours maximum during the qualifying period (ibid., p.14)). Discontinuing the qualifying period would also remove what had proved to be a cause of frustration and a disincentive to the pursuit of further education.

But why had the Department proposed the three month qualifying period in the first place? The DHSS believed that a twenty-one hour rule without a three month qualifying period would have allowed some young people, staying on at school or college to take 'A' levels as a means of gaining entry to higher education, to qualify for benefit, 'so cutting across the principle that supplementary benefit is not an appropriate means of support for people engaged primarily in study outside the employment field' (SSAC 1982, Annex 2, para.6). The government's view has consistently been that the qualifying period helps ensure that a person claiming benefit while studying is genuinely in the labour market 'rather than a continuing student in disguise' (H.C. Standing Committee B, Social Security Bill, cols 577-8, 4.3.86, Mr A.Newton M.P.). Nevertheless, some concessions were introduced - for example, for those who fell ill during the qualifying period and for those who signed on after being on a government training scheme. Those in the latter category were allowed to count time spent during the previous six months on a YOP or YTS scheme towards the three month qualifying period (SI 1983 No.1000). This concession, which created something of an anomaly but was consistent with the government's promotion of youth training, is now in the IS regulations (SI 1967 No.1967 reg.9(2)).

So, it is possible for a person to undertake up to twelve (previously fifteen) hours per week study during the qualifying period in order to establish entitlement, after three months or more, under the twenty-one hour rule. During the three months the claimant will not be in 'relevant education' and so will have spent the requisite time on 'qualifying benefit' under the twenty-one hour rule. The three month period must precede the 'commencement date' of the course. This is interpreted to mean that the course (or at least the subjects taken) during the three month qualifying period must be *different* to the course following it - not just in terms of involving fewer hours (see Mesher 1988, p.53). The revised CSBO's guidance on the rule (CSBO 1982b) suggested that if the same subjects were taken at a different institution, or if part of the original curriculum had been dropped and new subjects added, the claimant should be treated as having started a different course. (See also *S Manual* (guidance on SB prior to April 1988), para.1300.) But there were complaints of wild inconsistencies in the interpretation by SBOs of the phrase 'different course' even after publication of the CSBO's guidance (*The Guardian*, 3.5.83).

The DHSS has explained (H.C. Education, Science and the Arts Committee 1983) that the intention behind the 'different course' requirement is to prevent 'manipulation of the rules, for example by a student who might embark on a full two year 'A' level course but make an artificial adjustment to the hours for the initial three months'. But the 'different course' requirement has clearly presented colleges with enormous difficulties in relation to providing courses which offer a sensible educational progression yet stay within the rule. Indeed, this aspect of the twenty-one hour rule has placed a severe limitation on the rule's potential to widen educational opportunities for the young unemployed.

Nevertheless, some have argued that the rule concerning different educational provision during the qualifying period ought not to be regarded as overly-restrictive. It has been claimed that if the autumn term could be used for a foundational and diagnostic course, the three month qualifying period might not be a severe obstacle. The Further Education Unit (FEU) of the DES has argued that programmes could be devised for the qualifying period, leading into a subsequent twenty-one hour course, provided that courses undertaken after the qualifying period are 'demonstrably different from those in the first three months' (FEU 1984, para.3.1). Of course, the major problem would lie in ensuring that there was continuity between the two courses. The FEU recommended, as one possibility, a 'modular approach' under which fresh units could be added after the qualifying period. The Unit asserted that such an approach to educational provision was consistent with an underlying trend in the continuing development of further education. But a note of realism was struck by the Welsh Office (in a letter to county councils, dated 10.9.82): 'At a time of increasing demand for full-time courses and of general financial constraint... there are limitations on the opportunities for making extra provision'. Colleges remained sceptical about the opportunities offered by the twenty-one hour rule, especially after the introduction of the qualifying period.

One major problem associated with the twenty-one hour rule has been lack of co-ordination between the DES and DHSS, as revealed by some of the oral representations made to the H.C. Select Committee on Education, Science and the Arts in April 1983. A DHSS spokesperson told the Committee (Q.731) that the Department would 'simply consult the Department of Education when we were considering making any changes to the rule, or we would expect them to approach us if they felt the rule was causing difficulties'. This hardly reveals evidence of a co-ordinated approach to the operation of the part-time education benefit concession. While on the one hand the FEU was exhorting colleges to respond enthusiastically to the opportunity the rules offered for devising new part-time courses, the main body of the DES was uninspiringly indicating (ibid., Q.744) that it had 'no objection' to provision being made under the twenty-one hour rule. But any lack of co-ordination at national level did not hamper the development of local co-operation between some DHSS offices and LEAs and colleges. In some cases local agreements were struck, easing considerably the administration of the twenty-one hour rule and associated provisions (Pelican 1983, pp.53-4).

While the operation of the rule relating to the qualifying period has caused much concern, and a varied response from LEAs and colleges, it has been claimed that it has not proved the major hurdle to claimants that some had expected it to be. The DES reported (*Administrative Memorandum 3/1984*): 'While demand fell in some areas, the introduction of the qualifying period does not seem to have led to an overall reduction in the number of unemployed people taking advantage of the concession'; and about 30,000 16 and 17 year olds were believed to be receiving SB under the rule in 1987.

Comment: the future of the twenty-one hour rule Much of the evidence on the effects of the twenty-one hour rule has emanated from one major study, *Studying on the Dole*. This revealed that the concession was under-exploited by claimants and education providers and that the regulations were a source of much confusion. This confusion, coupled with the educational and administrative problems surrounding the concession, meant that 'few... in the education service had any sense of excitement about the possibilities it offered' (Pelican 1983, p.14). However, the study also emphasised that development of courses to meet the requirements of the twelve and twenty-one hour rules - incorporating modular design, transferability of credits, 'negotiated curriculum', etc. - would be possible since it would not represent anything new for colleges. These suggestions were later included in the FEU's guidance to colleges on the rules, as we saw earlier.

More recently, the FEU (1986, para 83-91), in comprehensive guidance to further education institutions and LEAs on creating educational opportunities for the unemployed, maintains that it is possible to encourage and assist young people who are unemployed to learn in FE institutions without loss of benefit. It remains the FEU's contention (ibid., para.91) that despite the need for careful planning, curriculum design and development and flexible delivery of provision, if there is due commitment from teachers 'there should be few obstacles to valuable programmes of continuing education and training for most unemployed people seeking further opportunities in life and work'. The FEU stresses, however, that it is of central importance that college staff be familiar with benefit regulations, and guidance is offered. But, as Allbeson (1985, p.97) put it, the benefit rules became so complicated that educators saw 'the issue of benefit while studying as a problem rather than an opportunity'. (Senior and Naylor 1987 have explained the difficulties.)

The value of twenty-one hour-type provision rests in the albeit constrained educational opportunity it can offer the unemployed. For some young people, one of the few consoling factors in being unemployed lies in the opportunity for further education (Roberts et al. 1985; Pelican 1983). But it should not be assumed that all young people who enter part-time education do so simply because there is nothing better to do. Although it is necessary to be prepared to give up a course if and when a suitable job becomes available, most young people in the *Studying on the Dole* survey made a deliberate decision to attend and showed a high degree of commitment. But part-time study was still 'very much second best' to a job (Pelican 1983, p.43). The lack of proper support for young people in this situation has led to many such persons undertaking college studies 'using social security as student grants' (Roberts et al. 1985, p.189). The level of support offered to young people by SB has been subsistence level only, so: 'that (SB) should appear attractive to unemployed young people is an indication of the lack of alternatives for adequately-funded full-time study' (Pelican 1983, p.45). There is also the fact that twenty-one hour students often do not qualify for the bus pass provided to full-timers (Crutwell and Morris 1987, p.160).

Denial of benefit entitlement to young people seeking to extend their education raises the issue of dependence on the family for support: 'the price of continuing education at 16+ is... dependence' (NUS 1985a, p.16). If the student cannot depend on the state for support s/he will have to rely on her/his family, if this is possible. But this may present a continuing and overbearing financial burden for the family, barring the way to further education for some unemployed would-be entrants. It can be argued that the object of any policy towards young adults making the critical decision on which direction to take after leaving school should be to enable that decision to be based on their aptitudes and preferences, with financial considerations allowed to have but a neutral effect on the decision.

A problem for young people is that social security law requires a distinction to be drawn between those choosing a purely educational path and those seeking employment and studying only until employment arises. The wholly inadequate system of discretionary awards for persons continuing in non-advanced full-time education post-16 (cf. YTS trainees' allowances), coupled with the inability of many families to support young people not drawing benefit in their own right, has undoubtedly increased the attractiveness of being classed as following the second of these two 'paths'. But although there has understandably been interest in studying under the twenty-one hour rule, the conditions forming parts of the rule, such as the qualifying period, and the resultant curricular limitations, have limited its value to young people.

If, as the DHSS has suggested (HC Education, Science and the Arts Committee 1983) high levels of youth unemployment have made 'the dividing line between those young people whose primary commitment is their studies and those who are effectively in the employment field increasingly difficult to draw', one wonders whether the rather arbitrary and artificial distinction, based on weekly course hours, should not be removed altogether. The test could be simply availability for work, based on an active search for employment and willingness to take up any suitable offer of work. Robert Clay M.P.'s proposed (but defeated) amendment to the Social Security Bill in 1986 would have resulted in only those receiving education for twenty-four or more hours per week being excluded. This would have been an improvement, but would simply have substituted one, admittedly less unsatisfactory, dividing line for the existing one.

The draft Income Support (General) Regulations, issued in the summer of 1987, seemed to preserve the substance of the twenty-one hour rule. Thus the features of a rule which, according to the government, aimed to enable unemployed people to 'do something useful' while looking for a job, but which was subject to so many limitations, were to remain. But although it has been encouraging initiatives such as the 'Work-Related Further Education Programme' (see Dept. of Employment 1988b, paras 6.7-6.8), the government seems to think that youth training constitutes most of what is 'useful' in this context, and the vast majority of young people aged 16 and 17 have been denied the option of attending a course while drawing benefit, following the implementation of s.4 of the Social Security Act 1988. This move, aimed at, *inter alia*, increasing YTS participation, has, in the absence of real alternative sources of financial support, removed even the limited amount of choice that these unemployed young people currently enjoy.

As things stand, 18 year olds can qualify under the twenty-one hour rule. Those aged 19 or over who are not classed as students because their course is part-time may, if their course is non-advanced, or if they are on a course of training or instruction analogous to one for which a training allowance would be payable, and in either case they are prepared to terminate their course when notified of a vacancy, be eligible to be considered available for employment under the twenty-one hour rule. But the various restrictions, such as the three month qualifying period, remain. [3]

Education and benefits: concluding remarks

If any area of social security law has been deserving of the epithet a 'tangle' it is surely the rules relating to young people in education. The detailed and complex provisions, modified with alarming and disconcerting frequency, have presented problems for claimants, administrators and education providers alike. Amendment has been piecemeal. There has been no attempt to present a coherent policy on the benefit entitlement of those engaged in study.

In part, the problems can be blamed on the uncertain distinction between those unemployed but engaged in study and those continuing along an unequivocally educational path. The government, and benefit administrators, have gone to tortuous lengths to devise a system of rules and guidance enabling this distinction to be made without equivocation. The results, as seen in the regulations, are distinctions which are often inappropriate and arbitrary and which often hamper the fulfilment of educational aspirations.

Failure by the government to explore properly the relationship between social security and other forms of student support before instituting reform in this area has meant that changes in students' benefit entitlement have tended to be reactive, prompted by strains on the benefits system as a result of an increasing volume of claims from this group. Nevertheless, the present government would argue that moves such as withdrawal of students' social security and housing benefits during the short vacations are part of its long-term plans to remove student support from the social security system altogether, and thus do represent part of a coherent strategy. But unless the grants system can become more flexible, enabling grants to reflect individual need more accurately, which it is by no means clear will be the result of the reforms to the grants system envisaged by the 1988 White Paper, support for students must of necessity continue to be available under the social security for some time to come. This will certainly be the case for part-time unemployed students still able to receive benefit (which group is not included in the White Paper).

There have been a number of underlying influences on the reform of benefits for those attending courses at educational institutions. The cost of administering benefits, particularly high where students are concerned, has been one factor. Another has been the government's aversion to what it sees as the 'dependency culture', which it claims that the availability of benefits to young people breeds. In addition we have the work ethic, exemplified by the availability for work requirement, and the dependency assumption, which, as we have seen, has underlain most areas of social security entitlement for young people in the past and is clearly evident in the area of benefits and education - especially 'relevant education'. A further factor, which may well have served to inhibit improvements in the area of 'relevant education', has been government youth employment policy. Considerable effort and expense has been put into the development and promotion of the training programmes, while education for unemployed young people has, by comparison, been somewhat neglected by the government, despite the proven worth of academic qualifications in the quest for employment (see Gray, McPherson and Raffe 1983).

Improvements in the area of benefits and education can only be achieved if there is first a thorough and comprehensive reappraisal of state support for persons wishing to study at an educational institution. The 1988 White Paper on top-up loans for students was principally concerned with those attending courses which attract a mandatory award, and there needs to be a more broadly-based review and consequential reform. The aim should be, *inter alia*, to improve educational opportunity and remove financial disincentives to study from the young unemployed. The Beveridge Report (1942) suggested that social security provision for young people of school leaving age should be moulded around educational policy for this age group. But today, when education is a possible route into employment for the many 16-25 year old persons who are unemployed, it is necessary that social security entitlement be fully incorporated into plans for the development of post-16 education - unless, of course, the system of grants and awards is so drastically improved that virtually no-one taking a full-time course in an educational institution needs any longer to rely on welfare benefits.

Notes

[1] The position of someone attending university or college in preparation for resit examinations was considered in *CSSB/221/1986*. The claimant had been attending a full-time three year B.Sc Medical Science course and had to resit two of his five subjects - at the end of the following, fourth year. He claimed that he was not a student in this fourth year because he was not attending a full-time course. It was held to be a question of fact whether his studies were an extension of the three year course, in which case he might

still be a 'student', or sufficiently different in nature and content to constitute a course on their own.

[2] Not only are such 19 year olds not generally entitled to IS in their own right, but also their parents are not entitled to claim dependency additions or child benefit in respect of them. When the community charge (CC) or 'poll tax' is introduced in Scotland in April 1989 and in England and Wales in April 1990 these 19 year olds will, like others of their age, be liable for the personal community charge (see pp.88-9 above) and will presumably qualify for the 80 per cent. maximum CC rebate. But how will they find the remaining 20 per cent? CPAG (1989) believe that parents will be expected to pay, regardless of their own financial circumstances.

[3] There is also a twenty-one hour rule governing entitlement to severe disablement allowance (SDA), paid under s.36 Social Security Act 1975. Under s.36(4), a 16-19 year old cannot qualify for SDA if s/he is in full-time education. Under reg.8 of SI 1984 No. 1303, a person is to be treated as in full-time education for this purpose if, inter alia, his/her attendance is for not less than twenty-one hours per week, excluding 'instruction or tuition which is not suitable for persons of the same age and sex who do not suffer from a physical or mental disability'. There is no three month qualifying period.

7 Social security and youth employment policy

Introduction

At a time of rising unemployment, the post-1979 Conservative government centred its employment policies on the development of training programmes. Despite changes in these programmes during the 1980s, including the introduction of a new Employment Training scheme in September 1988, there has continued to be a scheme catering specifically for under-18 year olds; since 1983 it has been the Youth Training Scheme (YTS), which replaced the Youth Opportunities Programme (YOP) introduced by the Labour government in 1978. (For the background to the introduction of these schemes see Loney 1983.) Many young people aged 18 or over have been involved in another important scheme, the Community Programme.[1] Increasingly, these schemes have dominated the lives of young labour market entrants (see Chapter 1 above). Although unemployment has declined in recent years (at least in official terms) the percentage fall in youth unemployment has been matched by an almost equal percentage rise in YTS participation.

For reasons which will be explained below, young people in the labour market and unable to secure employment have increasingly been channelled into government training schemes. A training allowance has acted as a financial incentive to participation. Even though the level of allowance has been well below average wage rates for young people, it has consistently exceeded standard social security rates. Moreover, restricted benefit entitlement (under the disqualification and forty per cent. rules (see below)), has provided a disincentive to refusing to participate in a training scheme or prematurely leaving one. Such restriction is not unprecedented. As briefly discussed in Chapter 3 and considered further below, an element of compulsion was built into the juvenile instruction schemes of the inter-war years by making receipt of instruction a condition of entitlement to unemployment benefit.

For 16 and 17 year olds seeking but unable to secure employment there has not, in recent years, exactly been financial neutrality between the choices open to them. Full-time study on minimal educational maintenance allowances or discretionary awards (of usually no more than £15 per week), or part-time study on supplementary benefit of £18.75 (the short-term non-householder rate prior to April 1988) (see Chapter 6), have compared unfavourably in financial terms with the YTS. The Scheme offers an allowance, which in 1987-88, stood at £28.50 (or £35 in the second year, or first year if the trainee was 17). In 1987 the government announced that because it was guaranteeing all 16 and 17 year old people a YTS place, the 'option of unemployment' would be removed from them.

Section 4 of the Social Security Act 1988 has raised the minimum age of entitlement to income support (IS) from 16 to 18 years. This is, in fact, a measure of great significance. For one thing, it has removed the long-standing link (only marginally weakened by the introduction of waiting periods under the 'terminal dates' rules introduced in November 1980 - see Chapter 4) between the school leaving age and the minimum age of entitlement to 'safety-net' means-tested benefit. The practical effect of the reform has been the removal of entitlement from 90,000 young people and an annual net saving of £84 million (Social Security Bill 1987, Explanatory Memorandum) (taking into account, perhaps, increased YTS expenditure, if the government's aim of maximum take-up of the two year YTS is realised).

Savings in public expenditure are not the only motive, however. The reform offers a potent illustration of the fact that the government's rationalisation and reform of social security, outlined in the Green Paper and White Paper of 1985 and enshrined in the Social Security Act 1986 and pursuant regulations, is intended to foster 'self-reliance' (Green Paper 1985, Vol.2, para.2.70) and 'give people greater encouragement to help themselves - by working' (White Paper 1985, para.9.26). During the second reading debate on the 1988 Act Conservative M.P.s talked of the immorality of allowing young people to 'move effortlessly, and seemingly without shame, on to supplementary benefit' (S.Burns M.P., *H.C. Hansard*, Vol.121, col.678, 2.11.87), or 'to leave school, do nothing and claim social security' (V.Bottomley M.P., col.726). One M.P. suggested that benefit payments had 'done much to sap the moral fibre of our young people' (J.Arnold M.P., col.726). Ministers were more restrained, but it was patently clear that the government was intent on applying the long-standing work ethic principle with considerably increased vigour so far as young people were concerned - receipt of training being regarded, in this context, as the equivalent of working. Work and training incentives have, accordingly, been strengthened.

Social Security Act 1988

The complete removal of entitlement to income support from the under 18 age group had been on the cards ever since Lord Young, then Employment Secretary, said that if young people failed to avail themselves of the opportunity of youth training the government would be prepared to consider ending supplementary benefit entitlement for persons of this age (see *The Guardian*, 24.3.87). In June 1987 plans for not including independent entitlement to income support for under 18 year olds in the reformed benefits scheme after April 1988 were announced in the Queen's Speech, a prior indication having been given by the Prime Minister in the House of Commons in April 1987 (*H.C. Hansard*, Vol.114, col.787, 23.4.87).

Therefore, by the time the Social Security Bill was published in November 1987, disentitlement of the 16 and 17 years age group was firmly on the political agenda. Yet the Manpower Services Commission's Youth Task Group and the Secretary of State for Employment had previously, in 1982, considered that the independent right of school leavers not entering the training scheme to receive SB should not be removed altogether (SSAC *Second Annual Report, 1982/3*, para.4.15). Such removal, it was feared, might have a damaging effect on the launch of the new YTS. Instead, a forty per cent. reduction of SB for up to six weeks (changed to thirteen weeks maximum in October 1986) was applied to those unreasonably refusing, or failing to avail themselves of - interpreted to include leaving - a place on the YTS. Between December 1983 and September 1984 1,076 persons had their SB reduced for refusing a YTS place and 9,336 for prematurely leaving the scheme (*H.C. Hansard*, Vol.69, cols 165-6, 4.12.84). Between April and March 1985 benefit was reduced in 1,122 YTS refusal cases (*H.L. Hansard*, Vol.483, col.729, 28.11.85). There were, however, repeated claims by the Secretary of State for Employment, Lord Young, that these reductions did not represent compulsion:

> It seems to me that we are saying to young people: "Here is the opportunity of a place for training to help you on your way through life; or you have the opportunity of a job. But if you consistently and wilfully refuse a place on the scheme, the State, in all its majesty, will reduce your benefit by up to forty per cent for up to six weeks." For that to be considered compulsion is a distortion of the use of the English language (*H.L. Hansard*, Vol.468, col.729, 25.11.85).

In a sense, the removal of entitlement from 16 and 17 year olds represented something of an official about-turn for the government. Ministers had two years previously been confirming that this age group would retain independent entitlement (e.g., A.Newton M.P., *H.C. Hansard*, Vol.89, col.434, 20.12.85, and the White Paper 1985). Conservative M.P. Ralph Howell's attempt, during the committee stage of the Social Security Bill in March 1986, to have the minimum age of entitlement to IS set at 18, was unsuccessful. Moreover, despite the indication in the Queen's Speech that 16 and 17 year olds were to lose entitlement (referred to above), the Income Support (General) Regulations (SI 1987 No.1967), circulated in draft in the autumn of 1987, appeared to make provision for this age group.

The Social Security Act 1988 received the Royal Assent on 15 March 1988. With effect from 12 September 1988 (SI 1988 No.1226), the minimum age of entitlement to IS was raised from 16 to 18, by an amendment to s.20(3)(a) of the Social Security Act 1986. (Note that some claimants, essentially couples where one partner was under 18 on 11 September 1988, were granted transitional protection: SI 1988 No.1229.) In some circumstances 16 and 17 year olds *may* be entitled to IS for a prescribed period (IS (General) Regulations 1987 (SI 1987 No.1967), as amended by SI 1988 No.1228). Persons in the following categories have legal entitlement even though only 16 or 17 years old:

(a) persons exempt from the requirement to be available for work, such as lone parents, pregnant women, certain persons in relevant education (reg.13(2)(a)-(e)), carers and those in receipt of a YTS allowance - *all these persons can, in effect, draw IS indefinitely,* provided the various conditions of entitlement remain satisfied (reg.13A(1)-(3)(a) and Sch.1A Pt.I);

(b) registered persons (i.e. registered for work/YTS training) who are: married partners of persons (i) aged not less than 18 or (ii) registered (for work or youth training) or (iii) in one of the categories in (a) (above); certain persons leaving care or prison or living away from home during a programme of resettlement; orphans; at risk of physical or sexual abuse if living at home; etc. *This group may initially be entitled to IS* (and their parents will not be entitled to child benefit, where relevant) *only until the 'relevant date'* - which in most cases means until the end of the child benefit extension period - unless either starting work or joining the YTS first (reg.13A(1),(2),(3)(b), and (7)). The child benefit extension period is twelve or sixteen weeks, depending on the young person's 'terminal date' (see Chapter 4). (Regulation 7D of the Child Benefit (General) Regulations 1976 (SI 1976 No.765), as amended by SI 1988 No.1227, prescribes the duration of the extension period.) [2]

During this extension period, child benefit in respect of those 16 and 17 year olds not entitled to IS in their own right will be paid to parents who request payment in writing, provided the young person is registered for work or training and not in full-time (twenty-four hours or more per week) work, and immediately before the extension period the parents were in receipt of child benefit for the young person in question.

There is, in addition, a discretionary power, in s.20(4A) of the Social Security Act 1986, under which the Secretary of State can award IS to a 16 or 17 year old who is otherwise not entitled to it. The award may be made to a person 'if it appears to the Secretary of State that severe hardship will result to that person unless income support is paid to him'. [3] Payment will almost certainly cease if a change of circumstances removes the threat of severe hardship (s.20(4C)).

As the expectation was that school leavers without work would opt for training rather than a full-time search for employment, and given that the only compensation for removal of benefit rights would be the guarantee of a training place plus an allowance, the government decided to pay a 'bridging allowance' of £15 per week to those opting for the YTS but forced to wait for a place to become available. Provision for this has been made in the Employment Act 1988. But the allowance is only available to those who have been in work or in receipt of training under the YTS, and is paid for a maximum of eight weeks in any twelve month period, on condition that the applicant is available for work or further training.

Youth employment and restricted social security: the 1988 Act in context

Reference was made above to the expectation that there would be 90,000 fewer young people entitled to IS as a result of the above reforms. These individuals have now disappeared from the unemployment statistics. Clearly, the government stands to gain political capital from this apparent fall in youth unemployment. For many years the YTS has similarly masked the true level of youth unemployment (trainees are not classed as unemployed in the statistics, as we saw in Chapter 1). Now no people aged 16 or 17 years appear in the statistical returns for unemployed people. (The government has apparently stopped counting them, even though a very small proportion of 16 and 17 year olds remain entitled to IS.) But what other reasons were there for the reform? What influence has the continuing emphasis, in social security policy, on maintaining work incentives had? From both historical and international perspectives, how unique is Britain's recent restriction of social security in the management of youth unemployment?

1. *Reductions in public expenditure or state provision*

It has become almost trite to state that the containment of, and targeted reductions in, public expenditure have been fundamental to Conservative economic policy in the post-1979 period. There was a saving to be made, albeit a very small one in public expenditure terms, of £84 million from the removal of independent entitlement to IS from most persons in the 16 and 17 years age group. We saw in Chapters 4 and 6 how, since 1980, reductions in the entitlement of school leavers, students (whose benefits have proved particularly costly to administer), boarders and others, have been prominent features of the rationalisation of the social security system. The restrictions affecting young people are part of a wide-ranging assault on the role of the welfare state and a reining-back of public expenditure. Moreover, the political context in which these reforms have taken place has been one where the middle-classes, who tend not to be reliant on social security, have enjoyed considerably more influence than the working-classes, who form the bulk of claimants (see Introduction).

2. *The work/training ethic*

A point which was frequently made from the government benches during the parliamentary debates on the Social Security Bill was that the availability of benefits to under 18 year olds reduces their incentive to work and raises, among many of them, expectations of state provision which discourage self-reliance.

The work ethic has, of course, been perhaps the most pervasive influence on the development of poverty relief over the years. It was reflected in the policy of the Poor Law, which directed that the able-bodied should be set to work if they were to obtain poor relief. It continued in the Poor Law Amendment Act 1834 principle of 'less eligibility' and the 'workhouse test' which rested on the belief that poverty resulted from laziness or immorality and that the poor would not work if conditions were made too favourable for them. The work ethic was reflected in the level of benefits paid under the unemployment insurance scheme (introduced in 1912 following the National Insurance Act 1911) and successor schemes (see Chapter 3), whose allowances were well below most minimum wage levels. Up to a point - for an aim was also to protect the insurance fund - it was also reflected in the disqualification rules under which voluntary unemployment was penalised by suspension of benefits for six weeks (from 1930 a *maximum* of six weeks).

These latter two manifestations of the work ethic have continued to this day. Indeed, they have been considerably tightened up recently through a more penetrative application of the 'available for work' condition for receipt of benefit (under the RESTART interview for those aged 18 or over) and extensions to the maximum period of disqualification from unemployment benefit - which means, in most cases, a forty per cent. reduction in income support as well - to thirteen weeks in 1986 (s.43(2) Social Security Act 1986) and, subsequently, to twenty-six weeks (SI 1988 No.487). The Employment Secretary's 1988 White Paper entitled *Training for Employment* promised further measures, mostly of an administrative nature, to ensure that claimants are genuinely available for work (Department of Employment 1988a, Chaps 7 and 8). In fact, measures contained in the Social Security Bill published in December 1988 would require claimants to be not only available for work but also actively seeking it.

In the government's view, young people who are not continuing their education should be receiving training for employment. The government regards participation in training as representing a willingness and, indeed, a firm desire on the part of young people to enter the world of work. Accordingly, those opting out of training have been treated in a similar fashion, in terms of benefit entitlement, to those becoming or remaining voluntarily unemployed, as demonstrated above. Now, the Employment Act 1988, in amending and extending the grounds for disqualification for not entering or not remaining on a training scheme, has offered a more comprehensive and clear-cut basis for such disqualification, and one which is expressed in almost identical wording to that relating to voluntary unemployment. New sub-paragraphs (e), (f) and (g) of s.20(1) of the Social Security Act 1975 provide for disqualification: where a person loses a place on a scheme through 'misconduct' or where s/he has 'voluntarily left... without good cause'; or where a person 'has, without good cause, refused or failed to apply for [a vacant training place of which she or he has been notified]... or refused to accept that place...'; or where a person 'has neglected to avail himself of a reasonable opportunity of a place on an approved training scheme'. The equation of training with work is further emphasised by this reform and, of course, by the removal of independent IS entitlement from most 16 and 17 year olds - in respect of which John Moore M.P., then Secretary of State for Social Services, argued: 'unemployment for young people need not exist. They have every incentive, including financial incentives, to avoid it, and now they have every opportunity as well' (*H.C. Hansard*, Vol.121, col.655, 2.11.87).

The theory that unemployment may, in some cases, be benefit-induced, has been a factor behind the benefit restrictions and conditions referred to above and has provided justification for keeping benefit rates well below average earnings. The theory has been stated thus:

> Benefit induced unemployment describes the classic response of "rational economic man" to unemployment benefit... The response is to prolong the duration of unemployment - whether for leisure or job search - and thereby reduce the time spent at work (Casson 1979, p.39).

Casson argues that benefit-induced unemployment cannot be discounted from any serious study of youth unemployment. His argument runs as follows:

> ...benefit induced unemployment has been disputed on the grounds that many people are habituated to work, and have a strong desire for regular employment. For these people work confers status and satisfies a need

for independence and financial security. However, if there are any people in a position to indulge in periodic unemployment without great risk, and without a positive preference of leisure and variety in working life, they are probably young people (ibid., p.41).

Discussion of benefit-induced unemployment is concentrated on two inter-related issues: first, the amount of benefit which is provided; and secondly, the rules, such as the 'availability' rule, under which it is administered.

A. *Level of benefits* Benjamin and Kochin (1979, p.525) postulated that if, in the inter-war years, juveniles' benefits had been as high relative to wages as adults' had been, the unemployment rate among juveniles would have more than doubled. As shown in Chapter 3, the unemployment insurance scheme was far less supportive of unemployed juveniles than of adults. Juveniles faced stiffer contributory requirements and suffered greater restrictions in relation to the period of time for which benefit could be paid. Benjamin and Kochin concluded that in the inter-war years '...the low level of juvenile unemployment was due largely to the insulation of this group from the influence of the unemployment insurance scheme' (ibid.). Sadler (1983, p.20) claims that Benjamin and Kochin's argument that relatively high levels of benefit might have led to large numbers of workers opting for unemployment was

> incorrect for it does not take account of the qualitative differences in benefits, the loss of manhood and the demoralising effect of unemployment which, together, constituted a major disincentive to voluntary unemployment.

Garside (1979, pp.530-1) accused Benjamin and Kochin of failing to consider the severity of the eligibility rules and the way they were administered. In relation to the current system, Layard (1986, pp.50-3) argues that the way benefits are administered may have more impact on work incentives than the level of benefits.

While Casson's argument, cited above, might lead one to doubt the disincentive effects described by Sadler, Casson himself refutes the hypothesis which states that high rates of unemployment prevail when benefit rates are high relative to expected income from unemployment, at least when that hypothesis is applied to youth unemployment. He says (1979, p.96) that 'the application of the hypothesis to youth unemployment is based on the assumption that for young people the benefit constitutes a relatively high proportion of the average wage'. Partly because most young people have to rely on means-tested benefit rather than unemployment benefit (due to lack of opportunity to 'clock-up' contributions), and IS scale rates tend to favour married people with dependants (at perhaps two-thirds of normal net income compared with one-third in the case of 16 and 17 year old people) (ibid.), young people are proportionately worse off out of work than adults. As Casson says: 'Although the young worker does not have the same commitments as the older worker, it is clear that his loss of income is, in proportional terms, much greater' (ibid.).

Single people (which classification covers a majority of young people) have a much lower 'replacement ratio' than married people. [Note: the replacement ratio is the ratio of replacement income (while unemployed) to the normal income (when in work).][4] In January 1986 the ratios were:
Single (aged 18 or over)   38%
Married, no children   48%
Married, two children   58%
(Layard 1986, p.47). The replacement ratio in relation to single people aged under 18 is likely to have been even lower. Casson concludes (1979, p.96) that on the basis that the position in the U.K. is fairly typical of EEC countries, 'it appears that state subsidies to the unemployed are unlikely to account for the high rate of unemployment among young people'. However, Casson says that given the lack of sufficient data on the effects of subsidies which young people receive from their families, a comprehensive test of the benefit-induced unemployment hypothesis is not yet possible.

But analysis not quite as technical as Casson's indifference-curve representation of the benefit-income-leisure relationship, and his hypothetical analysis, has cast wider doubt on the work disincentive effect of benefit levels. A Manpower Services Commission study has concluded that few longer-term claimants fail to seek employment because they feel they are better off on benefit (SBC *Annual Report for 1979*, 1980, paras 5.25-5.26). A Department of Employment Study in 1978 tested the theory that 'if the gap between net earnings and available benefits has reduced, employment may have become relatively less attractive to youngsters'. The finding was that 'Changes in the levels of social security relative to the net earnings of young people were found not to be associated significantly with changes in youth unemployment' (*Department of Employment Gazette* 1978, pp.908-16). The conclusion was that there was 'no obvious need to introduce... hypotheses (such as the effect of... unemployment benefit) in order to account for changes in unemployment in this particular category'. Similarly, the Academy of Social Sciences in Australia has agreed that 'increases in the real value of unemployment benefits... cannot be regarded as a major cause of the increase in junior unemployment' (Henderson 1977, p.H.19). Department of Employment figures show that while the rate of youth unemployment rose between the years 1966-76, the rate of SB as a percentage of net average earnings of young people fell (*Department of Employment Gazette* 1978, p.915). In a recent survey only six per cent. of teenage workers would have been better off on SB (Bradshaw et el. 1987, p.15).

In recent years benefit levels have been well below average earnings and the desired income of young people when starting work. A survey of unemployed 17 year olds conducted in 1982 found that the starting pay which would be the lowest acceptable averaged at just under £37 compared with income while unemployed of about £17 for those living with parents, and about £20 for those living independently (Banks et al 1984, p.344). It is hard to imagine any work disincentive operating in the light of these figures. Moreover, in this 1982 survey 54 per cent. of the sample indicated that they would be prepared to take any job that was offered (ibid.). Research undertaken by Social and Community Planning Research in 1984 revealed that young people regard the level of wages offered as secondary, in terms of job attractiveness, to the kind of work being offered and whether it is expected to be interesting (Hedges and Hyatt 1985, para.6.5.2(b)). This reinforces the argument that benefit/wage relativities are unlikely to have much of an effect on work incentives and thus unemployment levels, a conclusion reached by Professor Layard (1986, p.50) who shows that the replacement ratio has not risen much since the mid-1960s, whereas unemployment has increased six-fold. (See also Sinclair 1987, p.274. Sinclair, while concluding that the precise effect of any reduction in benefit levels on unemployment is difficult to predict accurately, states that there might be a fall in the duration of unemployment among young people out of work for a short period (ibid., p.273). But he rejects the case for a comprehensive reduction in benefits put forward by Patrick Minford of Liverpool University.) The government appears to have conceded that fears of a reduction in net income if they take a job are not a factor which is influencing the unemployed, especially the long term unemployed, when making decisions about working.

The argument that social security benefits are not deterring young people from seeking employment is further reinforced by research findings indicating an extreme reluctance on the part of some young people to register as unemployed (Roberts et al. 1981, p.8 - see below).

Finally in this section on rates of benefit, it is worth noting that parents' and young persons' own judgement of the role which benefits should play seems to be in favour of variation in benefits according to the claimant's real level of motivation towards work. The rate paid to a school leaver, of £16.50, in 1984, was seen as inadequate for a young 'work seeker' but rather more generous for someone who was 'work shy' (Hedges and Hyatt 1985, para.6.5.2(d)). But it might be argued that the low levels at which benefit is set are designed to deter the latter even though there may be injustice to the former as a result. It may also be noted here that regardless of any effect of benefits on work incentives, parental pressure to work exercises a powerful influence on young people's motivation (Banks and Ullah 1987, p.55).

B. *Availability of benefits* (i) The 'work test' Whilst on the whole there seems to be agreement that current benefit rates, especially those relating to young people's entitlement, have had little impact on the incentive to work, some argue that the conditions governing availability of benefit can have a profound effect.

Professor Layard (1986) argues that during the 1960s and 1970s the requirement that people on benefit be genuinely and actively looking for work was less and less strictly applied - as evidenced, in his view, by a decline in the rate of denial of benefit. He suggests that by the early 1980s Britain had, in this respect, an 'open-ended benefit system' which had 'made it easy for long-term unemployment to soar' (pp.52, 64). This open-endedness, Layard suggests, stemmed partly from new administrative arrangements - in particular the separation of job placement and benefit payment functions, with the former being handled by job centres and the latter by benefit offices. The result of this change, and of new signing-on arrangements, he suggests, was that 'the payment of benefit became more automatic' and there was a significant 'erosion of the work test' (ibid., pp.52-3). But even if Professor Layard's assessment is sustainable, recent changes in the administration of benefits, in particular the more strictly applied availability test, together with the more restrictive policy in relation to young people's entitlement, have made it more difficult for young people to obtain benefits. Thus, as Creedy and Disney (1985, p.15) say: 'The strict enforcement of the eligibility conditions would seem to reduce the importance of moral hazard for policy purposes'. (The 'moral hazard' refers to the possibility of benefits discouraging a person from working - see below.)

Support for maintaining the emphasis on the work ethic is likely is likely to come from those who point to the experience of abolishing the 'genuinely seeking work test' in 1930. Abolition is said to have resulted in an 'accumulation of spurious claims from people who were not genuinely in the labour market, or who, for other reasons, had no moral title to benefit' (Davison 1938, p.9). Yet today, as Ogus and Barendt (1982, p.498) point out, 'not only is there doubt about the precise nature of the "voluntary unemployment" problem, there is also. as might be expected, doubt about its scale'. Nevertheless, through its Social Security Bill published at the end of 1988 the government is seeking to reinstitute a form of 'genuinely seeking work' test.

A Department of Employment Research Paper, by Banks and Ullah (1987), has provided much useful evidence on the attitudes of young people towards employment. The researchers questioned school leavers one year, and subsequently two years after leaving school. Few saw any advantages to being unemployed, and there was no significant increase in unemployment, although there was some increase in labour market withdrawal - attributed largely to reduced motivation to look for work due to pessimism about the prospects of finding a job. Despite claims from some academics that benefits reduce the incentive to work (above) the chief disadvantage to being unemployed which the young people in this survey identified was lack of money.

(ii) <u>Non-registration</u> In common with other studies, research by Roberts et al. (1981), uncovered evidence of a great deal of interest in work on the part of young people - the vast majority of those questioned were truly available for and actively seeking employment. But given the high rate of non-registration for work these researchers felt compelled to ask the question: 'If they are genuinely interested in employment, then why on earth should they decline to register and draw the dole?' (ibid., p.20).

One reason that is put forward, perhaps less frequently these days than in the past, is the stigma attached to 'signing-on'. Roberts et al. certainly found this to be one influencing factor (ibid., p.26); and Hedges and Hyatt (1985, para.6.5.2(c)) reported that 'A number of young people felt quite strongly aware of the stigma attached to claiming'. Yet Roberts et al. found that young people growing up in areas where unemployment is more persistent are 'not taught to regard registering as a stigma. They learn, by example, to treat social security as a right' (1985, p.29).

Other reasons for non-registration include optimism about obtaining employment in the near future, avoidance of the 'hassle' of claiming, and, in some cases, sheer ignorance of the right to benefit (ibid., p.26-7). Hedges and Hyatt (1985, para.6.3.2) found that 'General awareness of benefits available to 16-19's was patchy at best, and often poor', although most young people living at home and their parents were aware that some form of state support was available, even if there was some confusion as to whether it was unemployment benefit or supplementary benefit. There was evidence to suggest that in London, where earnings tend to be much higher than in the provinces but where SB/IS rates are the same as elsewhere, some young people did not consider it worth their while claiming (Roberts et al. 1981, p.30). Moreover, young benefit recipients' possible contributions to the family income would be insignificant:

> With parents and/or siblings in employment - in decently paid jobs by south-east standards - the contribution to household budgets of young Londoners who receive social security are often incidental. This is a different situation from districts like Liverpool's Granby, where adult unemployment is more common, and wages are relatively low: in these circumstances even small sums are welcome (ibid.).

C. *Comment* So far as benefit levels are concerned, it has been argued that their suppression or reduction do not improve work incentives and that higher wages could have more impact in this regard. It was claimed in 1985 that depression of youth wages would have to be very severe indeed to bring them near to the £16.50 per week then paid to non-householders aged 16-17 years or the £21.45 paid to non-householder 18-20 year olds (Allbeson 1985, p.90). Over 40 years ago Lush (1941, p.29) argued that the creation of work incentives ought not to involve reduction of benefits:

While unemployment retains its present proportions and wage scales remain at their present level it will be very difficult for those men with no skill to find employment at wages which will exceed the present allowances. The solution will not be found in a reduction of such allowances which are recognised to be subsistence allowances, but rather in a higher level of wage rates.

In the context of work incentives and young people today, Allbeson (1985), in a similar vein, commented:

> the 'incentive effect' of lower benefit levels for young people is evidently being taken very seriously by the government - even though there is considerable evidence that higher wage levels for young people would do far more to achieve the government's aims.

A good example of the seriousness with which the Conservatives regard the 'incentive effect' of benefit reductions can be seen in the government's reform of the SB board and lodgings rules in 1985, with the introduction of time limits of two, four or eight weeks for young claimants (see Chapter 4). The Secretary of State for Social Services (1985a, p.6) stated that the pre-April 1985 system of board and lodging allowances

> discourages young people from finding employment... young, able bodied people are allowed to settle down in expensive board and lodging accommodation for long periods of time. This does nothing to help them obtain jobs because the accommodation is often far more expensive than they could afford when they are in work. For example, the average gross earnings in April 1984 for men under 18 was about £63 a week and for those aged 18-20 about £100 a week. At the end of 1983 ordinary board and lodging limits averaged £66 a week for a single person, with the highest limits at £110 per week. In this situation there are clearly problems of incentives.

The government rejected the SSAC's argument that although SB board and lodging payments might often be higher than average earnings for young people aged under 18 years, only 6,700 of this age group claimed as SB boarders - most lived at home with their parents (SSAC 1985, p.18). The SSAC said that they could

> understand the Government's concern here, but we suspect that most unemployed young people are only too anxious for a job, and that a different kind of accommodation market becomes available once a youngster is in work (ibid.).

The Committee members were 'reluctant to see restrictions being placed on all claimants in order to make an impact on a few...'(ibid.). But the government remained unconvinced.

Little evidence has been produced by the government in support of its argument that social security benefits have acted as a disincentive to work where young people are concerned. There seems, overall, to be little reason to suppose that benefit levels have affected the level of youth unemployment to any degree.

So far as the conditions under which benefits are made available are concerned, it is more difficult to draw conclusions about the disincentive effect. In some cases reductions in the availability of benefits will lead to an *apparent* fall in the level of unemployment; the removal of most 16 and 17 year olds' entitlement to income support under the Social Security Act 1988 is a prime example. These young people will be drawn towards the YTS, which offers an allowance for trainees. It is the promotion of youth training which has led to fewer and fewer young people being officially classed as unemployed. The government might, instead of removing benefit entitlement, have limited its duration to a fixed period - say six months. In the summer of 1987, there was talk of such a development taking place - the introduction of a six months 'job search allowance' modelled on a similar provision in Australia (see *The Times*, 23.6.87). Such a scheme might push any 'workshy' school leavers towards seeking work or training. The YTS 'bridging allowance' for school leavers waiting for a place on the scheme falls a long way short of this. Furthermore, although, as shown above, the Secretary of State now has a power under s.20(4A) of the Social Security Act 1986 to order that IS be payable for a predetermined (by him) period to young people who would otherwise not qualify, this, along with the prescribed categories of exception from the new minimum age of entitlement of 18, will only apply to a relatively small number of them.

Creedy and Disney (1985, p.115) point out that

> Of all the issues concerning unemployment insurance, the moral hazard question - the extent to which the insurance system discourages the claimant from remaining in employment or seeking employment - has generated the most heat.

Yet it would appear that at the very least there is considerable doubt about the precise significance of the 'moral hazard' aspect of social security, where young people are concerned. The evidence suggests that there is little justification for the introduction of such stringent benefit restrictions, especially when the numbers whose benefits have been reduced for refusing a YTS place are so small; only nine people who refused places on the YTS were subjected to the thirteen week disqualification rule in May 1987, causing a parliamentary

Opposition spokesperson to comment that the Bill to remove entitlement from 16 and 17 year olds represented 'something of a sledgehammer to crack a nut' (R.Cook M.P., *H.C. Hansard*, Vol.121, col.666, 2.11.87). Various measures had already been taken, including the payment of the YTS allowance, the thirteen week disqualification from, or reduction of, benefit, and significant benefit concessions to claimants who were former YTS trainees and families whose members included a YTS trainee.[5] It could be argued that these measures ought to have been sufficient for the government to have achieved its objective.

3. *Historical precedents*

> Now Parliament has made some provision - possibly not as much as some people think it ought to have done - that persons shall not get the dole without doing some work... the Minister is to say to the boy: "Here is a course of instruction which you can take; if you do not take it you will not get the dole" (per Scrutton LJ in *Jones v London County Council* (1932), at pp.455-6, referring to s.15(2) Unemployment Act 1930).

It is not all that often in discussion of social security policy that a direct historical precedent can be invoked, but during the period of high unemployment between the wars governments adopted youth employment measures which, like today's, involved training to replace idleness, reinforced by a strong element of compulsion.

During the inter-war years, Beveridge (1930, pp.211-16) was a keen advocate of training for young people. Later he recommended (1942, para.131(ii)) that 'for boys and girls there should ideally be no unconditional benefit at all; their enforced abstention from work should be made an occasion of further training'. The measures adopted in the 1920s and 1930s, discussed below, had largely been responses to high levels of youth unemployment. Unemployment was not a problem after the Second World War (see Chapter 1), but the high levels of youth unemployment in recent years have given Beveridge's recommendation renewed relevance. Indeed, it was cited verbatim by one Conservative M.P. when arguing in favour of the Social Security Bill in 1987 (N.Hamilton M.P., *H.C. Hansard*, Vol.121, col.705, 2.11.87).

State intervention to manage breaks, caused by unemployment, in the transition from child to adult worker is not only a recent phenomenon:

> The State has, throughout the history of British capitalism, always taken an interest in 'surplus labour' - an interest expressed in a diversity of institutions ranging from skill centres to workhouse (Clarke and Willis 1984, p.8).[6]

Churchill, referring to the 'evils of unemployment', wrote to Asquith in 1908: 'Youth must be educated and disciplined and trained from fourteen to eighteen' (cited in Gilbert 1966, p.251). Similar views were expressed between the wars when youth unemployment became an important focus of political and popular concern (Rees and Rees 1982, p.13).[7] The inter-war measures included the establishment of juvenile unemployment centres, originally under the auspices of the Board of Trade, in which a somewhat rudimentary form of training and instruction was offered to young people. Their title was changed to junior instruction centres in 1929 to help give them a more positive image. Comparisons between their regime and YTS provision today are not particularly appropriate. For one thing, the courses provided in the 1920s and 1930s were not attended by the number or proportion of young unemployed people receiving training under the YTS; and for another, recent schemes have been much better financed than inter-war juvenile instruction. The emphasis in juvenile instruction was on the acquisition of practical skills rather than on specific vocational training - which has increasingly been the emphasis of YTS provision.

According to Davison (1938, p.121), the young persons attending instruction centres 'were given what amounted to a new start in life', and 'new discoveries were made in the art of blending practical and academic instruction'. But Rees and Rees (1982, p.19) describe the typical curriculum as 'predominantly practical without being vocational: for the boys, woodwork, metalwork, boot repairing and leatherwork; for the girls, cookery, dressmaking and home nursing'. Later on this 'basic diet' was supplemented by physical education, games, and in some centres by drawing, painting, drama, civics, maths, English, and history (ibid.). The curriculum in one area, Salford, seems fairly typical:

> ... six hours physical training, games, swimming and life-saving instructions. Four hours handicraft training. Three hours general education, i.e. English Empire History, Empire Geography, general talks on character and such topics. One hour simple Arithmetic (Royal Commission on Unemployment Insurance 1931, p.34).

(One of the subjects studied was 'The World's Greatest Men!)

Despite the completely different content and focus of inter-war 'instruction' compared to 1970s and 1980s 'training', an element of compulsion represents a common theme. Moreover, the arguments voiced in favour of compulsion in the 1920s and 1930s were very similar to those recently presented by supporters of reduced benefit provision for 16 and 17 year olds. For example, the Commissioner for Special Areas in England and Wales said in 1936 that young males could only be saved from themselves by a measure of compulsion... suitable young men who are fit and able to take up a course of instruction, which offers good prospects of employment on completion, should not be permitted to stay home in idleness (cited in Davison 1938, p.110).

Attendance at a juvenile unemployment centre or junior instruction centre became a condition for receipt of unemployment benefit by unemployed juveniles after 1920 (Unemployment Insurance Acts 1920 and 1930). Under s.15(2) of the Unemployment Act 1930 it was the duty of the Minister of Labour, if there was an approved course of instruction which the juvenile could reasonably be expected to attend,

> to cause notice in writing in the prescribed form to be given to him informing him that such a course is available, and that if he fails without good cause to attend the course he will be disqualified for receipt of benefit.

The Unemployment Act 1934 empowered the Minister of Labour to make regulations compelling all employers to notify juvenile employment exchanges of all departures of people aged under 18 years. Although these regulations were never made, it is worth recalling that a few years ago employers participating in the YTS received similar instructions from the DHSS. The 1934 Act also empowered the making of regulations (which in the event were not made - see Chapter 3) requiring unemployed juveniles between the ages of 14 and 18 who were in receipt of unemployment assistance to attend courses of instruction provided by local education authorities. (A duty to make provision for such courses had been placed on local education authorities in 1934.)

The element of compulsion in present training programmes has already been discussed. Here there is an obvious parallel with the above measures in the inter-war years.

Finally, it should be noted that not only was there concern about the possible effects on young people of a period of idleness resulting from unemployment. There was also perceived to be a threat of general social disintegration as a result of the demoralisation and disaffection of unemployed youth (Rees and Rees 182, p.17). Such a perception may have influenced government thinking in recent times as well.

4. *Developments abroad*

Government spokespersons frequently cite in support of their case for reducing benefits provision in Britain the non-availability of social security benefits to school leavers in many other industrialised countries. (See, for example, the reference to the system in the Federal Republic of Germany by Dame Jill Knight M.P. - *H.C. Hansard*, Vol.121, col.682, 2.11.87.)

In the Federal Republic of Germany, benefit is not available to unemployed school leavers. Here, as in Austria and Switzerland, a dual system of vocational training and apprenticeship has operated for a number of years. By law, young West Germans without jobs or training apprenticeships must attend classes for a minimum of eight hours per week after they leave school, until they are 18 years old. (See Koditz 1985, pp.99-103, for extracts from various regulations governing compulsory attendance at vocational institutions in the Federal Republic of Germany.) Not surprisingly, few West Germans leave school and go straight into unemployment (Mitton et al. 1983, p.32). An equal allowance is paid to those who remain at school or enter apprenticeship or training, unlike in Britain, where trainees are better off than persons at school or in further education and where there are, in effect, financial incentives to leave school.

Sweden and Denmark are said to have

> largely solved problems of unemployed sixteen to eighteen year olds by removing most of them from the labour market... both countries accept the notion that such youngsters should be seen as citizens in training rather than young workers (Boucher 1983, p.50).

In these countries there is a strong element of compulsion in relation to entry to training programmes - 'they cannot simply receive social security payments to do nothing' (ibid.). In Australia many politicians have supported the idea of work-for-the-dole schemes. Social Security Minister Brian Howe, who has already announced that school leavers could face waiting periods for receipt of benefit, appears, according to some observers, to be planning to force young people in that country into some kind of training or education programme as a condition of entitlement to unemployment benefit (Presdee and White 1987, pp.1-6, 20). Already, Australian benefits provision for young people aged under 18 has been well pegged back in order to maintain work incentives (Carney and Hanks 1986, p.118).

Although the element of compulsion - which these benefit restrictions represent - varies from one country to another, the significant common factor, mirrored of course in Britain, is its increase across the countries surveyed. That social security and employment policies may be further inspired by developments abroad is a strong possibility, in view of the keen interest in the U.S. Workfare programme displayed by the U.K. government over the past few years.

Conclusions

Underlying the decision to remove independent entitlement to income support from young people aged 16 and 17 years is a combination of traditional capitalist notions about a 'minimal' welfare state and the work ethic, which have been given particular prominence in recent years through policies developed in response to unprecedentedly high levels of youth unemployment. One effect of the YTS has been to weaken considerably the 'welfare' element of provision for young unemployed people. Removal of entitlement to income support suggests that 'welfare' may be about to lose out to 'workfare'.

As to the consequences of the removal of IS entitlement from the under-18s, it is certain that this age group's freedom of choice, already limited by the availability of training allowances well in excess of educational maintenance allowances and discretionary awards, has been seriously diminished. In a sense, the YTS has become Hobson's Choice for this age group. Those electing either to study or to engage themselves in a full-time search for a job face a prolonged period of economic dependence on the family, with all the undesirable potential consequences described in Chapter 5.

It has been suggested that a guaranteed state income represents a form of recognition, on the part of society, of the position of young people as citizens with a role to play in society which unemployment has served to deny them (Marshall 1976, p.57; Fragniere 1985, pp.2-3; and see Part IV below). But some argue that what has been happening is the increasing marginalisation of young people and their channelling into 'institutional constraints' such as training (Finn 1984, p.60). Young people, it is said, are being perceived as a fringe category and are being denied welfare rights - which are considered to be an element of citizenship (Marshall 1976). Some might argue that a training place plus allowance is a 'welfare right'. But welfare rights, if they are to be an element of citizenship, must not be based on compulsion, for this surely works to the negation of citizenship in a democratic society. (cf. the philosophy of 'workfare' - discussed in Chapter 8).

When the YTS was introduced in 1983 to replace the YOP it was expected that its attractiveness to young people would guarantee their participation. Ministers were convinced of this, and abandoned plans to remove benefit entitlement from 16 year olds. They were also wary of stirring up the sort of controversy that might have jeopardised a successful launch of the YTS. Now attitudes have hardened, and the government feels that the moral and political climate is right for the removal of benefits support. The political ease with which this reform was achieved via the Social Security Act 1988 (despite four standing committee days on clause 4) may persuade ministers to promote further reductions in benefits for those aged 18-24 - who, like 16 and 17 year olds, have suffered progressive benefits reductions since 1980 - once the new training programme (Employment Training) for this age group has sufficient places. However, the tightened up availability rules in the Employment Act 1988, set out above, and the Social Security Bill (when enacted), may be regarded by the government as sufficient to combat voluntary unemployment and non-participation in training.

Trainees participating in Employment Training receive an allowance amounting to a set amount more than the trainee would be entitled to in weekly benefits support:
(i) single people aged under 25 entitled to IS - £11.95 more
(ii) married people without children entitled to IS - £11.25 more
(iii) others - £10 more
In addition, travel expenses in excess of £5 per week are re-imbursed, and certain other expenses, such as child care costs of up to £50 per week incurred by lone parents, are met. If the trainee has an entitlement to IS s/he will receive it as part of the allowance - thus preserving free school meals entitlement for her/his children (see Department of Employment 1988a, para.5.29). The government may later claim that given the 'generous' allowances there is little reason for any unemployed person aged over 18 not to participate in training. But there continues to be little evidence that training schemes offer a real solution to long-term unemployment, and it is likely that only a demographic trend - a decline in the numbers of under 25 year olds in the 1990s - will have any impact in this regard.

The government has recently said that 'the objective must be to establish... training as a normal start to working life for all young people who chose not to remain in full-time education after age 16' (ibid., para.8.17). This, of course, raises questions about the job displacement effect of the training schemes. But, more especially, it suggests that denial of benefit entitlement to those who refuse to take part in the training programme will remain an inextricable part of the government's youth employment policies.

Notes

[1] The Community Programme (CP) offered part-time work in the community to those aged 18 or over who had been unemployed for twelve months or more. It was abolished in 1988. CP workers were held, by the House of Lords (*Chief Adjudication Officer v Brunt* (1988)) to be ineligible for unemployment benefit in respect of the days of the week when not engaged on the Programme. Prior to that decision, the government had, in any event, amended the appropriate regulations on the 'full extent normal rule' (see Bonner et al. 1988, pp.418-420).

[2] In March 1989 the Social Security Minister, Mr Nicholas Scott, announced that further exemption categories were to be introduced, at a date to be

determined (see *The Guardian*, 14.3.89). Benefit would be paid, probably for a set period, to 16 and 17 year olds living away from home and deemed to be estranged from their parents. Another proposed concession, resulting from mounting evidence of hardship caused by the removal of entitlement from most of this age group (see e.g. 'Young people leaving care facing hardship', *Municipal Review & AMA News*, March 1989, p.252), was disregarding in full for IS purposes payments by local authorities to young people leaving care. A further change would be that the IS personal allowance for 16 and 17 year olds would be increased to the same rate as that applicable to the 18-24 age group. (See further, note 3 below.)

[3] One of the concessions anounced in March 1989 (see note 2 above) was that 16 and 17 year olds seeking emergency accommodation at night shelters would automatically be considered for IS under the 'severe hardship' provision.

[4] Replacement ratios tend to form the basis of most assessments of the effects of benefits provision on work incentives. Economists have used replacement ratios in various ways to test these effects. One way involves exploring the relationship over time between the unemployment rate and replacement ratio. Another compares the latter with exit from unemployment probabilities. These are discussed by Creedy and Disney (1985, pp.115-17) who regard such tests as having offered inconclusive evidence so far.

[5] These include: allowing time on the YTS to count towards the three month qualifying period under the twenty-one hour rule (see Chapter 6); not applying the non-dependant deduction from HB where a trainee is concerned; and exemption for the trainee from the conditions of registration and availability for employment under the SB (Conditions of Entitlement) Regulations 1981 (SI 1981 No.1526) and now IS (General) Regulations 1987 (SI 1987 No.1967) (both as amended).

[6] Under the Poor Relief Act 1601 (43 Eliz. c.2) the overseers of the poor were obliged to set children whose parents could not support them to work so that they might contribute to their own maintenance, or to send them into an apprenticeship to learn a skill (Oxley 1974, pp.73-4 - see also Nicholls 1904, pp.190-1). Later, under the workhouse system, children of the poor growing up in workhouses were, at an appropriate age - generally 14-16 - sent out to work (often domestic service) or into an apprenticeship (Oxley 1974, p.95).

[7] For discussion of youth unemployment and government policy between the wars, see: Beveridge 1930; Davison 1938, Chapter VI; Garside 1977 and 1979; and Benjamin and Kochin 1979.

PART IV
CONCLUSIONS

8 Conclusions

Throughout the past two decades youth unemployment, probably more than any other single factor, has been responsible for focusing public attention on young people. Media reports and study after study have highlighted the potentially disastrous social consequences for young people of the poverty and alienation resulting from unemployment. The government has chosen to tackle the problem by concentrating its youth employment policy around its Youth Training Scheme. But the scheme has been viewed cynically by many commentators as an attempt to minimise recorded levels of unemployment and 'contain' the young unemployed. The way that government economic and social policies appeared to be reinforcing the reduction in personal choice caused by unemployment, with young people increasingly shunted towards the youth training programmes, and the extended transition to adulthood for unemployed working-class youth, suggested that there was a new official perception of 'youth'. Increasingly that perception seemed, to many, to be based on a dependency assumption and the notion of the subservience of youth rather than on its independence and citizenship.

In no sphere of social policy has this official perception been more clearly demonstrated than in the field of social security. From a governmental point of view the most direct effect of steeply rising youth unemployment has been the concomitant increasing demand for social security from young people. The resultant strains and stresses to which the administration of social security has been subjected have not only helped to prompt a programme of rationalisation, they have also brought to the surface many of the inherent deficiencies in those parts of the benefits system which affect young people in particular.

When youth unemployment began its steady rise in the late 1960s and early 1970s, the social security system to which young people increasingly turned for support was ill-designed for the task facing it. It had developed piecemeal over the preceding decades. It was devoid of a coherent underlying policy on young people's entitlement, although this is not surprising given the fact that youth unemployment on such a scale was virtually unprecedented in Britain and a truly coherent policy of this nature had, accordingly, never seemed necessary or important. Assumed dependency on families, and the expectation that families were able and willing to accept a measure of responsibility for the maintenance of their aged 16-plus unemployed offspring, had long underlain aspects of the social security system. Although by the late 1960s young people had acquired considerable independence in society, as Britain's unemployment problem worsened the social security system increasingly forced young people to depend on their families.

If social security was going to ameliorate the effects of unemployment on young people and meet societal expectations of independence for this age group, there was, perhaps, no better opportunity to devise an appropriate form of provision than that offered by the social security reviews of 1984-5, instituted by the then Secretary of State for Social Services, Norman Fowler M.P. Indeed, one of the reviews was devoted entirely to benefits for children and young people. The findings of this review were not published separately, and the reviews as a whole contained no positive proposals for a coherent strategy on benefits for young people. The problem of differentials between benefits and other sources of state financial assistance for young people, and the lack of co-ordination between the DHSS and other departments (such as the DES) responsible for various services for this age group, were not addressed. It will be recalled that Beveridge saw the development of benefits provision for young people as dependent upon the direction of education policy for this age group. This issue has never been addressed properly by government in Britain.

The development of the YTS, with its training allowance, brought a new element into the equation. Those participating in education or training, engaged in employment or simply unemployed had widely differing incomes. As a result, there were financial disincentives to study and financial pressure to opt for a place on a training scheme. When the decision to remove IS entitlement from the 16 and 17 years age group was taken, scant government concern for those in education was in evidence. Indeed, most of those who would previously have been entitled to SB under the twelve or twenty-one rules while studying are not entitled to IS if their part-time study and claim for benefit commenced after 11 April 1988. This reduced educational opportunity seems particularly unfortunate in view of the existence of firm evidence of the importance attached to qualifications by employers when recruiting young people (Gray et al. 1983). Similarly, when the demand for social security from students increased, the government's response was to cut back benefits support rather than reform comprehensively student grants to widen opportunity. Only belatedly has such reform been announced, and even so the proposals are far from comprehensive, as shown in Chapter 6.

The government's record on student financial support offers another illustration of the insufficiency of co-ordination between the DHSS and DES in relation to young people. Recent reforms to benefits important to household formation have also highlighted the problem of poor inter-departmental co-ordination in relation to young people's support. For example, the board and lodging payments reforms of 1985-86 demonstrated that there was 'no sign of any intention to develop an integrated housing and benefit policy for single people' (Berthoud 1986, para.127).

The lack of a clear strategy on benefits support for young people, and the piecemeal development of social security as a whole throughout much of this century, have undoubtedly contributed to the rather confused and incoherent state of young people's social security benefits in Britain. The entitlement of young people, since 1980 in particular, offers a striking illustration of the social security system's complexity. One effect of this complexity is that among many young people and their parents, confusion or ignorance about entitlement is still much in evidence (Hedges and Hyatt 1985).

Simplification of the system was one of the objectives behind the Social Security Act 1986 reforms (see Green Paper 1985, paras 2.70-2.71). It would, the government argued, be in the interests of claimants and administrators alike. All claimants would receive a 'reasonable level of help'; the system would not need to 'provide in detail for every variation in individual circumstances' (ibid.). Family responsibilities and other circumstances of need were to be recognised; the IS premiums and family credit rules make provision accordingly.

Indeed, simplification of the system, and the government's aim of targeting resources on need more effectively, were, in effect, to go hand in hand. Single unemployed young people (other than those on a training scheme) have, throughout the post-1979 period, been viewed by government as a low priority for support. It was not surprising, therefore, that the government chose to effect several key areas of simplification at the expense of young people:- the new age 25 dividing line in IS personal allowances; removal of entitlement from most 16 and 17 year olds; removal of short vacation benefit entitlement from students; reforms to Easter school leavers' benefits; abolition, in respect of under-25 year olds, of the non-householder's contribution; and so on. In defence of these and other reforms, which were clearly designed principally to cut administrative costs and the amount paid out in benefits and to increase work/training incentives, the government was able to raise its 'more effective targeting' argument:

The abolition of the householder distinction and the introduction of the 25 age point have enabled the Government to concentrate more resources on older people - including pensioners and disabled persons living in other people's households (White Paper 1985, para.3.10).

This was a familiar argument. The government had stated, when reforming the twenty-one hour rule in 1982, that if SB became a generalised form of support for 16-18 year olds this would 'divert resources from other social needs which we judge to be of higher priority' (SSAC 1982, Secretary of State's statement, p.3).

Some have regarded the singular treatment of young people under the rationalisation of social security, with this age group, as one M.P. put it, 'systematically, deliberately and consistently attacked by the Government's policies' (Dafydd Wigley M.P., H.C. Standing Committee B, col.479, 27.2.86), as part of a 'centrally constructed strategy aimed at remoralising and containing the young' (Davies 1986, p.2). Others have simply viewed young people as being an 'easy political target' (Allbeson 1985, p.98). As one M.P. put it, 'The most convenient client group from which... money could be extracted with the least political pain was the unsuspecting under 25 group' (Archy Kirkwood M.P., H.C. Standing Committee B, col.677, 6.3.86).

In some respects there is a clear ideological basis to the Conservatives' rationalisation of social security and, in particular, their concentrated assault on young people's benefits. Many of the official statements in connection with the government's training policy and the raising of the minimum age of entitlement to IS, refer to the need to break the 'culture of dependency' prevalent among young people who move straight from school to life on the dole. Financial independence, the government might argue, should be earned rather than expected from the state. Removal of entitlement, which will have the effect of steering thousands of young people towards the YTS, will inculcate a spirit of self-reliance, according to government thinking. As we saw in Chapter 7, this is reflective of a new work ethic (under which being trained is regarded as the equivalent of working) which has, in the minds of its proponents, a moral foundation.

What about Davies' (1986, pp.125-7) argument that current government policy on youth, involving benefit reductions and expansion of youth training, is also aimed at containing the young? It could be argued that reducing young people's independence and increasing their dependence on their families, as recent social security reforms have probably done, or forcing them into training, might be likely to inflame protest amongst them. But, on the contrary, channelling young people into courses of instruction or training, as has happened in the 1920s and '30s and 1970s and '80s, is said to alleviate some of the more dangerous consequences of unemployment and idleness - from individual criminality to a threat to the smooth operation of society.

Paradoxically, the strict application of an availability for work test to those taking courses of education, and the lack of adequate grants for those on full-time courses, have actually been discouraging young people from spending their time usefully.

The fact is, that while the young unemployed are being put to work on training programmes the basic feeling of powerlessness to effect real change in their lives (Shostak 1983, p.145) will remain. Here, then, is another paradox, since the government argues that by entering training rather than 'sponging' off the state young people will gain a new sense of purpose.

What also surely lies behind the singularly detrimental treatment of young people under social security in Britain in recent years, and throughout this century, is adult policy makers' perceptions about young people, their role in society, and the way they make the transition to adulthood. There has always been a sense in which governments, reflecting a broad social consensus, will refrain from encouraging premature conferment of adult status while at the same time seeking not to restrict young people's natural progress towards independence. It has been suggested (Wringe 1981, p.92), that society does not wish to accord independent status to young people until they have reached an age at which they can be expected to manage their own lives successfully. Moreover, there is evidence that many young people do not actively seek to live independently of their families until they are aged 25 or over; the government argued that this justified the age 25 split in IS rates (Green Paper 1985, Vol.2, para.2.73).

Nevertheless, British law has tended to adopt an inconsistent approach towards young people (Ogus and Barendt 1982, p.430). This is, perhaps, a result of there being 'contradictory sets of societal objectives for and notions about youth' (Price and Burke 1985, p.50). The position of young people in western society is said to be 'exceptionally confusing' (Wringe 1981, p.92). Nowhere, perhaps, is this better illustrated than in the field of social security. Partly for historical reasons, for example the tradition of family means-testing in the British social security system, it is now possible to distinguish between different young people who, at the same age, are child dependants because they are in full-time education, or entitled to benefit in their own right but in effect treated as partial dependants, or on a training scheme, treated as young adults, and entitled to their own non-means tested allowance (see Cooper 1985, pp.104-5). The social security system's treatment of young people is bedevilled with anomalies, inconsistencies, and crude distinctions; no wonder that it often appears that, as Bennett and Tarpey (1984, p.31) say, there are 'contradictory messages at present being directed at young people'. As if to confirm the ambiguous position of young people, parts of recently reformed social security law now refer to a new category of claimant - 'young people'. But this change appears to be cosmetic, for the most part. In the IS (General) Regulations (SI 1987 No.1967), the appropriate regulation (reg.14(1)) states that a 'young person' means 'a person aged 16 or over but under 19 who is treated as a child for the purposes of (child benefit)'.

But why, under our benefits system, is an 18 year old who is in full-time non-advanced education a 'child' while one who is unemployed is not? It might appear to be because education is regarded as synonymous with dependency. The technical reason is that those in full-time education are not available for work. Yet it seems unlikely that society regards an 18 year old as less of an adult because s/he is a student. Nevertheless, s/he is so treated under the state's system of support for young people in Britain. The result of distinctions such as those referred to above is glaring anomalies which, as the NUS pointed out (1984, para.2) 'militate against the exercise of the right choice for the right reasons' by young people and their families.

Furthermore, the long-standing dependency assumption (defined in the Introduction), which has been applied with increasing intensity to the young unemployed in recent years, has reinforced the protracted transition to adulthood experienced by (usually working-class) youth as a result of unemployment. It has thus contributed to the normalisation of delayed entry to adulthood. By contrast, despite the depressed nature of many young workers' wages, which some argue that government policy has helped foster (Rees 1985, pp.236-7; Lewis 1985), a good number of young people in work have benefited from increasing material satisfaction and independent status. The lifting of certain restrictions on the employment of young people if the Employment Bill published at the end of 1988 is enacted further emphasises the extent to which a divide exists between the adult/independent status accorded young people who are working and the state of childhood dependency accorded the young unemployed. The likelihood of employers recruiting from a small pool of youth labour in the 1990s raises the prospect of greater material rewards for the young employed in contrast to the enforced dependency and poverty of the, albeit fewer, young unemployed.

The dependency assumption relating to young people represents a continuity in British social security law and policy. Many manifestations of it were highlighted in Chapters 3 and 4 - such as the Minister of Labour's exercise in 1925 of his discretionary power to exclude from benefit single persons living with relatives to whom they could reasonably look for support, the household means test of the 1930s, the payment of child benefit to parents of young people continuing their education and the restrictions on board and lodging payments for claimants aged under 26. There is also the age 25 divide in IS personal allowance rates. This dependency assumption operates via such age divisions. Many of these age barriers to higher rates of support (apart from perhaps the minimum age of independent entitlement to the major benefits which has logically been linked to the minimum school leaving age - until the Social Security Act 1988) create rather artificial distinctions in status. Even the government, when deciding, in effect, that age was to be an even greater determinant of need, under the Social Security Act 1986 reforms, accepted that 'there is no age dividing line relevant to all claimants' (Green Paper 1985, Vol.2, para.2.73). Thus the age dividing lines appear rather crude means of attributing adulthood or childhood status to individuals under social security law. Moreover, while it is accepted that there are apparent inconsistencies in social expectations of certain ages, it is by no means clear that British social security law reflects those expectations accurately.

Whilst the divergent definitions of adult status in our law, including social security law, may reflect cultural norms and values, as Thane (1981, p.7) suggests, it may be that, certainly in recent years, it is mostly the cultural norms and values of the middle-classes that have held sway. Social class may well have had a major influence on the political context in which policies surrounding the dependency assumption, and the welfare state in general, have been developed.

For example, the traditional assumption that children of the middle-classes are more likely to continue in education, and so remain in some measure dependent on their parents, is repeatedly borne out by social class analysis concerning participation in higher education. (The latest figures show that only 6.9 per cent. of students in higher education have parents in manual occupations: DES 1988, para.2.18.) It is possible, therefore, that given the predominant influence of the middle-classes (compared with the working class) over the development of public policy in Britain (reasons are given in Le Grand and Winter 1987, especially at pp.153-4), public policy has proceeded along the avenue of increasing the period of dependency on families by working-class unemployed youth because this extended period of dependency is culturally acceptable to the middle-classes and unlikely to be opposed by them. It is also the case that because there are relatively few middle-class beneficiaries of benefits, and yet they may 'as taxpayers... perceive themselves as contributing heavily to the funding of the welfare state', the middle-classes will 'perceive an interest in reducing welfare state activities' (ibid., p.151). Le Grand and Winter conclude that the Conservative government of 1979-83 'favoured government services which were exclusively used by the middle-classes' (ibid., p.166).

Student grants as well as benefits have, in real terms, been cut back, and in 1988 proposals for student 'loans' were announced. The government may have been treading dangerously and risking middle-class support. On the other hand, the government may believe that the support for its policy of reduced state provision and curtailed public expenditure runs so deep that cutbacks in state support for students may result in minor registrations of protest but will not shake the fundamental basis of its middle-class support. Nevertheless, the middle-classes are users and managers of important parts of the welfare state and this, along with widespread ideological support for the welfare state (King 1987, p.169), may have prevented a more fierce assault being made on social security provision, even though it has not prevented the formulation and publication of plans to remove students' entitlement to social security in 1990-91.

But for the working-class, the increasingly protracted transition to adulthood of the young unemployed, which social security cutbacks have probably intensified, runs counter to social expectations of a brief transition to adult independence. This independence was traditionally achieved via employment. The consequences for families of the increased duration and degree of dependence of young unemployed people on their families in recent years may be poverty, stress and even disintegration. Enforced dependence may be contributing to the clearly identified psychological health problems of the young unemployed, as we saw in Chapter 5.

Reform

It would appear that comprehensive reform of state income support for young people in Britain is urgently required. The object would be to eradicate many of the problems which currently bedevil it, especially the anomalies and inconsistencies, the hampering of independence, the inhibition of freedom of choice and the lack of coherent policy objectives. Any replacement system would have to avoid all the false assumptions, especially those concerning dependency, which underlie the existing status of young people within the social security system. It would have to offer much greater support to young people and their parents or relatives, in respect of the transition of young people to adulthood. It should be accepted that, as Cooper said (1985, p.105):

> ...benefit arrangements ought to take some account of the fact that the combined effect of the raising of the school leaving age to 16 years and the lowering of the age of majority to 18 years has left a foreshortened transitional period between childhood and adulthood during which the individual has grown in ability to take on adult responsibilities.

In general, there needs to be greater knowledge and clearer understanding on the part of policy makers of the nature of the transition to adulthood, and this should inform the preparation of future arrangements for social security and other areas of state support for young people.

It is important that any arrangements for state financial support offer young people a measure of independence. Conservative policy is that personal independence must be achieved through the individual's own efforts: 'social security must be designed to reinforce personal independence, rather than extend the power of the state' (Green Paper 1985, Vol.1, para.6.6). But it is hard to see how young unemployed people, unable to achieve personal independence through employment, are going to be able to achieve it without adequate state support. Moreover, one research report (Hedges and Hyatt 1985, para.6.4.1) has noted that there is a widespread belief that because many young people simply cannot get jobs, society as a whole should take responsibility for them. In the long term, the government's YTS may help a number of young people to gain employment and thus begin to attain adult independence. But for those 16 and 17 year olds affected by the raising of the minimum age of entitlement to IS, there is, in the short term, a loss of independence. The age 18-24 age group, for whom rates of benefit are lower than before April 1988 (excepting those with transitional protection), are adults in every other sphere than social security, and it is vital that their independent status is reinstated. The SSAC recently (*Sixth report, 1988*, para.2.20) expressed

> regret that the decision to introduce differential benefit rates for those young (18-24 year old) adults would make it difficult for young men and women to leave home, whether to seek work, to escape domestic tension or simply to establish their independence.

It would be desirable that equal support be offered to those participating in education and training, so that young people living in poor circumstances do not suffer both financial disincentives to study and pressure from families to take the more 'lucrative' option. Also, it seems perverse to offer so little to persons in education (other than those receiving mandatory awards) in comparison to the amount available to those able to draw benefits. This is not an argument for reducing the level of benefits, but rather for increasing support for those in education, especially in view of the importance attached to qualifications by recruiting employers.

Equal support for those in education, training or a full-time search for work has been recommended in various sets of proposals (see below). But such a system of support would give rise to problems. If the training allowances are set too low (as some suggest they are at present) the schemes might be felt to be exploitative. If they are set too high, then matching the rate paid to persons in education to that paid to trainees is prohibitively expensive, as calculations by the Social Democratic Party (SDP 1985) demonstrated. (Also, they might encourage enrolment at college by the academically unmotivated.) Youthaid's recommended 'Youth Allowance', which they envisage would be paid for between two to four years to all young people aged 16-19, at perhaps £30 per week, would cost an estimated £1,200 million per annum at 1984 rates of unemployment (Youthaid 1984). Tom Clarke M.P.'s proposed 'cost of living allowance net of essential expenses for all persons aged 16-19', which his private member's Young Persons' Rights Bill would have provided for (*H.C. Hansard*, Vol.41, cols 556-573), would also have been very expensive, since Mr Clarke appeared to envisage an allowance higher than the YTS allowance. He was concerned to remove what he described as the 'chaotic system of benefits, awards and bursaries for training and education' (col.559); but his Bill did not progress beyond its second reading stage in the House of Commons.

In fact, the majority of recommendations for reform of young people's benefits envisage a totally new system of support. Richard Silburn (1984, p.32), for example, has said that the young unemployed constitute a large group of claimants 'for whom some more appropriate income maintenance measures separate from the means-tested SB are badly needed'. This argument remains valid despite the beginnings of an expected decline in youth unemployment. The SSAC (*Third Report, 1984*, para.6.20) have argued in favour of the introduction of a 'comprehensive youth benefit', saying that the ambiguity in the position of 16 and 17 year olds might best be solved

> not via inclusion in/exclusion from an adult system of benefits but by creating a different system of support for the years between 16 and 18 which takes into account also the different types of educational assistance which are available.

Recently, the SSAC (1987b, para.28) called for 'a concerted re-appraisal of training and benefits' and said that 'the whole structure of State support for 16-18 year olds needs to be reviewed and rationalised'. The Committee have not felt able to produce detailed recommendations on support for young people.

But during the committee stage of the Social Security Bill in 1986, Dafydd Wigley M.P. saw 'an opportunity to try to establish a comprehensive approach to the problem of young people who should be given specific assistance' (H.C. Standing Committee B, col.480, 27.2.86). Mr Wigley tabled an amendment which stated that 'Young persons' support will be payable to every young person who has reached the age of 16 years, but not yet reached the age of 22 years'. Young persons' support was to be paid to persons in nine separate categories, including unemployed, in full-time education and in training. The Secretary of State was to be empowered to set individual rates for each of the nine categories - in view of the wide differences in between them in terms of the degree of need. For example, relatively more support for those who were permanently incapacitated than for the self-employed or employed would clearly be required. (Subsidy to the employed might, in fact, have resulted in depressed wage levels.) Mr Wigley's proposals, which were narrowly defeated, had the merit of comprehensiveness and, by stipulating payment direct to the young person in every case (unlike educational maintenance allowances and child benefit at present), uniformity.

The alternative to the introduction of a wholly new system of support for young people would be modification of the existing system. Stephen Cooper of the Policy Studies Institute has argued (1985, pp.108-10) that the objectives of a system of support for young people should be: to encourage education and training; to facilitate the process of maturing to greater independence and developing the capacity to assume more adult roles; and to enable freedom of choice to develop (with the system being made sufficiently flexible to cater for those making 'non-standard choices'). These objectives, Cooper argues, could be met by adapting the present system. He envisages: equalisation of the amount of educational maintenance allowances (EMAs)/discretionary awards with training allowances; mandatory EMAs/discretionary awards paid to parents until the young person is 16 and then paid direct to the young person at age 17; and retention (which would now mean re-instatement) of SB/IS rights for all young people, including those in part-time education (but in such a case, paid at a lower rate than allowances for those in full-time education/training, to encourage full-time study etc.). Cooper's suggestion that there should be 'one budget for allowances for young people, even if this was administered by separate agencies for the different schemes' would seem to offer only a partial solution to the problem of lack of both coherence and co-ordination in the provision of benefits and allowances for young people.

Another important issue is that of *citizenship*. A workshop conducted under the auspices of the Council for Cultural Co-operation in Delphi, in April 1985, took as its theme 'Young people as active citizens in society and the world of work'. (A Commission on Citizenship, under the patronage of the Speaker of the House of Commons, was launched in Britain in November 1988; it too is concerned with recognition of 'active citizenship' among young people, especially those such as the unemployed whose contribution to society often receives little recognition.) Discussion at Delphi centred around notions concerned with a commitment by society to the needs and aspirations of young people - especially the unemployed. One of these concerned 'an income, guaranteed or earned, through which society recognises youth's contribution to the life of the community' (reported in Fragniere 1985, pp.2-3). The importance of this income, in terms of it being an element in a 'new active citizenship' for young people, would be that it would constitute 'evidence that society does truly recognise the role of the young and is not merely shouldering the burden they represent' (ibid.). Thus there is almost certainly a link between the provision of state support for young people and the concept of citizenship. As Marshall wrote (1976, p.57), social security confers 'rights created by the community itself and attached to the status of its citizenship'. Clearly this aspect of the role of any system of state support for young people ought not to be overlooked. But as things stand in Britain today, an increasing degree of economic dependence on their families is being inflicted on young people not in employment, not only by long-term unemployment itself but also by reductions in independent social security entitlement (and not significantly affected by the training schemes). This dependence (which the government seems to want in place of dependence on the state) has had the potential to leave the young unemployed gaining little from the 'citizenship' which has, in general, increasingly become available to young people. The inability of the young unemployed to experience this 'citizenship' may have served to enlarge the divide between those in secure employment and those struggling to find their first real job.

If the young unemployed are to be recognised as equal citizens then the trend towards what some regard as their economic, social and political maginalisation, to which youth training and reductions in social security entitlement have contributed, must be reversed. Youth unemployment has hampered the integration of young people into the adult community and produced a new official perception of youth as a 'problem minority... a fringe category' (Fragniere 1985, p.2). Regardless of whether a combination of economic recovery and demographic trends produces a significant reduction in youth unemployment in the 1990s, there needs to be a new, wider, concept of citizenship in Britain. Marshall (1976, p.60) has referred to certain welfare rights as being 'part of the mechanism by which the individual is absorbed into society (not isolated from it)'. Any reform of state support for young people, including social security, should aim to offer the young unemployed improved status as citizens.

But the problem here is that in a market system citizenship may rest on, inter alia, the ability of the recipient to reciprocate for public/social services received (Parker 1975, pp.146-7). It will be recalled from Chapter 6 that the government, when seeking to justify removal of students' entitlement to social security and the introduction of 'top-up loans', said that 'it is undesirable that students should learn to depend upon a wrong understanding of the reciprocal obligations of the citizen and the state' (DES 1988, para.2.12). The government appears attracted to the notion that citizenship primarily connotes obligations, which therefore condition the rights attached to it, as exemplified by the philosophy of 'Workfare' in the United States (see Meade 1987; Plant 1988). But improved citizenship for the young unemployed will not be achieved by pursuing policies to promote 'self-reliance' or via 'workfare' schemes when, in reality, the former means dependence on parents and delayed adult independence and the latter means denial of personal autonomy.

The prevailing economic and political climate is providing unfavourable conditions for the much-needed comprehensive reform of young people's social security benefits. The extra resources which would inevitably be required would mean increased public expenditure; but the present government is committed to holding it back. Furthermore, the government wants to minimise the role of the state as provider (see King 1987). So firmly embedded are notions of self-reliance and the work ethic in Conservative thinking on social welfare that it is by no means certain that, even if the resources were available state financial support for young people would be extended. Any expectations of improved financial support raised by the government's statement that it 'fully accepts the importance of a coherent approach to the needs of young people, co-ordinating activity by all Government Departments concerned' (SSAC 1987b, Secretary of State's Statement, para.6), must be tempered by awareness of the government's self-imposed constraints on public expenditure. During the committee stage of the Social Security Bill in 1987, Mr Nicholas Scott M.P., Social Security Minister, referred to the difficulties standing in the way of any review of young people's benefits and said that the government could not promise to institute such a review in the near future (H.C. Standing Committee E, col.380, 3.12.87). The future seems, therefore, to hold the promise of further piecemeal reductions in entitlement rather than comprehensive reform.

It has been said that 'No one would pretend that there is a simple, or even a single, solution to the many inconsistencies and injustices in the present pattern of financial provision for young people' (Bennett 1985, p.13). But it is to be hoped that there will, in the near future, be the political will to resolve a good many of the considerable problems inherent in young people's social security benefits which have been identified in this book. Rather than ameliorating or eradicating some of these problems, the Social Security Acts of 1986 and 1988 and pursuant regulations have almost certainly exacerbated them.

There are many continuities in the historical development of social security for young people in Britain. Some of them are specific to this age group, such as the dependency assumption relating to parents and young people. Others are more universal in scope, such as the work ethic. These continuities may be expected to characterise the development of social security in the future (under Conservative, Labour or Democrat control) as in the past. But there are, at the present time, important transitions in the role of the welfare state. These threaten a break with the liberal tradition in social welfare provision and leave the future of state support for young people in a state of some uncertainty.

Bibliography

Allbeson, J., (1985) 'Seen but not heard: young people', in Ward, S., (ed) *D.H.S.S. in Crisis*, London, Child Poverty Action Group.

Allbeson, J., and Smith, R., (1984) *We don't give clothing grants any more* London, Child Poverty Action Group.

Atkinson, P., and Rees, T.L., (1982) 'Youth Unemployment and State Intervention', in Rees, T.L., and Atkinson, P., (eds) (below).

Ball, R.M., (1988) 'Student vacation workers and the labour market', *Youth and Policy*, No.23, p.30.

Banks, M., Ullah, P., and Warr, P., (1984) 'Unemployment and less qualified urban young people', *Employment Gazette*, 343.

Banks, M.H., and Jackson, P.R., (1982) 'Unemployment and risk of minor psychiatric disorder in young people: cross-sectional and longitudinal evidence', 12 *Psychological Medicine*, 789.

Banks, M.H., and Ullah, P., (1987) *Youth Unemployment. Social and psychological perspectives*, Research Paper No.61, LOndon, Department of Employment.

Bates, I., et al. (1984) *Schooling for the Dole?* London, Macmillan.

Benjamin, D.K., and Kochin, L.A., (1979) 'What went Right with Juvenile unemployment Policy between the Wars: A Comment', 32 *Econ. History*, 523.

Bennett, F., and Tarpey, M.R., (1984) 'The long term reform of social security', *Poverty* No.62, Winter 1985/86.

Berthoud, R., (1986a) *Selective Social Security*, London, Policy Studies Institute.

Berthoud, R., (1986b) *Supplementary Benefit Board and Lodgings Payments. The effect of time and price limits*, Research Paper 86/5, London, Policy Studies Institute.

Berthoud, R., (1987) *Help with Board and Lodging Charges for People on Low Incomes. Comment on the D.H.S.S. consultation document*, London, Policy Studies Institute.

Berthoud, R., (1988) 'New Means Tests for Old: The Fowler plan for social security', in Brenton, M., and Ungerson, C., *Yearbook of Social Policy 1986-7*, London, Longmans.

Beveridge, W.H., (1930) *Unemployment, A problem of Industry*, London, Longman.

Beveridge, W.H., (1942) *Social Insurance and Allied Services*, Cmd 6404, London, HMSO.

Beveridge, W.H., (1944) *Full Employment in a Free Society,*, London, Longman.

Blackstone, W., *Commentaries on the Laws of England*, Vol.1, - cited in Mnookin, R.H., (1978) (below).

Bloxham, S., (1983) 'Social Behaviour and the Young Unemployed', in Fiddy, R., (ed.), (below).

Bonner, D., Hooker, I., Smith, P., and White, R., (1988) *Non-Means Tested Benefits, The Legislation*, 2nd ed., London, Sweet and Maxwell.

Boucher, L., (1983) 'Transition from School to Work for 16-18 year olds in Sweden and Denmark', in Watson, K., (ed.) (below).

Bradshaw, J., (1984) 'Benefits for Children and Young People', in *Fabian Tract,* No.498, *Social Security: The Real Agenda*, London, Fabian Society.

Bradshaw, J., Lawton, D., and Cooke, K., (1987) 'Income expenditure of teenagers and their families', *Youth and Policy* No.19, 15.

British Youth Council (1988) *Young People and the Community Charge (Briefing Paper)*, London, British Youth Council.

Brown, J.C., (1984) *Family Income Support - Part II: Children in Social Security*, London, Policy Studies Institute.

Bruce, M., (1965) *The Coming of the Welfare State*, (2nd ed.), London, B.T. Batsford.

Burghes, L., and Stegles, R., (1983) *No Choice at 16: a study of educational maintenance allowances*, Poverty Pamphlet No.57, London, Child Poverty Action Group.

Carney, T., and Hanks, P., (1986) *Australian Social Security Law, Policy and Administration*

Carver, K., and Martin, G., (1987) *Taken for Granted. The Student Rented Sector and Related Finances in South Manchester*, Manchester, U.M.I.S.T. Union.

Cashmore, E.E., (1984) *No Future. Youth and Society*, London, Heinemann.

Casson, M., (1979) *Youth Unemployment*, London, Macmillan.

Catelanis, R.,(1985) *What does work mean at the age of the young*, Paper for the Public European Parliamentary Hearing on Youth Unemployment (at the Hague, 3-4 September 1985), Strasbourg, Council of Europe.

C.H.A.R. (1984) *Bare Boards*, London, C.H.A.R. (Campaign for the Homeless and Rootless).

Charles, I., (1985) 'The Norweigan Solution: Further Education, An Offer You Can't Refuse', in Fiddy, R., (ed.), (below).

Chief Adjudication Officer (1985) *S Circulars 17/85, 51/85* , London, HMSO.

Child Poverty Action Group - see CPAG.

Chiozza Money, L.G., (1912) *Insurance Versus Poverty*, London, Methuen.

Church of England Board for Social Responsibility (1985) *Reform of Social Security. Response of the Board for Social Responsibility*, London, Board for Social Responsibility.

Clarke, J., Cochrane, A., and Smart, C., (1987) *Ideologies of Welfare. From Dreams to Disillution*, London, Hutchinson.

Clarke, J., and Willis, P., (1984) *Introduction*, in Bates., I., et al., (above).

Coffield, J., Borrill, C., and Marshall, S., (1983) 'How Young People Try to Survive Being Unemployed' *New Society*, 2 June.

Coffield, J., Borrill, C., and Marshall, S., (1986) *Growing Up at the Margins*, Milton Keynes, Open University Press.

Coleman, J.C., (1979), 'Current Views of the Adolescent Process', in Coleman, J.C., (ed.), *The School Years. Current Issues in the Socialisation of Young People*, London, Methuen.

Coleman, J.C., (1980) *The Nature of Adolescence*, London, Methuen.

Cooper, S., (1985) *Family income support part 2: the education and training benefits*, London, Policy Studies Institute.

Courtney, G., (1986) *England and Wales Youth Cohort Survey. Preliminary results from the 1985 Survey. First Summary Report, 1986*, London, Social and Community Planning Research.

Courtney, G., (1988) *England and Wales Youth Cohort Study. Report on Cohort 1, Sweep 1*, Sheffield, Manpower Services Commission.

CPAG (Child Poverty Action Group) (1984) *CPAG's Evidence to the Social Security Reviews. 1984, Changed Priorities Ahead?*, London, Child Poverty Action Group.

CPAG (Oppenheim, C.) *et al* (1989) *Ability to Pay? A Critical Summary of the Government's Proposals for Poll Tax Rebates*, (forthcoming) London, CPAG.

Creedy, J., and Disney, R., (1985) *Social Insurance in Transition, An Economic Analysis*, Oxford, Clarendon Press.

Crowther (Committee, The) (1959) *Report of the Minister of Education's Central Advisory Council, '15-18'*, London, HMSO.

Cruttwell, A., and Morris, J., (1987) 'The 21-Hour Students', *Youth in Society*, No.130, September.

C.S.B.O. (1982a) *Memorandum 10*, London, DHSS.
C.S.B.O. (1982b) *Memorandum 15*, London, DHSS.
Cusack, R., and Roll, J., (1985) *Families Rent Apart* , Poverty Pamphlet No.65, London, Child Poverty Action Group.
Davies, B., (1982) 'Towards an integrated view of youth policy', *Youth and Policy*, No.18, Autumn.
Davies, B., (1986) *Threatening Youth. Towards a national youth policy*, Milton Keynes, Open University Press.
Davison, R.C., (1938) *British Unemployment Policy. The Modern Phase since 1930*, London, Longmans.
Deacon, A., (1976) *In Search of the Scrounger*, Occasional Paper on Social Administration No.60, London, Bell.
Deacon, A., (1981) 'Unemployment and Politics in Britain since 1945', in Sinfield, A., and Showler, B., (eds) (below).
Deacon, A., and Bradshaw, J., (1983) *Reserved for the Poor - The Means Test in British Social Policy*, Oxford, Martin Roberton.
Department of Education and Science - see DES.
Department of Employment (1971-74) *Department of Employment Gazette*.
Department of Employment (1980-88) *Employment Gazette*.
Department of Employment (1981) *A New Training Initiative: A Programme for Action* , Cmnd 8455, London, HMSO.
Department of Employment (1988a) *Training for Employment*, Cm 316, London, HMSO.
Department of Employment (1988b) *Employment for the 1990s*, Cm 540, London, HMSO.
Department of the Environment (1981) *Single and Homeless*, London, HMSO.
Department of Health and Social Security (see DHSS).
DES (1982) *Administrative Memorandum 2/82*, 24 August, DES, London.
DES (1983) *Young People in the 1980s*, London, HMSO.
DES (1984) *Administrative Memorandum 3/84*, 10 July, DES, London.
DES (1985a) *Education and Training for Young People*, Cmnd 9482, April 1985, London, HMSO.
DES (1985b) *The Development of Education into the 1990s*, Cmnd 9524, London, HMSO.
DES (1987) *Higher Education: Meeting the Challenge*, Cm 114, London, HMSO.
DES (1988) *Top-up Loans for Students*, Cm 520, London, HMSO.
DHSS (1972) *Supplementary Benefits Handbook* (3rd ed.), London, HMSO.
DHSS (1976) *Report of the Working Party on Homeless Young People*, London, HMSO.
DHSS (1978) *Social Assistance. A Review of the Supplementary Benefits Scheme*, London, HMSO.
DHSS (1981-87) *Social Fund Manual*, London, HMSO.

NOTE: 1985 Green Paper and White Paper on Reform of Social Security cited under Secretary of State for Social Services.

DHSS (1985) *Housing Benefits Guidance Manual*, London, HMSO.

DHSS (1986a) *Help with Board and Lodging Charges for People on Low Incomes. A Consultation Document*, London, DHSS.

DHSS (1986b) *Supplementary Benefit for Certain Children and Young People. An Explanatory Note*, London, DHSS.

DHSS (1987) *The Social Fund Manual - Draft Guidance and Directions for DHSS Social Fund Officers. A Consultation Paper*, London, HMSO.

Dilnot, A.W., Kay, J.D., and Morris, C.N., (1984) *The Reform of Social Security*, Oxford, Clarendon Press.

Dow, P., (1948) *National Assistance*, London, Shaw and Sons.

Essen, J., and Ghodsian, M., (1977) 'Sixteen-Year-Olds in Households in receipt of Supplementary Benefit and Family Income Supplement', Appendix B to SBC *Annual Report 1976*, London, HMSO.

Evans, J., and Thrower, C., 'A Home from Home', *Youth in Society* No.112 (March).

Evason, E., (1985) *On the Edge. A Study of poverty and long-term unemployment in Northern Ireland*, London, Child Poverty Action Group.

Family Poverty Studies Centre (1988) *Young People at the Crossroads: Education, Jobs, Social Security and Training*, London, Family Policy Studies Centre.

Farley, M., (1982) 'Trends and Structural Changes in English Vocational Education', in Rees, T.L., and Atkinson, P., (eds) (below).

Fiddy, R., (ed.) (1983) *In Place of Work: Policy and Provision for the Young Unemployed*, Lewes, Falmer.

Fiddy, R., (1985) 'The Emergence of the Youth Training Scheme', in Fiddy, R., (ed.) (below).

Fiddy, R., (ed.) (1985) *Youth Unemployment and Training. A Collection of National Perspectives*, Lewes, Falmer.

Finer (Committee, The) (1974) *Report of the Committee on One-Parent Families*, Vols 1 and 2, Cmnd 5629 and 5629-1, London, HMSO.

Finn, D., (1984) 'Leaving School and Growing Up: Work Experience in the Juvenile Labour Market', in Bates, I., et al., (above).

Fletcher, R., (1973) *The Family and Marriage in Britain*, (3rd ed.), Harmondsworth, Penguin.

Fragniere, G., (1985) *Strategies for Solving the Malaise*, Paper for the Public European Parliamentary Hearing on Youth Unemployment (at the Hague, 3-4 September 1985), Strasbourg, Council of Europe.

Franey, R., (1983) *Poor Law. The mass arrest of homeless claimants in Oxford*, London, CHAR/CPAG/CDC/NAPO/NCCL.

Further Education Unit (1984) *FEU Guidance Note No.3. Curriculum Implications of the 12/21 hour rules*, London, FEU, London.

Further Education Unit (1986) *Opening Doors. Creating further education opportunities for the unemployed*, London, FEU.

Garraty, J.A., (1978) *Unemployment in History*, New York, Harper and Row.

Garside, W.R., (1977) 'Juvenile Unemployment and Public Policy Between the Wars', 30 *Econ. History Rev.*, 322.

Garside, W.R., (1979) 'Juvenile Unemployment Between the Wars: A Rejoinder', 32 *Econ. History Rev.*, 529.

George, V., (1973) *Social Security and Society*, London, Routledge and Kegan Paul.

Gilbert, B.B., (1966) *The Evolution of National Insurance in Great Britain. The Origins of the Welfare State*, London, Michael Joseph.

Gilbert, B.B., (1970) *British Social Policy 1914-1939*, London, B.T.Batsford.

Glennerster, H., (1984) 'The 16-18 Age Group', in Silburn, R., (ed.) (below).

Gray, J., McPherson, and Raffe (1983) *Reconstructions of Secondary Education*

Hamilton, S.F., and Claus, J.F., (1985) 'Youth Unemployment in the United States', in Fiddy, R., (ed.) (above).

Harris, C.C., (1983) *The Family and Industrial Society*, London, George Allen and Unwin.

Harris, J., (1972) *Unemployment and Politics. A Study in English Social Policy 1886-1914*, Oxford, Clarendon Press.

H.C. - see House of Commons

Hedges, A., and Hyatt, J., (1985) *Attitudes of Beneficiaries to Child Benefit and Benefits for Young People*, London, Social and Community Planning Research.

Henderson, R.F., (ed.) (1977) *Youth Unemployment. Academy of the Social Sciences in Australia. Second Symposium, 7th & 8th November 1977*, Melbourne, University of Melbourne.

Hendry, L.B., (1983) *Growing Up and Going Out. Adolescents and Leisure*, Aberdeen, Aberdeen University Press.

Hirsch, D., (1983) *Youth Unemployment. A background paper*, London, Youthaid.

Horton, C., (1985) *Nothing Like a Job*, London, Youthaid.

House of Commons Education, Science and the Arts Committee (1983) *Minutes of Evidence*, 20 April, London, HMSO.

House of Commons Education, Science and the Arts Committee (1986a) *Minutes of Oral Evidence*, 18 November, London, HMSO.

House of Commons Education, Science and the Arts Committee (1986b) *First Report 1986-87. Student Awards*, 16 December, London, HMSO.

House of Commons Fifth Standing Committee on Statutory Instruments (1984) *Draft Supplementary Benefit (Requirements) Amendment and Temporary Provisions Regulations, 1984*, Wednesday 12 December, London, HMSO.

House of Commons Second Statutory Instruments Committee (1982) *Report of proceedings, 27 July 1982*, London, HMSO.

House of Commons Select Committee on Employment (1983) *The Youth Training Scheme, Minutes of Evidence*, 20 April, HC 335, London, HMSO.

House of Commons Social Services Committee (1986a) *Evidence Presented to the Committee, 22 January 1986*, London, HMSO.

House of Commons Social Services Committee (1986b) *First Report, Session 1985-86. Reform of Social Security*, HC 180, London, HMSO.

Housing Benefit Review Team (1985) *Report of the Review Team*, Cmnd 9520, London, HMSO.

Jewkes, J., and Jewkes, S., (1938) *The Juvenile Labour Market*, London, Victor Gollancz.

Jewkes, J., and Winterbottom, A., (1933) *Juvenile Unemployment*, London, George Allen and Unwin.

Jones, G., (1987) 'Leaving the Parental Home: An Analysis of Early Housing Careers', 16 *J. Social Policy*, 49.

Judd, J., (1988) 'A la carte on the campus', *The Observer*, 6 November.

Kallen, D., (1983) 'Youth, Education and Unemployment - a European Overview', in Watson, K., (ed.) (below).

Kay, F.G., (1972) *The Family in Transition. Its Past, Present and Future Patterns*, Newton Abbot, David and Charles.

Kemp, P., and Raynsford, N., (1985) *Housing Benefit: The Evidence. A collection of submissions to the Housing benefit Review*, London, Housing Centre Trust.

Koditz, V., (1985) 'The German Federal Republic: How the State Copes with the Crisis - a Guide through the Tangle of Schemes', in Fiddy, R., (ed) (above).

Land, H., (1975) 'The Introduction of Family Allowances', in Hall, Land, Parker and Webb, *Change, Choice and Conflict in Social Policy*, London, Heinneman.

Land, H., (1987) *Social Policy and the Family*, (unpublished) Paper presented at Conference on 'The goals of social policy: past and future', University of London, 17-18 December 1987.

Latey (Committee, The) (1967) *Report of the Committee on the Age of Majority*, Cmnd 3342, London, HMSO.

Layard, R., (1986) *How to Beat Unemployment*, Oxford, Oxford University Press.

Le Grand, J., and Winter, D., (1987) 'The Middle Classes and the Defence of the British Welfare State', in Goodwin, R.E., and Le Grand, J. (eds) *Not Only the Poor. The Middle Classes and the Welfare State*, London, Allen and Unwin.

Lewis, P., (1985) 'Less Work, Less Money, Less Hope', *Poverty*, No.62, Winter 1985/6.

Lewis, P., and Willmore, I., (1985) *The Fowler Review. Effect on Young People*, London, Youthaid.

Lister, R., (1980) *Moving Back to the Means Test*, Poverty Pamphlet No.47, London, Child Poverty Action Group.

Lister, R., (1982) 'Income maintenance for families with children', in Rapoport, R.N., Fogarty, M.P., and Rapoport, R., (below).

Loney, M., (1983) 'The Youth Opportunities Programme: Requiem and Rebirth, in Fiddy, R., (ed) (above).

Longfield, J., (1984) *Ask the Family. Shattering the Myths about Family Life*, London, Bedford Square Press.

Loosemore, J., (1980) 'Policy and Discretion in Supplementary Benefit Decisions', 130 *New Law Journal*, 495.

Lush, A.J., (1941) *The Young Adult*, Cardiff, University of Wales.

Lynes, T., (1962) *National Assistance and National Prosperity*, Welwyn, Herts, The Codicote Press.

Lynes, T., (1980) 'Benefit Fraud', *New Society*, 3 April.

Macnicol, J., (1978) 'Family Allowances and Less Eligibility', in Thane, P., (ed.) *The Origins of British Social Policy*, London, Croom Helm.

Macnicol, J., (1980) *The Movement for Family Allowances, 1918-1945*, London, Heinemann.

Malpass, P., (1985) 'Beyond the Costa del Dole', *Youth and Policy* No.14, p.13.

Marshall, T., (1976) 'The Right to Welfare', in Timms, N., and Watson, D., (eds), *Talking about welfare - readings in philosophy and social policy*, London, Routledge and Kegan Paul.

Mathews, R., (1985) 'Out of house and home? - the board and lodgings regulations', *Poverty* No.62, Winter 1985/6.

Mesher, J., (1984) *CPAG's Supplementary Benefit and Family Income Supplement: The Legislation*, 2nd ed., London, Sweet and Maxwell.

Mesher, J., (1985a) *CPAG's Supplementary Benefit and Family Income Supplement: The Legislation*, 3rd ed., London, Sweet and Maxwell.

Mesher, J., (1985b) 'The Poor Law Strikes Back: 1909-1948-1984', in Hoath, D., (ed.) *75 Years of Law at Sheffield 1909-1984. The Edward Bramley Jubilee Lectures, 1984*, Sheffield, Faculty of Law, University of Sheffield.

Mesher, J., (1987) *CPAG's Supplementary Benefit and Family Income Supplement: The Legislation*, 4th ed., London, Sweet and Maxwell, London.

Mesher, J., (1988) *Income Support, The Social Fund and Family Credit: The Legislation*, 1988 Edition, London, Sweet and Maxwell.

Middlemass, K., (1981) 'Unemployment: The Past and Future of a Political Problem', in Crick, B., (ed.) *Unemployment*, London, Methuen.

Miller, D., (1969) *The Age Between. Adolescents in a disturbed society*, London, Cornmarket/Hutchinson.

Ministry of Labour (1927 et seq.) *Gazette*, London, Ministry of Labour.

Ministry of Labour (1932) *Report for 1931*, Cmd 4044, London, HMSO.

Ministry of Labour (1934) *Memorandum on the Establishment and Conduct of Courses of Instruction for Unemployed Boys and Girls (England and Wales)*, London, HMSO.

Ministry of Labour (1946 et seq.) *Ministry of Labour Gazette*, London, Ministry of Labour.

Ministry of Social Security (1967a) *Annual Report, 1966*, Cmnd 3338, London, HMSO.

Ministry of Social Security (1967b) *Circumstances of Families*, London, HMSO.

Mitton, C., Willmott, P., and Willmott, P., (1983) *Unemployment, Poverty and Social Policy in Europe*, Occasional Papers on Social Administration No.71, London, Bedford Square Press.

Mnookin, R.H., (1978) *Child, Family and State. Problems and Materials on Children and the Law*. Boston and Toronto, Brown and Co.

Moroney, R.M., (1976) *The Family and the State, Considerations for Social Policy*, London, Longmans.

Murphy, M., and Sullivan, O., (1986) 'Unemployment, Housing and Household Structure Among Young Adults', 15 *J. Social Policy*, 205.

NAB - see National Assistance Board.

NACAB (1988) *The Right Way?*, London, National Association of Citizens' Advice Bureaux.

National Assistance Board (1951-61) *Annual Reports*, 1950-60, London, HMSO.

National Advisory Councils for Juvenile Employment (1929) *Reports on Age of Entry into Unemployment Insurance. Majority and Minority Reports*, Cmd 3427, London, HMSO.

National Council for One Parent Families (1985) *The Insecurity System*, London, National Council for One Parent Families.

National Union of Students - see NUS.

NCC (National Consumer Council) (1976) *Means Tested Benefits*, London, NCC.

NCC (National Consumer Council) (1984) *Of Benefit to All*, London, NCC.

NEDO (National Economic Development Office) (1988) *Young People and the Labour Market. A challenge for the 1990s*, London, NEDO.

Nicholls, Sir G., (1904) *A History of the English Poor Law. Vol. 1. A.D. 924 - 1714*, Westminster, P.S. King and Son.

Nicholson, J., (1980) *Seven Ages*, London, Fontana.

NUS (1984) *Submission to the Review of Benefits for Children and Young People*, London, NUS.

NUS (1985a) *Grant us a Living. A discussion document, Student Financial Support*, London, NUS.

NUS (1985b) *Response of the National Union of Students to the Green Paper 'The Reform of Social Security'*, London, NUS.

NUS (1986) *Proposed Changes in Student Benefit Entitlement. Submission by the National Executive Committee of the National Union of Students to the Social Security Advisory Committee*, London, NUS.

NUS (1988) *The White Paper and the Effects of Benefit Loss*, London, NUS.

O'Kelly (1985) 'The Principle of Aggregation', in Silburn, R., (ed.) (below).

Ogus, A.I., and Barendt, E.M., (1982) *The Law of Social Security*, 2nd ed., London, Butterworths.

Oxley, D., (1974) *Poor Relief in England and Wales 1601-1834*, Newton Abbot, David and Charles.

Parrish, A., (1986) *The Road to Nowhere - the Effects of the Board and Lodging Regulations on young people in Birmingham*, Birmingham, Department of Social Administration, University of Birmingham.

Parker, J., (1975) *Social Policy and Citizenship*, Oxford, Clarendon Press.

Parker, R., (1982) 'Family and Social Policy: An Overview', in Rapoport, R.N., et al., (below).

Pelican, J., (1983) *Studying on the Dole*, London, Youthaid.

Piachaud, D., (1979) *The Cost of a Child*, Poverty Pamphlet No.43, London, CPAG.

Plant, R., (1988) 'The fairness of workfare', *The Times*, 16 November.

Platt, S., (1985), 'Recent research on the impact of unemployment upon psychological well-being and para-suicide ("Attempted Suicide")', in Berryman, J.C., (ed.), *The Psychological Effects of Unemployment*, Leicester, The University of Leicester.

Price, R.H., and Burke, A.C., (1985) 'Youth employment: Managing tensions in collaborative research', in Rapoport, R.N., (ed.), *Children, Youth and Families. The action-research relationship*, Cambridge, Cambridge University Press.

Prosser, T., (1979) 'Politics and Judicial Review; the Atkinson case and its aftermath', *Public Law*, 59.

Raffe, D., (1983) 'Can there be an effective youth unemployment policy?' in Fiddy, R., (ed.) (above).

Randall, G., (1988) *No Way Home: homeless young people in Central London*, London, Centrepoint (Soho).

Rapoport, R.N., Fogerty, M.P., and Rapoport, R., (1982) *Families in Britain*, London, Routledge and Kegan Paul.

Rapoport, R.N., and Rapoport, R., (1982) 'British families in transition', in Rapoport, Fogarty and Rapoport (above).

Rees, A.M., (1985) *T.H. Marshall's Social Policy*, 5th ed., London, Hutchinson.

Rees, G., and Rees, T.L., (1982) 'Juvenile Unemployment and the State between the Wars', in Rees, T.L., and Atkinson, P., (below)

Rees, T.L., and Atkinson, P., (eds), (1982) *Youth Unemployment and State Intervention*, London, Routledge and Kegan Paul.

Rimmer, L., (1981) *Families in Focus*, London, Study Commission on the Family.

Rimmer, L., and Wicks, M., (1983) 'The Challenge of Change: Demographic Trends, the Family and Social Policy', in Glennerster, H., (ed.) *The Future of the Welfare State: Remaking Social Policy*, London, Heinemann.

Roberts, K., Dench, S., and Richardson, D., (1985) *Youth Labour Markets: the class of '83*, University of Liverpool - now published as Department of Employment Research Paper No.59.

Roberts, K., Duggan, J., and Noble, M., (1981) 'Ignoring the sign: young, unemployed and unregistered', *Employment Gazette*, August, 353.

Roberts, K., Noble, M., and Duggan, J., (1981) *Unregistered Youth Unemployment and Outreach Careers Work. Final Report. Part 1. Non-registration*, Department of Employment Research Paper No.31, London, Department of Employment.

Roll, J., (1986) *Family Trends and Social Security Reform. Briefing Paper*, London, Family Policy Studies Centre.

Rowell, M.S., and Wilton, A.M., (1982) *The Law of Supplementary Benefit*, London, Butterworths.

Rowell, M.S., and Wilton, A.M., (1986) 'Supplementary Benefit and the Green Paper', *J. Social Welfare law*, 14.

Royal Commission on the Poor Laws and Relief of Distress (1909) *Report* (Majority), Cmd 4499; *Minority Report* (S. & B. Webb), London, HMSO.

Royal Commission on Unemployment Insurance (1931) *Appendices to the Minutes of Evidence*, London, HMSO.

Rust, T., (1982) 'SB and Part-Time Education', *L.A.G. Bulletin*, 53.

Sadler, B., (1983) 'Unemployment and Unemployment Benefits in Twentieth Century Britain: A Lesson of the Thirties', in Cowling, K., et al., *Out of Work. Perspectives of Mass Unemployment*, Coventry, University of Warwick.

Sallis, J., (1986) 'The right to be irrelevant', *Times Educational Supplement*, 10 January.

Save The Children Fund (1933) *Unemployment and the Child*, London, Longmans.

Sawdon, A., Pelican, J., and Tucker, S., (1981) *Study of the Transition from School to Working Life, Vol.1. (2nd ed.) and Vol.2*, London, Youthaid.

SBC (Supplementary Benefits Commission) (1976-80) *Annual Reports, 1975-79*, London, HMSO.

Schostak, J.F., (1983) 'Race, Riots and Unemployment', in Fiddy, R., (ed.), (above).

Scottish Office (1988) *You and the Community Charge*, Edinburgh, Scottish Office.

Scottish Youth Advisory Committee (1945) *The Needs of Youth in These Times*, Edinburgh, HMSO.

SDP (Social Democratic Party) (1985) *Tertiary Education for All*, Green Paper No.25, London, SDP.

Secretary of State for Social Services (1984) *The Housing Benefits Amendment Regulations 1984*, Cmnd 9155, London, HMSO.

Secretary of State for Social Services (1985a) *Reform of Social Security*, Green Paper, Vols 1-3, Cmnds 9517-9519, London, HMSO.

Secretary of State for Social Services (1985b) *The Reform of Social Security. A Programme for Action*, White Paper, Cmnd 9691, London, HMSO.

Secretary of State for Social Services (1985c) *Statement on the Supplementary Benefit (Requirements and Resources) Miscellaneous Provisions Regulations 1985*, Cmnd 9467, London, HMSO.

Secretary of State for Social Services (1986) *The Supplementary Benefit (Conditions of Entitlement) Amendment Regulations 1986 (Etc.). Statement by the Secretary of State for Social Services*, Cmnd 9814, London, HMSO.

Secretary of State for Social Services/Social Security Advisory Committee (1986) *The Supplementary Benefit (Requirements and Resources) Miscellaneous Provisions (No.2) Regulations 1985. Report by the Secretary of State for Social Services and the Report by the Social Security Advisory Committee*, Cmnd 9791, London, HMSO.

Senior, B., and Naylor, J., (1987) *Educational Responses to Adult Unemployment*, London, Croom Helm.

Shelter (1985a) *Board and Lodging: Evidence of Abuse*, London, Shelter.

Shelter (1985b) *SB Board and Lodgings Payments. Final Report*, London, Shelter.

Shelter (1985c) *The Board and Lodgings Cash Victory. Information Sheet*, London, Shelter.

Showler, B., and Sinfield, A., (eds) (1981) *The Workless State*, Oxford, Martin Roberton.

Silburn, R., (1984) 'Supplementary Benefit', in Fabian Tract No.498, *Social Security. The Real Agenda*, London, Fabian Society.

Silburn, R., (ed.) *The Future of Social Security. A Response to the Social Security Green Paper*, London, Fabian Society.

Social Security Advisory Committee - see SSAC (below).

Sofer, A., (1985) 'Young idea - and so wrong', *The Times*, 25 November.

Sorrentino, C., (1981) 'Unemployment in International Perspective', in Showler, B., and Sinfield, A., (above).

SSAC (1981-1988) *First Report, 1981*; *Second Report, 1982/3*; *Third Report, 1984*; *Fourth Report, 1985*; *Fifth Report, 1986/7*; *Sixth Report, 1988*, London, HMSO.

SSAC (1982) *The Supplementary Benefit (Requirements and Resources) Amendment Regulations 1982 (Etc.)*, Report of the SSAC and Statement by the Secretary of State for Social Services, Cmnd 8598, London, HMSO.

SSAC (1983) *The Supplementary Benefit (Requirements, Resources and Single Payments) Amendment Regulations 1983 (Etc.)*, Cmnd 8978, London, HMSO.

SSAC (1984) *Report on the Draft Housing Benefit Amendment Regulations 1984*, Cmnd 9150, London, HMSO.

SSAC (1985) *Report on the Proposals for the Supplementary Benefit (Requirements and Resources) Miscellaneous Provisions Regulations 1985*, Cmnd 9466, London, HMSO.

SSAC (1986a) *The Supplementary Benefit (Conditions of Entitlement) Amendment Regulations 1986 (Etc.). Report by the SSAC*, Cmnd 9813, London, HMSO.

SSAC (1986b) Cmnd 9836 - see SSAC/Secretary of State (below).

SSAC (1987a) *Help With Board and Lodging Charges for People on Low Incomes. Response of the SSAC to a consultation document from D.H.S.S.*, London, SSAC.

SSAC (1987b) *Proposals for Regulations Regarding Benefits for Children and Young People*, Cm106, London, HMSO.

SSAC/Secretary of State for Social Services (1986) *The Supplementary Benefit (Miscellaneous Amendments) Regulations (Etc.)*, Report by the SSAC/Statement by the Secretary of State, Cmnd 9836, London, HMSO.

Stewart, G., Lee, R., and Stewart, J., (1986) 'The Right Approach to Social Security: The Case of the Board and Lodgings Regulations', 13 *J. Law and Society*, 371.

Street, D., (1981) 'Welfare Administration and Organizational Theory', in Marshall Jnr., G.T., and Zald, M.N., (eds), *Social Welfare and Society*, New York, Columbia University Press.

Study Commission on the Family (1983) *Families in the Future*, London, Study Commission on the Family.

Swain, G., (1985) 'Faltering Steps Towards Adulthood', *Forum* 2/85, Strasbourg, Council of Europe.

Thane, P., (1981) 'Childhood in History', in King, M., (ed.) *Childhood, Welfare, Justice*, London, B.T. Batsford.

Townsend, P., Abel-Smith, B., and Land, H., (1984) 'Conclusion', in Fabian Tract No. 498, *Social Security: The Real Agenda*, London, Fabian Society.

UAB (Unemployment Assistance Board) (1938) *Report for the Year Ended 31st December 1937*, Cmd 5742, London, HMSO.

UAB (1939) *Report for the Year Ended 31st December 1938*, Cmd 6021, London, HMSO.

UNESCO (1981) *Youth in the 1980s*, Paris, UNESCO.

University of Liverpool (1938) *Report on Co-operation between the Unemployment Assistance Board, The Local Authority and Voluntary Associations in Liverpool*, Liverpool/London, University Press of Liverpool/Hodder and Stoughton Ltd.

Watson, K., (1983) 'Introduction - Youth, Education and Employment: the Challenge of the 1980s', in Watson, K., (ed.) (below).

Watson, K., (ed.) (1983) *Youth, Education and Unemployment - International Perspectives*, London, Croom Helm.

Warnock, M., (1978) *Special Educational Needs. Report of the Committee of Enquiry into the Education of Handicapped Children and Young People*, Cmnd 7212, London, HMSO.

WECVS - see West-End Co-ordinated Voluntary Services (below).

Welsh Office (1982) *Letter to Chief Executives of County Councils* (on the 21 hour rule), 10 September.

West-End Co-ordinated Voluntary Services (1986) *Enforcing Vagrancy*, London, WECVS.

White, M., (1985) *Long Term Unemployment and Labour Markets*, London, Policy Studies Institute.

Williams, S., et al. (1981) *Youth Without Work. Three Countries' Approach to the Problem*, Paris, O.E.C.D.

Wilson, E., (1977) *Women and the Welfare State*, London, Tavistock.

Wringe, C.A., (1981) *Children's Rights. A philosophical study*, London, Routledge and Kegan Paul.

Wynn, M., (1972) *Family Policy: A study of the economic costs of rearing children and their social and political consequences*, Harmondsworth, Penguin.

Young Homelessness Group (1985) *Moving On, Moving In*, London, CHAR.

Youthaid (1984) *Proof of Oral Evidence to the Review of Benefits for Children and Young People*, London, Youthaid.

Youthaid (1986) *Benefits for School Leavers. Response to Proposals for Change*, London, Youthaid.

Index

Adulthood
   See Childhood-adulthood divide; Independence; Transition to adulthood

Assumptions (in social security), about
   dependency, 5-6, 53-4, 66, 103, 111-2, 172-3
   families, 5-7
   household formation, 7
   parenthood, 7
   transition to working life, 7-8

Beveridge Report
   and young people, 54-7

Board and lodging payments
   claims for, numbers, 77-8
   income support, 84-5
   reform of, 76-86

Care
   young people, leaving, 43, 45, 74, 163 (n.2)

Child benefit, 64-5, 102-3

Childhood-adulthood divide, 3-4
See also Transition to Adulthood

Citizenship
and the unemployed, 12, 161, 177-8

Community charge ('poll tax')
students, 124-5
young people, and generally, 88-90, 141-2 (n.1)

Education
benefits for students etc. *See* Education & benefits
participation in, impact on demand for social security, 28-32
persons in 'relevant education', 30
school leavers, as claimants, 29-30
students, as claimants, 31-2

Education and benefits
'advanced' education, meaning of, 117
claimants, numbers - *see* Education
non-advanced education, meaning of, 62, 130-1
part-time education, 118, 133-4, 137-40 - *see also* twenty-one hour rule, below.
'relevant education', 70, 130-40
school leavers (and 'terminal date'), 70-1
students, 62-3, 116-30, 140-1, 173-4
twenty-one hour rule, 130, 132-40

Families
tension within, 79, 84, 109-110

Family allowances 56-8

Family formation
and young people, 96-7, 108-9

Family responsibility 10, 53, 66, 103, 105, 111

Furniture payments
See Single payments; Social fund

Government policy
    comment on, 167-74

History of social security
    Beveridge Report - *see* Beveridge Report
    household means test, 50
    inter-war period, 47-54
    National Insurance Act 1911, 46-7
    1945-1966, 57-61
    1966-80, 62-5
    unemployment assistance - *see* unemployment assistance
    unemployment insurance - *see* unemployment insurance

Household formation
    by young people, 43-4, 96, 108

Householders
    young people as, 74
    See also Income support; Supplementary benefit

Housing benefit 69, 73, 86-90
    See also Non-dependant deduction; Education & benefits, students

Income support
    age, minimum, of entitlement, 69-70, 145-7
    basis of assessment, 68
    board and lodging payments - *see* Board and lodging payments
    householder/non-householder distinction, removal of, 74-6
    students - *see* Education and benefits, students
    young couples, 98-100
    young parents, 98-102

Independence and young people 104-112, 174-5

Juvenile instruction
    See Youth employment policy

National assistance 59-61

National insurance 58-9

Non-dependant deduction 73-4, 107

Population
    young people, in 1990s, 27

Reform
    comprehensive, of young people's benefits, needed, 174-9
    reviews of social security 1984-5, 68, 168
    Social Security Act 1986, 1-2, 68-9
    See also Housing benefit and Income support

'Relevant education'
    See Education and benefits

Severe Disablement Allowance 142 (n.3)

Single payments
    bedding, 94
    claims for, numbers, 91-2
    furniture, 90-94
    reform of, 90-94

Social fund
    administration, 68
    budgeting loans, 95
    community care grants, 95
    furniture, 94-5
    generally, 94-5
    maternity, 101-103

Students
    See Education and benefits

Supplementary benefit
    aggregation, 63-4
    board & lodging payments - see Board and

lodging payments, reform of
householder/non-householder, 63, 71
minimum age of entitlement, 62
non-householder's contribution, 72
persons in education - *see* Education and benefits
scale rates, 64, 71
school leavers - *see* Education and benefits
students, 117-120
young couples, 97-8
young parents, 97-8

Transition to adulthood 39-45, 171, 174

Unemployment
See Youth unemployment

Unemployment assistance 50-4

Unemployment benefit
'full-extent normal' rule, 162 (n.1)
young people, eligibility, 62
students, 121

Unemployment insurance 46-9, 52-4
and see History of social security - National Insurance Act 1911, inter-war period

Values
underlying, in social security, 8-10, 111
See also Work ethic/incentives, Family responsibility

Work ethic/incentives
generally, in social security, 8-10, 51-2, 148-157
availability of benefits, 152-4
level of benefits, 150-2

Workfare 178

Young people
   defined, 2-3, 171-2
   poverty, and, 105-108
   the state, and, 11

Youth employment policy
   (including youth training)
   between the wars, 157-9
   other countries, in, 160
   participation in training schemes, numbers, 27
   social security, and, 11, 143-63, 167-8
   transition to adulthood, and, 42-3

Youth Opportunities Programme
   See Youth employment policy

Youth Training Scheme
   See Youth employment policy

Youth unemployment
   from 1900-39, 18-22
      levels, 18-19
      regional variations, 20
      duration, 20-1
      reaction to, 21
   from 1939-88, 22-28
      regional factors, 25
      ethnic minorities, and, 25, 27
      gender, and, 25
   influence on social security, 32-3
   present and future, 26-28
   transition to adulthood, and, 41-5